Questions of Phenomenology

John D. Caputo, *series editor*

PERSPECTIVES IN
CONTINENTAL
PHILOSOPHY

FRANÇOISE DASTUR

Questions of Phenomenology

Language, Alterity, Temporality, Finitude

TRANSLATED BY ROBERT VALLIER

FORDHAM UNIVERSITY PRESS
New York ■ 2017

This book was first published in French under the title *La phénoménologie en questions: Langage, altérité, temporalité, finitude*, © Librarie Philosophique J. Vrin, Paris, 2004.

Ouvrage publié avec le concours du Ministère français chargé de la Culture–Centre National du Livre.

This work has been published with the assistance of the French Ministry of Culture–National Center for the Book.

Cet ouvrage a bénéficié du soutien des Programmes d'aide à la publication de l'Institut Français.

This work, published as part of a program of aid for publication, received support from the Institut Français.

Fordham University Press also publishes its books in a variety of electronic formats. Some content that appears in print may not be available in electronic books.

Visit us online at www.fordhampress.com.

Library of Congress Cataloging-in-Publication Data available online at http://catalog .loc.gov.

Printed in the United States of America

19 18 17 5 4 3 2 1

First edition

Contents

Part III: Temporality and History

Part IV: Finitude and Mortality

Abbreviations

The following is a list of abbreviations for works frequently cited throughout this book. Translations have frequently been slightly modified to suit the context.

AN	Eugen Fink, *Alles und Nichts* (The Hague: Nijhoff, 1959).
BQP	Martin Heidegger, *Basic Questions of Philosophy: Selected "Problems" of "Logic,"* tr. R. Rojcewicz and A. Schuwer (Bloomington: Indiana University Press, 1994).
BT	Martin Heidegger, *Being and Time*, tr. J. Stambaugh (Albany: SUNY Press, 1996).
CM	Edmund Husserl, *Cartesian Meditations: An Introduction to Phenomenology*, tr. D. Cairns (Dordrecht: Nijhoff, 1988).
Crisis	Edmund Husserl, *The Crisis of European Sciences and Transcendental Phenomenology*, tr. D. Carr (Evanston: Northwestern University Press, 1970).
CTP	Martin Heidegger, *Contributions to Philosophy: From Enowning*, tr. P. Emad and K. Maly (Bloomington: Indiana University Press, 2000).
EJ	Edmund Husserl, *Experience and Judgment*, tr. J. Churchill, J. Spencer, and K. Ameriks (Evanston: Northwestern University Press, 1973).

FCM	Martin Heidegger, *The Fundamental Concepts of Metaphysics: World, Finitude, Solitude*, tr. W. McNeill and N. Walker (Bloomington: Indiana University Press, 1995).
FTL	Edmund Husserl, *Formal and Transcendental Logic*, ed. and tr. D. Cairns (Dordrecht: Nijhoff, 1969).
GA	Martin Heidegger, *Gesamtausgabe* (Frankfurt: Klostermann,1916–).
GMD	Eugen Fink, *Grundphänomene des Menschlichen Daseins* (Freiburg: Karl Alber, 1979).
GPP	*The Basic Problems of Phenomenology: From the Lectures, Winter Semester, 1910–1911*, tr. I. Farin and J. Hart (Dordrecht: Nijhoff, 2006).
HE	Jan Patočka, *Heretical Essays in the Philosophy of History*, tr. J. Dodd and E. Kohák (LaSalle: Open Court, 1996).
Hua VIII	Edmund Husserl, *Erste Philosophie (1923/24)*, Zweiter Teil, *Theorie der phänomeno-logischen Reduktion*, ed. R. Boehm (The Hague: Nijhoff, 1959).
Hua XV	Edmund Husserl, *Zur Phanomenologie der Intersubjektivitat: Texte Aus Dem Nachlass*, Dritter Teile, *1929–1935*, tr. I. Kern (The Hague: Nijhoff, 1973) [Husserliana XIII].
ID	Martin Heidegger, *Identity and Difference*, tr. J. Stambaugh (Chicago: University of Chicago Press, 2002).
Ideas I	Edmund Husserl, *Ideas: General Introduction to Pure Phenomenology*, tr. W.R. Gibson (New York: Collier, 1962).
IP	Edmund Husserl, *The Idea of Phenomenology*, tr. L. Hardy (Dordrecht: Nijhoff, 1999).
ITC	Edmund Husserl, *On the Phenomenology of the Consciousness of Internal Time (1893–1917)*, tr. J. Brough (The Hague: Nijhoff, 1991).
KM	Martin Heidegger, *Kant and the Problem of Metaphysics*, tr. R. Taft (Bloomington: Indiana University Press, 1990).
LH	Martin Heidegger, "Letter on 'Humanism' (1946)," tr. F. Capuzzi, in *Pathmarks*, ed. W. McNeill (Cambridge: Cambridge University Press, 1998).
LI I	Edmund Husserl, *Logical Investigations*, vol. I, tr. J. N. Findlay (London: Routledge, 1970).
LI II	Edmund Husserl, *Logical Investigations*, vol. II, tr. J. N. Findlay (London: Routledge, 1970).

MFL	Martin Heidegger, *The Metaphysical Foundations of Logic*, tr. M. Heim (Bloomington: Indiana University Press, 1984).
MT	Eugen Fink, *Metaphysik und Tod* (Stuttgart: Kohlhammer, 1969).
ND	Eugen Fink, *Nähe und Distanz: Studien zur Phänomenologie*. Freiburg: Karl Alber, 2008.
OA	Paul Ricoeur, *Oneself as Another*, tr. K. Blamey (Chicago: University of Chicago Press, 1995).
PCT	Martin Heidegger, *History of the Concept of Time: Prolegomena*, tr. T. Kisiel (Bloomington: Indiana University Press, 1992).
PhP	Maurice Merleau-Ponty, *Phenomenology of Perception*, tr. C. Smith (London: Routledge, 2002).
TM	Hans-Georg Gadamer, *Truth and Method* (New York: Crossroads, 1988).
TN I	Paul Ricoeur, *Time and Narrative*, vol. 1, tr. K. Blamey and D. Pellauer (Chicago: University of Chicago Press, 1990).
TN III	Paul Ricoeur, *Time and Narrative*, vol. 3, tr. K. Blamey and D. Pellauer (Chicago: University of Chicago Press, 1990).
TO	Emmanuel Levinas, *Time and the Other*, tr. R. Cohen (Pittsburgh: Duquesne University Press, 1987).
VI	Maurice Merleau-Ponty, *The Visible and the Invisible*, ed. C. Lefort, tr. A. Lingis (Evanston: Northwestern University Press, 1968).
WE	Eugen Fink, *Welt und Endlichkeit* (Würzburg: Koenigshausen and Neumann, 1990).
WPh	Martin Heidegger, *What Is Philosophy?*, tr. J. Wilde and W. Kluback (Albany: NCUP, 1956).
ZS	Martin Heidegger, *Zollikon Seminars: Protocols, Conversations, Letters*, ed. M. Boss, tr. F. Mayr and R. Askay (Evanston: Northwestern University Press, 2001).

Preface

At the beginning of the twentieth century, with the publication of the *Logical Investigations*, the term "phenomenology" (which had first appeared in Lambert's *Nouvel Organon* in 1764) no longer named a particular discipline within philosophy, as had been the case with Hegel, but rather a new conception of what philosophy must be. The Husserlian enterprise has gained its profound and long-lasting fecundity from the idea, borrowed from the Ancients, that philosophical work must be done in common and requires the concordance of several thinkers. These thinkers are united not so much by the unity of a doctrine or by belonging to a school, but rather by the practice of a method. Husserl himself had strongly insisted on this idea, as had Heidegger; Merleau-Ponty perhaps expressed it most clearly in the Preface to the *Phenomenology of Perception*, stating that "phenomenology can be practiced and recognized as a manner or a style" and that it "exists as a movement" rather than as a completed system.[1]

Our task here is certainly not to provide an exhaustive inventory of this phenomenological movement, to which so many philosophers in the last century belong. What we propose instead is simply to provide a glimpse of this movement, placing the emphasis less on the proper names of thinkers than on the problems they share in common. The essays collected in this volume are dedicated to a small number of fundamental questions, which have created a dialogue among some of the most eminent stars in the phenomenological constellation, sometimes resulting in irreconcilable positions. Phenomenology was fortified by bringing new perspectives to these questions, but at the same time, and above all, these questions call phenomenology itself into question—they are the questions through which phenomenology tirelessly continues to question itself. Once again borrowing an expression from Merleau-Ponty, we can say that these fundamental questions—of language and logic, of the self and other, of temporality and history, of finitude and mortality—bring us to the "limits" of phenomenology, which are no different from the limits of philosophy itself.

The first of these questions concerns the relation of phenomenology, language, and logic, and so Husserl's thought must first be questioned. We might say that for Husserl, the path of logic is the royal road of phenomenology because, from the beginning, Husserl wanted to articulate what he calls, even in his last works, a "genealogy of logic."[2] In this perspective, the problem of judgment and the status of the predicative proposition are the privileged objects of phenomenological investigation in the broad sense—that is, as an investigation seeking to go directly to the things themselves rather than contenting itself with a "purely symbolic understanding of words," as Husserl says in his introduction to the *Logical Investigations*.[3] This call to go beyond the symbolic and toward the intuitive can be qualified as "phenomenological" in the broad sense, as demonstrated by Husserl's earliest works, marked as they are by the concern not only to overcome the psychologism of the epoch, but also to show, against formalism, that logical idealities do not hover in empty space, but are instead firmly anchored in the ground of experience. From the beginning, and until his last book, *Experience and Judgment*, published shortly after his death, and always in the genealogical perspective characteristic of his method, Husserl never stops questioning the pre-predicative experience at the origin of predicative activity that forms the substructure of our linguistic practice. In a certain way, this is the same genealogical enterprise that Heidegger undertakes when, in the years preceding the publication of *Being and Time*, he formulates the project that he calls a "phenomenological deconstruction." The goals of this latter are in effect to elucidate the derivative character of philosophical propositions and to show that the phenomenon of language can be generally understood only within the larger framework of an analytic of existence. But very early on, Heidegger calls into question the privilege Husserl grants to intuition because, for Heidegger, primary experience is not the experience of sensible matter, but rather of an original "meaningfulness" or "significance" of the world.[4] It is thus this turn from a phenomenology of seeing to a hermeneutic phenomenology that is at stake during the 1920s in the dialogue between Heidegger and Husserl—a difficult dialogue that will end in an outright rupture.

The primordial question for the constitution of phenomenology is the question of the status of language and of logical truth; but alongside it, we encounter the no-less-decisive question of the plurality of subjects. Because Husserlian phenomenology took the form of a transcendental theory of the subject (particularly in the first book of *Ideas* in 1913), the question of the relation to the other (a question almost totally absent in modern philosophy from Descartes to Kant) became crucial, and first of all for Husserl. Although the development of phenomenology as a transcendental science after the *Logical Investigations* requires Husserl to take the Cartesian method as a model (which he proposed to elaborate further), phenomenology is nonetheless always a theory of intersubjectivity rather than of a solipsistic and abstract subjectivity. Husserlian phenomenology was thus the first to give impetus to the development of this major problematic, which, for phenomenologists in the twentieth century, is the question of the relation to the other. In order to resolve this problem, we would have to leave behind the framework of a philosophy of consciousness and, as Heidegger argued, think an originary being-with-others rather than the ego's "constitution" of the other subject, as Husserl wanted. On the basis of these two different ways to account for the experience of the other, an opposition will be sketched out between those who, like Levinas, claim the radical "exteriority" and absolute priority of the other in relation to the self, and those who, like Merleau-Ponty and Ricoeur, attempt in contrast to demonstrate that the alterity of the other is already announced in the more originary alterity constitutive of the self itself.

But the question of the other is not the only question that brings us to the limits of a constituting phenomenology: the same is also true for what, in the lectures on internal time-consciousness, Husserl called the "secular cross" of epistemology—that is, the question of the relation of consciousness to time.[5] While remaining entirely within the framework of a theory of the subject, Husserl nevertheless managed to elucidate the structural identity of temporality and subjectivity. But in his analysis of existence, Heidegger was able to see what in temporality radically impedes an understanding of the being of the human in terms of substrate or subject. From this confrontation of the two analyses of temporality, Merleau-Ponty derives a new idea of the subject and is led to emphasize its character as ek-static, and no longer as synthetic, as the classical tradition would have it. Now, in this perspective, a phenomenology of the event—that is, of what in time radically escapes the grasp of concepts and the mastery of the subject—does not seem totally impossible; does this then mean that phenomenology is equally able to open itself to the plural dimension of history? To address this, we would again have to abandon the transcendentalism that, even in the later Husserl, thinker of the crisis of European humanity and of the deviations of modern rationalism, is unable to see the foundation of history in finitude and mortality. To this end, we would have to appeal both to Heidegger and his thought of an intrinsic historicity, not just of human being but also of Being itself, and also to Gadamer and Ricoeur, who developed, each in his own way, a historical hermeneutic that decisively breaks with the Hegelian idea of a totalization of experience in Absolute Knowledge, which can only be understood as an abolition of the historical dimension itself.

If a phenomenology of history is possible, then would this not mean that phenomenology would have to confront the truly crucial question that philosophy, throughout its entire history of seeking "eternal" truths, always wanted to avoid—namely, the question of death?[6] Eugen Fink, Husserl's last assistant, and Jan Patočka, Fink's Czech student, both drawing from the Husserlian source and yet profoundly marked by the Heideggerian problematic of being-in-the-world, are the thinkers in whose work an admirable phenomenology of finitude and mortality is developed. We might wonder if taking mortality as the point of departure for the thought of human finitude, and requiring that philosophy not presuppose any support on earth or in heaven (as Kant had already done), amounts to prohibiting any reference to the dimension of the divine. But we find in both Husserl and Heidegger a discourse treating this very dimension, without implying phenomenology's submission to any theology. If God returns to the very interiority of a thought of appearance for which "there is nothing behind the phenomena," as both Husserl and Heidegger claim,[7] it is as the entirely new and unheard of figure of a God denied eternity—because in Husserl, "god" is confused with the infinite process of temporalization, and in Heidegger, "god" becomes an ephemeral God who merely "passes by." This thought of a God who has lost transcendence and remains essentially withdrawn is, paradoxically, how phenomenology testifies to its rupture (more profound than a militant atheism or an avowed anthropocentrism) with the whole of the metaphysical tradition of the West.[8]

Questions of Phenomenology

PART I

Language and Logic

1

The Logic of "Validity"
Husserl, Heidegger, Lotze

If the name of Lotze is known to us, it is largely because he is mentioned in the *Prolegomenon to Pure Logic* alongside those great thinkers under whose authority Husserl placed himself—namely, Leibniz, Kant, and Herbart.[1] Husserl even dedicates a paragraph to explaining his connections to Herbart and Lotze, but in fact, with the exception of the last few lines, the paragraph is devoted entirely to Herbart's merits and errors. Lotze is credited only with the merit of having the great perspicacity to deepen some of Herbart's suggestions and for developing them in an original manner; but like Herbart, he is criticized for having confused specific ideality and normative ideality and for having seen a morality of thought in logic. This is why Husserl concludes the paragraph with a rather negative judgment: "[Lotze's] great logical work, however rich it may be in original thoughts . . . hereby becomes a jarring mixture of psychologism and pure logic."[2]

The brevity of this diagnostic is explained in a note in the first edition of the *Logical Investigations,* specifying that "in the next volume, we will have the opportunity to offer a critical examination of Lotze's theory of knowledge, and in particular the chapter he dedicates to real and formal meaning in logic." This note is replaced in the 1913 second edition by the following: "In edition I, I promised to deal with Lotze's epistemology in an Appendix to volume II of his work. This was not printed, owing to lack of space."[3]

We will therefore not find any more complete information about Lotze's importance for Husserlian thought in the text of the *Logical Investigations* itself; Husserl merely underlines that the investigations "have been crucially stimulated by the ideas of Bolzano (along with Lotze)."[4] In a later text, a 1903 review of Melchior Palagyi's book on *The Conflict of the Psychologists and the Formalists in Modern Logic*, Husserl defends himself against Palagyi's accusation (shared, moreover, by other logicians and philosophers, especially Rickert) that he had merely exploited Bolzano in the *Logical Investigations* without noting his dependence on him; but in this same text, Husserl also underlines Lotze's importance for his thought. Recalling that in the *Prolegomena*, he had explicitly designated Bolzano (along with Lotze) as the thinkers who had the most decisive influence on him, Husserl adds:

> With specific reference to my concepts of the "ideal" significations, and "ideal" contents of representations and judgments, they originally derive, not from *Bolzano* at all, but rather—as the term "ideal" alone indicates—from *Lotze*. In particular, *Lotze's* reflections about the interpretation of *Plato's* theory of forms had a profound effect on me. Only by thinking out these thoughts from *Lotze*—and in my opinion he failed to get completely clear on them—did I find the key to the curious conceptions of *Bolzano*, which in all their phenomenological naïveté were at first unintelligible, and to the treasures of his *Wissenschaftslehre*.[5]

Against those who accuse him of having used Bolzano without crediting him, Husserl emphasizes the primordial importance of Lotze, who alone allowed him to acquire an understanding of those "curious" Bolzanoian conceptions, especially the idea of "propositions in themselves," which initially seemed to him (and to Bolzano's many other readers) as some sort of "mythical entities suspended between being and non-being."[6] As we will see, the Lotzian interpretation of the Platonic theory of ideas allows Husserl to understand that propositions in themselves are indeed objects even though they do not have "existence," because they have "ideal" being or the value of "general objects," and not the real—that is, temporal—being of things.[7]

The clearest text concerning Husserl's understanding of his relation to the Lotzian theory of knowledge, however, appears later, in the 1913 "Draft of a Preface to the *Logical Investigations*," specifically in section 8, entitled, "Critical Differentiation from Lotze."[8] Husserl eventually published a much shorter text as the "Preface," but Eugen Fink preserved and published this sketch in 1939 as "a historical evidence of a particular *self-interpretation* of Husserl's phenomenology." Fink contends, moreover, that this self-interpretation is instructive in that it was developed more than ten years after the publication of the *Logical Investigations* and thus from a superior perspective on the problematic; as such it is able to elucidate what in 1900 was still only latent—namely, the final direction of the sense of the work.[9] Our concern is therefore to show that just as Husserl was not limited to exploiting Bolzano, for whom the "idealist meaning that essentially belongs to [the Husserlian] idea of pure logic remained foreign" because his theory of knowledge "rested upon the foundation of an extreme empiricism"[10] (that consequently weakens the interpretation given in 1913 of propositions in themselves as ideal objects),[11] so too is Husserl not limited to repeating Lotze because, although he had assimilated Lotze's theory of validity (*Geltung*) and theory of ideas, Husserl proposes a theory of knowledge as different from Lotze's as Aristotle's is from Plato's or Kant's from Lambert's.[12] Husserl specifies: "only those who confine themselves merely to the first volume and in so doing do not even think it through thoroughly could identify my anti-psychologism, my theory of ideas, and theory of knowledge (insofar as the latter can be judged at all from such minor indications) with Lotze's, or would even attempt to contrast them according to their general type."[13]

Readers of the *Logical Investigations* who limited themselves to a superficial reading of the *Prolegomena* were numerous, which is why many of them, particularly the neo-Kantians, considered the six investigations of the second volume to be a relapse into psychologism. If between 1886 and 1895 Husserl had been preparing to renounce the psychologism to which he had previously subscribed through a study of Leibniz and the latter's differentiation of "truths of reason" and "truths of fact," he owes his radical "conversion" to "logicism" (and the "Platonism" that accompanies it) to the study of Lotze's *Logic*. When Husserl mentions his previously held psychologistic point of view, as he does in the preface to the first edition of the *Logical Investigations* (which ends with a quote from Goethe: "There is nothing we judge more severely than the mistakes we've just made"),[14] he is referring less to the study of number as presented in the *Philosophy of Arithmetic*, which he continues to cite positively in the *Formal and Transcendental Logic* in 1929,[15] than he is to the conception of logic that he was then developing and that he had inherited from Brentano. Brentano saw logic as an art, a technique, or even "the doctrine of correct judgment."[16] For Brentano, logic is not a theoretical science whose unity resides in the field that it chooses to investigate, but rather a practical science, similar to medicine or architecture, whose unity resides in the goal it proposes. Logic as a practical science has judgment as its goal—that is, the affirmation or negation of a content of a representation—and it prescribes directives for achieving this goal. Because judgments are psychic acts, logic turns into psychology, from which it nevertheless differs, in that logic treats only correct judgments and disposes of a norm allowing it to recognize correct judgments.

Under Brentano's influence, Husserl had viewed logic as a part of psychology, and so he had been led to psychologize mathematics, as the subtitle of the *Philosophy of Arithmetic* indicates: "Psychological and Logical Investigations." But he did not publish the second volume of these investigations, dedicated to *logical* investigations (whereas the first volume concerned *psychological* investigations) because in the interim he had broken with the Brentanoian conception of logic and had come to see logic as a theoretical and a priori science that concerns not the judging mind but rather the kingdom of ideal meanings. Husserl was led to this new conception of logic by his reading of Lotze, as he underlines in the Draft:

> Little as Lotze himself had gone beyond pointing out absurd inconsistencies and beyond psychologism, still his brilliant interpretation of Plato's doctrine of Ideas gave me my first big insight and was a determining factor in all further studies. Lotze spoke already of truths in themselves, and so the idea suggested itself to transfer all of the mathematical and a major part of the traditionally logical world into the realm of the ideal.[17]

And although Lotze also battles against a psychological foundation of logic, in the next part of his account he nevertheless abandons the theory of ideas he had established in an apparently pure fashion and falls back into anthropomorphism. Husserl underlines, moreover, that Lotze's theory of knowledge is proven to be a failure by the very fact that he recognizes a marvelous character in the possibility of knowledge:

> Proper epistemology clarifies, and something clarified is both something become understandable and something understood—thus the extreme opposite of "wonderment." Reference is repeatedly made to both the nature of all minds—actually understood as a fact of reality—and over against this, the nature of real things in themselves. And the completely distorted problem of the real and formal meaning of the logical comes about through the fact that Lotze presupposes a metaphysical world of things that exists in-itself and, over against it—at least according to our usual knowledge-claim—a world of ideas, meant to represent these things, that belongs to minds existing in the metaphysical world, and that he understandably now struggles in vain to explain the basis of the correspondence between these two worlds within knowledge.[18]

Husserl refers here exclusively to the third book of Lotze's *Logic*, which treats "Of Knowledge" and which includes five chapters. In the second chapter, entitled "The World of Ideas," Lotze exposits his interpretation of the theory of Platonic ideas, which Husserl qualifies as "great," whereas the fourth chapter treats of "Real and Formal Significance of Logical Acts," offering a theory in which Husserl sees only a "mythological metaphysics"[19] and proof that Lotze lacks "this inner power to draw the consequences of what is claimed."[20] But despite this, Husserl concludes that Lotze's work "is nevertheless one of the most important of the past century for the theory of knowledge" and that "the present investigations owe much to him."[21]

Our first concern will therefore be to understand the Lotzian interpretation of the theory of ideas so that we can then demonstrate why it had been so decisive for the development of Husserlian phenomenology. But before reading the famous Chapter 2 of Lotze's *Logic Book III* in detail, we might first give some succinct biographical indications of this thinker who is today forgotten.

Rudolf Hermann Lotze was born on May 21, 1817, in Bautzen-an-die-Spree, not far from the current German borders with Poland and the Czech Republic. He studied medicine and philosophy in Leipzig and taught both subjects there until 1844, when he succeeded Herbart at Göttingen. He remained there until 1880, leaving for Berlin, where he died of pneumonia some months later, on July 1, 1881. Lotze had been the most famous German philosopher of his time, in both Germany and abroad. He influenced not only phenomenology, but also the neo-Kantianism of the Baden school of value-theory, founded by Rickert and Windelband, and today there are many questions regarding the influence he may have had on Frege, who was his student. Translations of his *Logic* and his *Metaphysics* influenced Bradley's English neo-Hegelianism and James's and Dewey's American pragmatism. His most famous works are a study on anthropology entitled *Mikrokosmus* (published in three volumes between 1856 and 1864) and the two parts of his *System of Philosophy*, published between 1874 and 1879, consisting of revised versions of his 1843 *Logic* and his 1841 *Metaphysics*. The 1843 version of the *Logic*, significantly rewritten in 1874, includes three books, respectively entitled "Of Thought," "Applied Logic," and "Of Knowledge." The third book has garnered the most interest, but the first book equally allows for an understanding of Lotze's extensive influence on modern formal logic. This is why the books were republished in 1989 by the Felix Meiner publishing house.

In his youth, Heidegger was very interested in Lotze's *Logic*, and in particular his interpretation of the Platonic theory of ideas.[22] In his Winter Semester course in 1925–26 on *Logic: The Question of Truth*, he devotes the long first part to examining the situation of contemporary logic and to the question of psychologism, which leads him to give a detailed exposition of the Lotzian theory of ideas.[23] He also makes an extended allusion to Lotze in the Summer Semester course of 1919.[24] In this course, Heidegger characterizes Lotze, taking up Husserl's terms, as a "hybrid figure" (*ein Zwittergebilde*) who conjoins past and present dangers (relapsing into a speculative metaphysics or the overemphasis on naturalism), but who also discovered a non-empirical sphere and thereby avoided the reification of the mind and the reduction of being to material reality.[25] Heidegger thus already sees Lotze as the one who, taking up the Fichtean theory of the primacy of practical reason, interpreted Platonic ideas not as *beings*, but as *values*, and thus overcame naturalism while grounding logic in ethics, which will be the determining motif for Rickert and Windelband.[26] No doubt because he had rallied to the Lotzian theory of value in his 1912 thesis on "The Doctrine of Judgment in Psychologism,"[27] Heidegger felt the need in 1927 in *Being and Time* to stigmatize severely the obscure "problematic" developed around that "verbal idol" (*Wortgötzen*), which is the term "validity" (*Geltung*).[28] But if, on the one hand, the theory of *Geltung* prepares the theory of value as that which constitutes what Rickert will call in 1892 "the object of knowledge" (*Der Gegenstand der Erkenntnis*), then, on the other hand, it also allows for the refutation of skepticism and thus for saving the identity of truth.

We now turn to Lotze's text itself, the famous third book of his *Logic*. The first chapter is called "On Skepticism," in which he shows that skepticism cannot mean an absolute negation of every truth because "doubt is possible only on the presupposition of some acknowledged truth."[29] In this, we see what will form the heart of the Husserlian critique of skepticism: skepticism is undermined by an internal contradiction because denying the existence of a truth implies a minimal belief in the truth of the proposition that negates the existence of truth. It is important for Lotze to show that "nothing but the connection of our representations with themselves can ever constitute the object of our investigations,"[30] because we can only compare the known with the known, not the known with the unknown—that is, representations with representations, but not a representation with the thing that it represents. It is because "all we know of the external world depends upon the ideas of it which are within us; it is so far entirely indifferent whether with Idealism we deny the existence of that world, and regard our ideas of it as alone reality, or whether we maintain with Realism the existence of things outside us which act upon our minds. On the latter hypothesis as little as the former do the things themselves pass into our knowledge. They only awaken in us ideas, which are not Things. It is then this varied world of ideas within us, it matters not where they may have come from, which forms the sole material directly given to us, from which alone our knowledge can start."[31]

Wherever they come from, whether from us or from things, representations constitute the only immediate given of knowledge, which implies that confidence in our reason, the idea that the truth can be found by means of thought alone, is the inevitable presupposition of every investigation. Doubting the reality of a relation between two representations means nothing other than wondering whether this relation will generally and always subsist each time that the two things in question present themselves to our consciousness. As a result:

> It is therefore not this presupposed reality of an external world which inserts itself here between our ideas as the standard by which their truth is to be measured; rather it is always only the representation, necessary for us, of a possible comportment of such a world, if it exists, thus of one of our own thoughts, which constitutes the standard against which we measure the truth, whether the latter is immediately evident or requires elucidation through other thoughts.[32]

We cannot even suppose without contradiction that another mind more perfect than our own—the mind of an angel, for example—would know things as they are in themselves because knowledge can never consist in anything but an ensemble of representations bearing *on* the thing, and cannot coincide with the being of the thing itself. Whoever wants knowledge of the things in themselves therefore wants something completely incomprehensible and contradictory to the very of idea of knowledge. This argument announces, albeit in an inverted fashion, the same argument that Husserl uses in the famous section 43 of *Ideas I* to deny God the power to know the thing in itself, whereas human intuition is said to procure only knowledge of the phenomenal. Because he no longer differentiates between *intuitus originarius* and *intuitus derivativus*, Husserl is led to abandon the idea that knowledge is symbolic representation and to claim instead that intuition directly attains the thing itself in its corporeity. Lotze, on the other hand, by eliminating the "metaphysical" question of knowing whether real things correspond to our representations of them, is led to seek the "fixed points" (*die festen Punkten*) within the world of our representations, points that comprise the first certainties able to account for the laws governing this constantly changing world.

At the end of this first chapter, however, Lotze declares (against Kant) that he fears claiming that we know only the phenomena and not the thing in itself because such a claim contains a prejudice that he would like to undo, a prejudice according to which "our knowledge which was intended by rights for the apprehension of the higher, the essence of things, has to be content with the lower, the phenomenon."[33] This would mean that knowledge is reduced to a means that in no way attains its final goal of understanding things as they are. This criticism of the opposition of the phenomenon and the thing-in-itself strongly resembles the Hegelian criticism of the Kantian critique that, viewing knowledge as a means or as an instrument, also presupposes the separation of knowledge and the absolute. And just as in the introduction to the *Phenomenology of Spirit*, Hegel concludes that we need not be "troubling ourselves with such useless ideas and locutions about cognition as 'an instrument for getting hold of the Absolute,' "[34] so too does Lotze close this first chapter on skepticism with these words: "let us leave entirely out of the question the opposition between our world of ideas and a world of things; let us look upon the former alone as the material we have to deal with; and let us endeavour to ascertain where within this world the primary fixed points of certainty are to be found, and how it may be possible to communicate a like certainty through the medium of these to other ideas which do not in themselves equally possess it. By following certain circuitous paths which will be found to be no deviation from our proper route, we may perhaps arrive at clearness on this subject."[35]

In the second chapter on "The World of Ideas," Lotze begins with the idea that the conception of truth as the agreement of our representations with the things is a prejudice, thus rejoining the Cartesian position stating that only the multiplicity of our *cogitationes* is indubitably given. The apprehension of the Heraclitean flux of these *cogitationes* leads the Sophists to proclaim with Protagoras the merely subjective value of the truth and, with the Eleatic dialecticians, to deny the identity of the content of any concept. Whence reaction of Socrates who, thanks to his "*gesunde Wahrheitssinn*," the salutary sense of the truth that he possessed, recalls that the concepts of the good, the just, and the unjust have one immutable meaning independent of any subjective appreciation. Plato is thus credited with having developed his theory of ideas as an extension of these Socratic convictions and with having proposed the attempt to exploit "the truth which belongs to the world of our ideas [representations] in itself, without regard to its agreement with an assumed reality of things outside its borders [with a presupposed world of transcendent things]."[36]

This inner truth can only consist in the stable element that always maintains itself in the ever-changing course of our representations. But if truth is constituted by what remains permanent amidst changing representations, then the identical content of the representation must be distinguishable from mere affection or impression. This implies a first "objectification" of the subjective, which happens through the intermediary of language and nomination, allowing us to say that our state of consciousness is perceivable by another.[37] Our affection is thus objectified in the form of an autonomous content that always means the same thing and that continues to mean it "independently of the fact of knowing whether or not our consciousness aims at it."[38] Yet this object is not a thing, but a concept, a predicate by means of which we determine a thing as being this or that:

> Perception shows us the things of sense undergoing changes in their qualities. But while black becomes white and sweet sour, it is not blackness itself which passes into whiteness, nor does sweetness become sourness; what happens is that these several qualities, each remaining eternally identical with itself, succeed each other in the thing, and the conceptions through which we think the things have themselves no part in the mutability which we attribute on account of their changes to the things of which the qualities are the predicates.[39]

These constitute "the first adequate and solid beginnings of a permanent knowledge."[40]

Plato had been the first to articulate this very simple and important idea: the whole-in-movement, the Heraclitean flux, is nothing without a truth that thoroughly traverses it. Invariable contents are nothing but what Plato determined as constant being, *aei on*—that is, as idea, the first true object of certain knowledge. Lotze thus credits Plato with the Cartesian method of examining the representations of consciousness for a fixed Archimedean point that forms the basis for the construction of certain knowledge—which leads us to think that Lotze's interpretation of Platonism does not take into account the proper meaning of the theory of ideas. But for us, what alone is important here is to understand from which theory of truth Lotze draws this interpretation of Platonism. What are these contents—sound in itself, color in itself—when no one perceives them? Are they something rather than nothing? They are *not nothing* because we can indeed distinguish sound from color and many other contents. But even if they are something (*Etwas*), they are *not beings* according to Lotze. How then can we distinguish what is neither in-itself nor in our representations as a "something" distinct from something else?

We must nevertheless recognize that just by distinguishing it, we are moving in "a certain element of affirmation" or "acquiescence" (ein gewisses Element von Bejahung). A little further on, he again specifies that "we undoubtedly have a conception of affirmation or position in an extremely general sense" (Es gibt allerdings einen sehr allgemeinen Begriff von Bejahtheit oder Position) that accounts for the recognition of this "being something," which Lotze cannot call "being" because his naturalism inclines him to identify being with material being.[41] Even the term "position" is inadequate because it lets us think that this posited something is produced by thought and thus refers to an activity, whereas acquiescence or consent is by nature the passive acknowledgment of something that is already there, independently of any thinking subject. This is why, in order to designate this, he chooses the German term *Wirklichkeit*, effective reality, to which he gives greater purview than *Sein*, being. Reality, in the general sense of what is recognized or that to which one consents, adheres, or affirms (*Wirklichkeit als Bejahtheit*) includes several forms:

> we call a thing Real [*wirkliche*] which is, in contradistinction to another which is not; an event Real which occurs [*geschieht*] or has occurred, in contradistinction to that which does not occur; a relation Real which obtains [lit: subsists] [*besteht*], as opposed to one which does not obtain [subsist]; lastly we call a proposition Really true which holds or is valid [*gilt*] as opposed to one of which the validity [*Geltung*] is still doubtful.[42]

Thus, being, occurring, subsisting, and valuing are all independent forms of reality and are in no way derived from one another. We cannot say of a proposition that it "is," or that it "occurs," and its content can be said to "subsist" only if the things that it puts into relation "are" in the sense of natural material being (the *Real* according to Husserl). We can say about it only that it "is valid" and that this "validity" is not derivative from some other, more original phenomenon: just "as little as we can say how it happens that anything *is* or *occurs*, so little can we explain how it comes about that a truth has *Validity*."[43]

Plato did not attribute to the ideas a reality similar to the reality of things, as many falsely believe; he wanted to teach only that "the validity of truths as such, apart from the question whether they can be established in relation to any object in the external world, as its mode of being, or not; the eternally self-identical significance of Ideas, which always are what they are, no matter whether or not there are things which by participation in them make them manifest in this external world, or whether there are spirits which by thinking them, give them the reality of a mental event."[44]

But because there was no Greek term other than *ousia* to designate the idea, he opened the door to a misunderstanding with great consequences. He was therefore led to use the expression *ontos on* to designate the really valid truth in its distinction from a pretended truth. And when he assigns them to a supra-celestial intelligible space (*noetos, hyperouranios topos*), this is not at all the same as hypostasizing the ideas, but rather simply shows that they do not belong to the real world, to space, and expresses their pure validity in contrast to other modes of reality.[45]

Despite Lotze's admiration for Plato and for the philosophical prowess that led him to discover universal truths that are not of the order of real being, but that nevertheless regulate the comportment of things, Lotze must nevertheless recognize an "imperfection" in the Platonic theory of the ideas, which underscores the artificial character of the interpretation he gives of it. This imperfection consists, in Lotze's opinion, in the fact that the Platonic ideas are concepts, whereas truths are essentially propositions—that is, relations of concepts. In effect, "they cannot be transferred to single concepts because none of them contains in itself an affirmation or assertion [*Behauptung*]."[46]

Recognizing universal truth, consenting or saying yes to it, supposes that it has the propositional form of judgment, whereas the isolated concept contains no affirmation and has only one meaning that cannot be considered as valid outside of the proposition of which it is but one element. Plato thus did not see that the fundamental concepts of his world of ideas necessarily had to be propositions. But, Lotze adds, he is not alone: Kant committed the same error. Although he had been the first to claim that "thinking is judging," he nevertheless developed, on the basis of the table of judgments, a theory of the pure forms of thought in the form of a table of categories—that is, of isolated concepts. In contrast, and in a manner more Fichtean than Kantian, Lotze gives himself the task, at the end of the second chapter, of looking for "the first fundamental propositions of knowledge," to which it will then be possible "to subordinate the multiplicity of ideas."[47]

The concern in this limited and merely introductory exposition was simply to examine in some detail Lotze's interpretation of the Platonic ideas as "validities." We may deduce from this analysis that Lotze clearly overlays onto Platonic thought elements foreign to it, borrowed from Cartesian and Fichtean subjective idealism.

As a conclusion, let us content ourselves with bringing this partial reading of the third book of Lotze's *Logic* back to the general problematic of objectivity. What does *Geltung*, validity, mean? Not only the particular mode of reality attributed to truth as expressed in propositional form, but also the objectivity of this truth as it is in itself, independent of the intended real object and the intending mind. This "in itself" of the true proposition constitutes the proposition as an "object of knowledge," according to Rickert. Yet this implies that the meaning of knowledge is fundamentally modified and that the relation of the knowing to the known changes direction. The objective validity of knowledge no longer derives from the adequation of the intellect to the thing, but uniquely from the identical, permanent, stable character of the contents of our representations. Validity (in the sense of universality—that is, validity for all thinking minds) is now grounded on this identity of truth in itself. A proposition is true not because it is thought identically by everyone, but rather because all thinking minds necessarily "recognize" it as such. Its character as a "truth in itself" grounds its objectivity and its universality, and not the contrary. Yet Husserl will break with this notion of "truth in itself" and with the "logicism" it implies after his idealist "turn" of 1905–7, which will lead him to fall in with the "moderns" and to think the "correlation" of noesis and noema as the correlation of objectivity and intersubjectivity.

Nothing stops us from arguing, as Heidegger did in his Winter Semester 1925–26 course, that with the *Logical Investigations*, Husserl rejoins Aristotle's theory of the reciprocal opposition of the known and the knower, and thus begins to escape the impasse to which the modern notion of object leads—the neo-Kantian impasse of the dissolution of the object in the notion of a "value" of truth with Windelband and Rickert—not at the level of the *Prolegomena*, where he follows Lotze and understands truth as validity, but rather at the level of the sixth *Investigation*, where a more profoundly phenomenological idea of truth sees the light of day—namely, that of the identity of the intentional and the intuited. For, as Heidegger underlines, with the Lotzian theory of *Geltung*, the final stage of the decadence of the question of truth is not yet achieved. That would require the radicalization of the notion of validity in value (*Wert*). Thus knowledge will subsequently no longer depend on one of the modes of reality distinguished by Lotze, which implies that its "object" will have become the "value" that the human subject recognizes in it. Thus philosophy, which has now become *Kulturphilosophie*, now no longer treats reality, but rather diverse values corresponding to diverse modalities of human behavior. This is why Windelband and Rickert will be led to see a "valuing" behavior in theoretical comportment itself and a system of values in Kantian philosophy, the three *Critiques* respectively concerning theoretical, practical, and esthetic values.[48]

2

The Project of a Pure Logical Grammar
Husserl

When we ask about the meaning and genealogy of the notion of a "philosophical grammar," we cannot but linger for a while over the fourth of Husserl's *Logical Investigations*, entitled "The Difference between Independent and Dependant Significations and the Idea of a Pure Grammar."[1] We can say, just as Heidegger does in his 1916 *Habilitationsschrift* on "The Doctrine of the Categories and of Meaning in Duns Scotus," that in our epoch, Husserl "restored honor to the idea of a pure grammar and showed that there are a priori laws of meaning that disregard the objective validity of meanings."[2] On the same page, Heidegger cites a passage from the introduction to the fourth *Investigation*, which reads:

> Modern grammar thinks it should build exclusively on psychology and other empirical sciences. As against this, we see that the old idea of a *universal*, or even an *a priori grammar*, has unquestionably acquired a foundation and definite sphere of validity, from our pointing out that there are a priori laws which determine the possible forms of meaning.[3]

We know that the attempts to establish a universal grammar had been multiplied since the Middle Ages and that this idea has taken on a new dimension in the framework of modern linguistics, particularly Noam Chomsky's research and his theory of a transformational generative grammar, in which he sees "a modern and more explicit version of Port-Royal's theory."[4] Husserl himself refers rather generally to the seventeenth-century French grammarians, but specifically mentions both Humboldt and Duns

Scotus (which is to say Thomas of Erfurt, since we know today that the *Tractatus de modis significandi sive grammatica speculativa*,[5] which medievalists had attributed to that "subtle doctor" Duns Scotus, is in fact the work of Thomas of Erfurt).[6] In this regard, we must also underline the fact that the young Heidegger was interested in the problems of contemporary logic (as demonstrated by his 1914 dissertation on "The Doctrine of Judgment in Psychologism," itself inspired directly by Husserl's *Prolegomena to Pure Logic*), which is why he became interested in scholastic thought, and in particular its logic, in which he discovers some phenomenological elements. Scholastic logic is not merely a "remake" of Aristotelian syllogistic logic, but is instead, in Husserlian terms, a formal apophantic logic—that is, a mode of transcendental reflection on the conditions of possibility for all language and all meaning.

Now, what characterizes the Husserlian undertaking is that it poses the problem in a new way, without relying on the tradition for support. In this regard, the principal idea of the fourth *Investigation* is that all formal logic in the current sense—that is, the logic of validity (a term Husserl borrowed from Lotze), which obeys the principle of noncontradiction, which itself seeks to avoid counter-sense (*Widersinn*) or formal absurdity and regulates formal or objective truth—presupposes a logic of meaning that prevents non-sense (*Unsinn*) and that is not concerned with objective validity, but instead only with the a priori laws that establish the conditions for the unity of meaning. There is thus a logic and laws of meaning presupposed by what we normally call logic and logical laws (which themselves concern the object, not its meaning). Husserl calls this sphere of laws, which leaves aside objectivity, a pure morphology of meanings, a pure logical grammar, or later, in the *Formal and Transcendental Logic*, a formal apophantic logic. In Husserlian language, the object of formal apophantic logic (from the Greek *apophansis*, "assertion") is the proposition qua simple meaning and not the proposition qua an assertion with objective validity.[7] The latter belongs to the purview of formal ontology, which is the objective correlate of formal apophantic logic. These two disciplines taken together constitute formal logic.[8] It is worth noting that nearly thirty years after the *Logical Investigations*, in the period of the *Formal and Transcendental Logic*, Husserl seldom speaks of pure grammar, but this certainly does not imply that he had abandoned the idea of a universal grammar (in the *Cartesian Meditations*, for example, written in the same period [1929], Husserl places pure grammar next to pure logic, ranking them among the a priori sciences that had been made possible by phenomenology); rather, what it implies is that his route into logical problems no longer passes through a meditation on language, as had been the case in the *Logical Investigations*.[9] Formal apophantic logic is here constituted by the pure morphology of judgments: the term "judgment" has replaced "meaning," implying that the perspective is now strictly logical, since judgment is the logical correlate of the notion of object, whereas meaning is normally the correlate of the notion of expression, as is made very clear in the first *Investigation* (on "Expression and Meaning," *Ausdruck und Bedeutung*).

The first *Investigation* proposes to establish the juncture between pure logic and language. As Husserl notes in the "Introduction," it is important in the framework of this investigation to consider the grammatical aspect of logical lived experience,[10] precisely because "objects which pure logic seeks to examine are, in the first instance, given to it in grammatical clothing."[11] Because "we naturally tend to seek logical distinctions behind expressed grammatical distinctions," we must clarify the relation between expression and meaning, and we must distinguish those cases where the analysis of meanings coincides with the grammatical analysis from those cases where the parallelism of thought and language breaks down.[12] Already in the framework of this first investigation, Husserl invokes the difference between non-sense (*Unsinn*) and counter-sense (*Widersinn*)—a distinction that separates what arises from the logic of meaning from what arises from the logic of validity—specifically when the concern is to show that meaning is not the object to which expression corresponds (which is Frege's point of view)[13] and that the absence of the object is not the same as the absence of meaning (which is Sigwart's point of view).[14] The limit-case of non-sense shows that an expression without meaning is not, properly speaking, an expression (for example, "Green is or"). But the other limit-case of counter-sense shows that there is not necessarily an object wherever there is meaning: "square circle" has a meaning, but it is a priori impossible to make it correspond to an object. We therefore see that meaning is placed, so to speak, "between" expression and the object and that the object is its logical correlate. For if in 1900 the analysis of language provides access to logical problems, this implies that the emphasis will be placed on the correlation of meaning and object.

The theme of the fourth *Investigation* is consequently not the edification of a universal grammar, but rather of a pure grammar capable of serving as a foundation for logic. Husserl specifies this in the 1913 second edition of the *Logical Investigations* by underlining that it would be preferable to amend the expression "pure grammar," which had been used in the first edition, in favor of the expression "pure logical grammar" [*reinlogische Grammatik*]:

> In the first edition, I spoke of "pure grammar," a name conceived and expressly devised to be analogous to Kant's "pure science of nature."

> Since it cannot, however, be said that pure formal semantic theory comprehends the entire a priori of general grammar—there is, e.g., a peculiar a priori governing relations of mutual understanding among minded persons, relations very important for grammar—talk of "pure logical grammar" is to be preferred.[15]

And in Note 2, which immediately follows, Husserl adds:

> After what has been said, no one would imagine that there could be a "universal" grammar in the sense of a universal science comprehending all particular grammars as contingent specifications.

Defining the pure theory of meanings as "pure grammar" could, in effect, be the source of various misunderstandings. As René Schérer notes in his book on *La phénoménologie des "Recherches logiques" de Husserl*, "we thought that Husserl was proposing a pure grammatical a priori, so we took him to task, either for logicizing language or for confusing the rules of grammar with the rules of logic."[16]

The first reproach had been specifically addressed to Husserl by Anton Marty in his 1908 book *Untersuchungen zur Grundlegung der allgemeinen Grammatik und Sprachphilosophie* (Investigations on the Foundation of General Grammar and Philosophy of Language), to which Husserl responded by adding the qualifier "logical" to the expression "pure grammar." For Marty, the grammatical, which arises from the empirical-psychological, had to be distinguished from the logical, which is invariable; and even if one could delineate a general grammar by examining different spoken languages, this general grammar would in no way be a priori, nor could it be understood as the pre-given framework of an ideal language. Husserl, on the other hand, feels closer to Humboldt's position,[17] which does not separate linguistic form from the cognitive act animating it, and which sees the originary layer of meaning in the inner linguistic form, given that spoken language cannot be reduced to a pure system of signs and that it carries a worldview within itself. Husserl's response to Marty, and to anyone who calls the "logico-grammatical parallelism" into question,[18] is that his delimitation of the logical sphere is too narrow, restricted only to the logic of validity, which leads him to demote logico-grammatical knowledge to the domain of the psychology of language:

> Nothing has so much confused the discussions of the question of the correct relation of logic to grammar as the constant confusion of two logical spheres, sharply distinguished by us as lower and upper, and characterized by way of their negative counterparts—the spheres of

nonsense and of formal absurdity respectively. The logical sphere, in the sense of the upper sphere oriented towards formal truth and objectivity, is certainly irrelevant to grammar. This is not true of all logic in general.[19]

This "logic in general" characterizes the sphere of pure logical grammar, whose rules, to the extent that they merely exclude non-sense, establish what has always been understood as self-evident. But *Selbstverständlichkeit*, the character of banal evidence, and its lack of practical utility for the lower sphere of logic must not obscure its importance for a philosophical point of view because, as Husserl emphasizes, "it is precisely behind the obvious that the hardest problems lie hidden, and this is so much so, in fact, that philosophy may be paradoxically, but not unprofoundly, called the science of the trivial."[20]

Only philosophers deal with the a priori, with the discovery of truths so fundamental that other sciences take them to be self-evident. Marty's objection thus arises from this "blindness" to ideas that prevents him from seeing the universality of the meaning-conferring act, which the linguist foregoes because he is interested only in the system of signs that comprise languages. But we must underline yet again that the pure morphology that Husserl considers does not encompass the whole of the a priori arising from universal grammar and that he judges it necessary to reinvigorate the idea of an a priori grammar (which had been abandoned by the era's linguists, who were too fixated on semiology and the empirical methods of comparative grammar) because he wants to react against the hegemony of psychology and reanimate the philosophical interest in the meaning of the a priori, which was threatened with extinction. This is why he takes "in large part fact and cause as the old doctrine of a general and reasoned grammar" that has the merit of distinguishing the purely grammatical or a priori (that is, ideal) form from the empirical form of language.[21] The pure morphology of meanings exposes this "ideal framework" (*ideales Gerüst*), which is "absolutely stable," even though it manifests itself more or less perfectly in empirical clothing, and which, were it not taken into account as "self-evident," would render general linguistics itself unable to rise to the level of a science, for science would then be unable to compare empirical languages or to inquire, for example, how Latin, Chinese, or German express "the" plural, "the" not, "the" categorical proposition, etc.[22] Husserl insists on the importance for linguistics to "possess the insight that the foundations of speech are not only to be found in physiology, psychology, and the history of culture, but also in the a priori."[23] In order to avoid any confusion with empirical grammar and to dissipate the misunderstanding that attributes him with the thesis of a logic based in linguistics, Husserl will call this a priori foundation of language "the grammatical" in the *Formal and Transcendental Logic:*

> It is therefore not without reason that theory of the forms of signification was characterized in my *Logical Investigations* as the "grammar of pure logic." And in a certain manner, furthermore, it is also not without reason that people often say that formal logic has let itself be guided by grammar. In the case of the theory of forms, however, this is not a reproach but a necessity—provided that, for guided by grammar (a word intended to bring to mind de facto historical languages and their grammatical description), guidance by the grammatical itself is substituted.[24]

We thus see clearly here that the consideration of pure grammar is restricted to the logical sphere of the a priori, since—from the "pure grammar" in the first edition of the *Logical Investigations,* to the "pure logical grammar" in the second edition, and then on to the "grammatical" in the *Formal and Transcendental Logic*—grammar has been elevated to the level of the analysis of the formal conditions of thought. Now that we have clearly seen the level where Husserl situates the task of logical grammar, it is time to define it more specifically—that is, to dive into a reading of the fourth *Investigation.*

In order to enter into the fourth *Investigation*, we must first understand that the question of pure logical grammar is an application of the logic of whole and parts, developed in the third *Investigation*:

> if we ask why our language allows certain verbal combinations and disallows others, we are to a large extent referred to contingent linguistic habits, to matters of mere fact concerning language, which develop in one way in one speech-community and another way in another. In part, however, we encounter the essential difference of independent and non-dependent, and closely involved therewith, the a priori laws of the combination and transformation of meaning, laws which must be more or less revealed in every developed language, both in its grammar of forms and in the related class of grammatical incompatibilities.[25]

Remember that the title of the fourth *Investigation* is "The difference between independent and dependent meanings and the idea of pure grammar." There is a narrow correspondence between the formal categories of the object (which was the theme of the third *Investigation*, concerning the difference between independent and dependent objects) and the formal categories of meaning, between "objective" logic and the logic of meaning, implying that the distinctions established concerning objects in the third *Investigation* will be directly transposed into the domain of meaning.[26] There is certainly a parallelism between meaning and expression, conforming to what was established in the first *Investigation*, but the object of the fourth *Investigation* is not the semantic relation itself, not the relation of signified to signifier; instead, the object is the logical problem of the a priori conditions, the structural laws of the semiological system of language insofar as language permits a meaningful discourse. Husserl clearly claims that "every developed language" obeys these laws, which does not imply that some languages are more logical than others, but rather that every language functions according to a logic. The existence of a narrow relation between thought and language (as Humboldt claims) or between logic and language (as Husserl claims) does not imply the existence of a separate layer of meanings "in themselves" or of an eminently logical language that would serve as a model for all other languages.[27] With respect to language, as Schérer correctly emphasizes, we must guard against confusing the distinction established in the *Prolegomena* between the normativity and the ideality of the laws.[28] Husserl's concern is thus to conduct a phenomenological study of the pure forms of meaning, which implies that not only the ideal unity of meaning, but also its subjective correlate (the meaning-conferring act) be taken into account.

Now that the properly phenomenological—and not merely semantic or formal-logical—level of the fourth *Investigation* has been indicated, I propose simply to give a very general glimpse of its content.[29] A linguistic expression—whether it be dependent, as is the case of a word that has a syntactic function in a sentence, or independent, as is the case of a sentence or a proposition—is an ensemble of phonemes whose unity is based in its meaning; inversely, a series of phonemes without meaning or unitary sense is not a linguistic expression. A nominal or adjectival expression (substance or predicate) is a dependent expression; only a complete proposition is an independent expression, and the first task of logical grammar is to establish the pure categories of meaning in their relations of dependence and independence. What is important at this level is to understand that the linguistic expression is a "whole" constituted of parts that are members or *moments* of this whole,[30] rather than discrete elements linked together in a merely de facto manner. The members or moments of a whole are inseparable from one another and from the whole: such is the case, for example, with the extension, surface, or color of a physical object of perception. Husserl views color and surface, or surface and extension, as united by a priori laws given in perception (an a priori that must be "synthetic" or "material," since the idea of color is not analytically contained in that of surface).[31] Such an a priori law is not the result of a cultural conditioning or an empirical psychological fact; it is a law based on the very meaning of color and extension: that color implies surface, and that surface implies extension, is an a priori law of the constitution of objects of perception, and no perception can contravene this law because the law is a part of the meaning of the perceptual object.

It is possible to apply this notion of the "whole" taken from the third *Investigation* to grammar by noting that an independent meaning or a proposition is a formal structural whole constituted by parts linked together by a priori laws regulating their meaning-function within the unified ensemble that the proposition itself is. What we therefore understand in an independent linguistic expression of the type "S is P" is that the parts are linked together by laws of composition, which we call *syntax*. The dependent terms have a unified nucleus of meaning, but this meaning is incomplete and needs to be completed in accordance with certain laws if it is to be integrated into the meaning-function of the complete proposition. In brief, a sentence will be grammatically well-formed and therefore potentially meaningful if and only if certain rules of the correct integration of partial meanings into a total meaning are observed. These rules are the laws of logical grammar, and they are presupposed by the laws regulating the objective validity or the truth of the propositions. The concern at this level is to distinguish non-sense from the counter-sense that constitutes a partial domain of what is endowed with meaning: "The combination 'a round square' really yields a unified meaning, having its mode of 'existence' or being in *the realm of ideal meanings, but it is apodictically evident* that no existent object can correspond to such an existent meaning. But if we say 'a round or,' 'a man and is,' etc., there exist no meanings which correspond to such verbal combinations as their expressed sense."[32]

And Husserl clearly characterizes the difference between *Unsinn* and *Widersinn* in section 12 of the fourth *Investigation*. In the case of *Widersinn*, the object does not exist, but the meaning does: "names such as 'wooden iron' and 'round square' or sentences such as 'all squares have five angles' are names or sentences as genuine as any."[33] But in the case of *Unsinn*, "the possibility of unitary meaning itself excludes the possible coexistence of certain partial meanings in itself."[34] Here, meaning itself can exist (and we can possess it) only as an indirect representation of a certain unitary meaning awakened in us by the words assembled; yet at the same time, we have apodictic evidence that such a meaning cannot exist. The laws of logical grammar aim only at guaranteeing the coherence of meaning, which is the necessary foundation for the objective validity of propositions—that is, for their logical validity in the strong sense.

The second task of logical grammar, after establishing the pure categories of meaning, concerns the laws of the composition of partial meanings into well-formed wholes. At the limit, no word can be taken independently of its relations to its possible grammatical functions within the complete sentence. When words are combined to form sentences, they are given certain syntactical forms, allowing for their integration into the whole. For this, a number of primitive forms of connection (such as attribute, conjunction, disjunction, etc.) and a number of purely syntactical forms (such as the subject-form and the form of the predicate) are necessary. This is the basis for the fundamental distinction between syntactical matter and form and for the recognition that the propositional form presupposes the forms of the subject and the predicate. The same term ("paper"), taken first as the subject of a proposition ("this *paper* is white"), and then as a predicate ("I write on *paper*"), preserves the same meaning even though its syntactical form has changed because this identical element preserves the reference to the same thing.[35] The meaning of the proposition, or what Husserl will call the state of the thing, the *Sachverhalt*, depends on the meaning of its components, which implies that the proposition is a categorical unity of a higher degree and that it is "grounded" on the meaning of its component parts, even though it gives them the syntactical form necessary for the production of a unified meaning. There are thus an infinite number of syntactical materials, even if the number of syntactical forms is limited. The unity of syntactical form and material is the *syntagma*. Each and every member of the proposition is a syntagma, and the proposition itself is a syntagma of a higher degree. Complex modal forms are constructed on the basis of the matrix "S is P," which is itself composed of infra-propositional syntagmae (for example, "is S P?" or "If S is P . . . ," etc.). It goes without saying that when the word appears in a sentence, its proper syntactical form has already been modified because a purely nonsyntactical material cannot be found in any process of language and because the pure material of an expression can be attained only through an ideal analysis. For example, if I want to examine the syntactical material of the sentence "the tree is green," I obtain "tree" and "green." But these are not totally unformed materials because if I vary "green" in the diverse syntactical forms that it can take on, I obtain a nucleus of nonsyntactical meanings (*Kernform*) that remain the same throughout its diverse syntactical functions. There are nonsyntactical forms of the substantive and of the adjectival.[36] Yet at this presyntactical level, it is still possible to distinguish between form and matter: if we compare two nonsyntactical forms, for example "red" and "redness," we discover that an identical material has taken on two different forms—namely, that of the substantive and that of the adjectival. These forms "animate" a pure *Kernstoff*, a material nucleus, which arises from pre-predicative experience and which constitutes material "in the amplified sense."[37] The union of this *Kernstoff* and *Kernform*, this nonsyntactical material and nonsyntactical form, constitutes the nonsyntactical material formed by the pure laws of syntax (*Kerngebild*). These are abstractions, and thus components dependent on the unity of the lower degree, the syntactical material of the sentence—the word. Syntactical form is thus something more general and formal than the word. The basic nonsyntactical forms are the substantive and the adjectival, but Husserl grants a "remarkable privilege" to the substantive.[38] Every adjective can be substantivized, but there is no adjectivalization "in the proper sense" of the substantive. Husserl refers here to the operation of substantivation that allows for the transformation of an adjective into a substantive (for example, "red" into "redness"), even though the "modified" meaning of this substantive continues to base itself on the meaning of the adjective from which it is derived.

The third task of pure logic is thus the constitution of a closed or self-contained system of basic syntactical forms and of a minimal number of independent elementary laws for combining these forms. It is here that we find the notion of a grammatical "operation" permitting the generation of sentences.

1. The fundamental forms of judgments or propositions allow laws to be established, which in turn allow subordinate forms of judgment to be derived by reiteration. So the form "S is P" is more original than the form "SP is Q," which can be obtained by converting P into an attribute. Husserl calls these operations whereby the predicate is transformed into a substantive "nominalization."[39] For example, the proposition "this paper is white," which has the form "S is P," can be transformed into the proposition "this white paper is in front of me," which has the form "SP is Q," and then transformed yet again into the proposition "this white paper in front of me is torn," which has the form "(SP)Q is R."
2. But it is possible to modalize the primitive form of the judgment "S is P" as, for example, the modals "if S is P," "because S is P," or "S may be P," etc. The process of modalization does not essentially transform the fundamental structure of judgment, which is merely modified by "doxic" qualities (the hypothetical, the optative, the causal, etc.). The task of logical grammar is simply to discover

the minimal number of laws of derivation and modalization of the primitive apophansis "S is P," and thus of taking account of all the possible forms of judgment that can make sense.

On the basis of this too brief and very formal exposition of logical grammar, and in order to conclude, I would like to raise a few questions. Let me first take up the questions posed by René Schérer at the close of his analysis of the fourth *Investigation*: "Can the idea of a general grammar escape the danger of transposing categories valid only in one language to all languages?" Because one can wonder whether "claiming that correspondence is always possible is not also to accept a confusion, initiated by Aristotle, of subjugating logic to grammar.[40]

To avoid falling into an arbitrary apriorism, which would moreover be a relapse into empiricism where a factual language would be illegitimately erected as an ideal model, we must clearly distinguish the plane where the grammarian is situated from the plane where the phenomenologist is situated and distinguish the level of the formal categories of language and of its parts of discourse (noun, verb, case, modality) from the level of syntactical functions (subject, predicate, object). Certain languages may indeed not have the formal categories of our languages and yet still possess the same syntactical moments. The semantic plane must also therefore be distinguished from the logical-syntactical plane.

There is, however, a certain correspondence between the phenomenological and the structural-linguistic analyses.[41] An example is Chomsky's transformational generative grammar, provided we do not keep its "psychologism"—the idea of linguistic universals referring back to a biological constitution of the human organism. For his notion of "linguistic competence" can and should indeed be separated from his Cartesianism and theory of "innate ideas." We can view that Chomsky's distinction between deep structure and surface structure corresponds to Husserl's distinction between empirical grammars and what he calls "the grammatical." Chomsky himself distinguishes the laws arising from deep structures (the a priori laws of meaning for Husserl) from the laws of transformation that differ with each language and that affect only surface structure. Only the first are "formal universals," the universal conditions that prescribe the form of human language.

Husserl insisted on the priority of the category of the substantive not only because the predicate can be converted into an attribute, but also because the proposition itself can be converted into a substantive and become the substrate of new judgments. The priority of the substantive thus expresses a fundamental structure of the logic of discourse. Here we have an analogy with Port-Royal's theory, which recognizes the same propositional structure as Husserl's, and which considers that all surface modification has the proposition as its foundation.[42] Chomsky relies on Port-Royal's *Grammar* and *Logic* in order to claim that nominal phrases precede verbal phrases in the deep structure.[43] There is thus a priority of nouns over verbs and, in this respect, a certain unity in the aims of both Chomsky and Husserl.

Yet it is precisely on this importance granted to nominalization that I would like to bring to bear one last question. In the fourth *Investigation*, Husserl already showed that this operation rests on the possibility of a modification of meaning (*Bedeutungsmodifikation*) whereby any word and any expression in general can be substituted for a categorematic ensemble, and he insisted on the fact that these modifications of meanings are part of the grammatical structure of every language. In this regard, he evoked the Scholastic *suppositio materialis*, which consists in what every expression can present through its own name and thus itself be named as a grammatical phenomenon.[44] This reference points us back to how the nominalists had understood the meaning-function, as a *suppositio* that, at least in the form that it had taken on in Ockham, implies that *dictio* (or *terminus*) *supponit pro re*—that the word or the concept is substituted for the thing. And it is certain that "every language" makes use of such a "*suppositio*" to the extent that it is meaningful—that is, to the extent that it aims at and "means-to-say" the "thing itself."[45] But we can wonder if every language is able to let this "*suppositio*" appear explicitly in its inner structure.

This is precisely what Johannes Lohmann examines in an article that is already quite old (but which has been largely overlooked, it seems to me, at least in France) concerning "Martin Heidegger's Ontological Difference, and Language."[46] Johannes Lohmann determines that Indo-European languages make use of the supposition (*supponierende Sprachen*) insofar as their nominal and verbal forms differentiate between a word stem, expressing the concept, and a flexional ending, expressing the relation of the concept to the object given in the context of each expression (inflected languages). In the grammatical form of words (nouns and verbs), these languages express the "ontological difference" between Being and beings—that is, the "supposition" or transformation of the simple conceptual meaning of the word into an objectively grounded meaning. In Indo-European languages, the ontological differentiation that determines the logico-ontological structure of the predicative proposition is materialized expressly in the verb "to be," the central focus from which Western philosophical thought has developed since the Greeks. For this verb[47] unites within itself the existential meaning and the purely logical, "synthetic" meaning of the copula.[48] Yet there are languages that know neither the verb "to be" nor the predicative structure of the proposition. This is notably the case with Chinese, on which Lohmann dwells at length. The Chinese word, which is a purely conceptual expression, has no need to receive formal objectification in the proposition, no need for the "supposition" or for the "syntactical form." The word thus remains in "ontological indifference," and is therefore diametrically opposed to the word in Indo-European languages. However, because Chinese places its directing concept at the center of the sentence, it ends up creating a proposition whose structure resembles the verbal phrase. Syntactical forms therefore express by means of the external relation of concepts, whereas this relation is internal in Indo-European languages. And so, just as Humboldt had believed, we are dealing with two opposed realizations of the possibilities of human language—which are also indissolubly possibilities of being human—each of which is perfect in its own way.

By emphasizing the universality of nominalization, Husserl thus had the merit, as J. N. Mohanty points out,[49] of making us aware of the necessity of this operational law, which had been viewed by many philosophers since Nietzsche and his critique of metaphysical grammar as a falsification leading to the postulation of substrates and imaginary entities. This necessity is effectively the necessity of philosophical thought insofar as it is born of and remains inseparable from the structure of certain determinate languages. The *reflection* on what human language is no doubt requires that the predicative form of the proposition appear as an a priori structure. But this does not at all mean that every language is effectively structured according to this model, even if a language can always be translated into it: the example of Chinese shows that this structure is expressed by means that do not refer to morphology—that is, by means that are not reflected in spoken language. We can thus wonder whether pure logical grammar is a mere product of reflection like every empirical grammar and whether the "essence" of a language that it discovers is, like every *eidos*, posterior to the relation whose meaning it unveils, or as Merleau-Ponty already emphasizes in his critique of the early Husserl's phenomenology of language, posterior to life and to the deep *diachrony* of language.[50]

3

The Problem of Pre-Predicative Experience
Husserl

From the *Logical Investigations* to the *Cartesian Meditations*, Husserl always saw in phenomenology a new "critique of reason," giving himself the task of "the elucidation of knowledge"[1]—the title of the sixth *Investigation*—redefining it later, in the transcendental perspective developed in the *Paris Lectures* in 1929, as a "theory of knowledge."[2] Beyond this essential definition of phenomenology as phenomenology of knowledge, the permanence of the theme of the foundation (*Fundierung*) of the formal sciences must be underlined, as we see it throughout Husserl's entire itinerary, from the *Philosophy of Arithmetic* to *Experience and Judgment* via the *Logical Investigations* and the *Formal and Transcendental Logic*. From his first work onward, and even before the term "phenomenology" was invoked, Husserl's concern was to thematize the field of the formal, to describe its laws, and to trace its genesis by leading theoretical formations back to the originary experiences from which they drew their meaning. It is true that this "genetic" investigation had initially been characterized using Brentano's vocabulary as a "psychology," so in this regard it is essentially important that in the Introduction to his manifesto on genetic phenomenology (that is, *Experience and Judgment*), Husserl explicitly reiterates his refusal to characterize his genetic problematic as psychological because the project of a genetic psychology is fundamentally distinct from a genetic phenomenology of judgment.[3] As Husserl strongly emphasizes, the concern of a genetic phenomenology is to return to the most originary evidence of experience, which cannot be accomplished by means of psychology, even a pure psychology limited to the strict interiority of inner perception.[4] Such a psychology certainly has genetic pretensions, but even "in the best of cases" it can lead back only to "mundane" or "worldly" [*mondains*] subjective operations, to the lived experiences of subjects who are of our world, which is itself already the result of a history, and thus only to an experience that is already mediated by the idealizations arising from the modern natural sciences, the Galilean mathematization of nature. Psychology is therefore unable to achieve a return to properly originary experience because this return supposes an *Abbau*, a dismantling of these idealizations;[5] that is, it supposes nothing less than the methodical deconstruction of the *epistēmē* in order to lead it back to its originary source in *doxa*. For it is a question of legitimating the latter, under the name of pre-predicative experience,[6] and not considering it as a domain of evidence inferior in rank to science or judicative experience. This does not mean, however, a devaluation of science; the concern is rather to elucidate (*aufklären*) the hidden presuppositions on which scientific idealizations rest. Husserl therefore does not propose to submit the content of exact knowledge to a new examination by means of his regressive inquiry (*Rückfrage*), but rather to procure for us a full understanding of the scientific ideal, which implies that he retrace the total itinerary leading from pre-predicative evidence to predicative evidence, and that he return to the origin of the idealized world itself.[7] Yet this origin of the pre-given world, which contains within itself an entire sedimented history, is not immediately accessible by reflection, but is only indirectly implicated in the deposits and sediments that give the world its current, actual meaning. This origin is also subjective, but the subjectivity concerned here is a "veiled subjectivity," not actually disclosable, which can appear only at the end of a deconstruction, precisely because it is at the origin of idealizing constructions—that is, because it is an "operant" (*leistende*) subjectivity, bearing within itself all the operations through which the world is what it is for us. This original subjectivity is therefore not psychological, but "transcendental"—that is, it leads us back to the ultimate source of all formations of knowledge.[8] Consequently, the project of a genesis of logic must be given its full scope from the outset. The genealogy of formal logic that Husserl undertakes in the form of an elucidation of predicative judgment constitutes only a part of a much larger task—namely, the task of the phenomenology of constitution, whose goal is to exhume the hidden origin of the world—not just our factual world or the real world, but any possible world in general.

Experience and Judgment, which is one of Husserl's last texts dedicated to the problem of the genealogy of logic, can certainly be considered as a prolongation of the *Formal and Transcendental Logic*, and more specifically, as the systematic implementation of the genetic investigations of section II ("From Formal Logic to Transcendental Logic") in which the evidence of pre-predicative experience was already opened as the ground of judgment. In section 86 of this text, Husserl had noted that truth does not belong exclusively and properly to the predicative sphere, but rather, insofar as it is the truth of existence, is already part of the intentionality of experience. And his concern had been to seek the origin of the superior, categorial (and thus conceptual and grammatical) syntax (with which the formal analytic is concerned) in the "first syntaxes in themselves" of the judgment of experience.[9] But it seems that there is a clear difference of level between these two texts, since the originary layer of the *Lebenswelt* is not yet the ultimate ground in which logic, as conceived in the last chapters of *Formal and Transcendental Logic*, must be founded. For *Experience and Judgment*—whose editor, Ludwig Landgrebe, relates in the foreword the "complicated history of its genesis"[10] and reconstitutes the multiple stages of its elaboration from 1910–14 (dates of the oldest manuscripts) to 1935 (concerning the preparation of the introduction)—integrates the results of Husserl's very last investigations—namely, those exposed in the *Crisis of European Sciences and Transcendental Phenomenology*. *Experience and Judgment* therefore represents an advance in understanding the genetic theme as the fundamental theme of Husserlian phenomenology, and, on the basis of this recognition, I would like now, in a merely indicative manner, to bring to the fore some axes of reflection that could serve as supports for one possible reading of this last text by Husserl.

The principal problems to be addressed by the total itinerary that Husserl proposes to follow and that leads him from pre-predicative experience to predicative thought and to general judgment seem to me to be those of the relation of passivity to activity, of the individual to the general, and of the temporal to the supratemporal.

I will begin with this last pair, temporal and supratemporal, because it may be the problem that best allows us to understand the opposition between originary experience and the provision of knowledge. Husserl's concern is to take account of the irruption of the immanent but irreal and supratemporal moment of knowledge,[11] which remains identical across all of its real repetitions. It is the operation of objectification, an active operation of the ego, that creates such an identity in predication, and insofar as this identity is at the origin of the firm positing of beings, it alone constitutes a durable possession,[12] communicable and usable in a future beyond the momentary situation.[13]

It is a question therefore of understanding the passage from objectification, which has already taken place in pre-predicative experience and which ends up at the construction of "real" objects, to those objects in the strong or "pregnant" sense, which are "objectivities of understanding" or "categorial objectivities" produced in predicative activity. Husserl emphasizes that the principal difference between these two kinds of objects is a difference of temporality because "the necessary relation to time is always present" and "belongs originally to all objects."[14] But if the time of natural objects is objective time, then the time of the objectivities of understanding, which are not individualized as real objects in a point of time, is only a contingency of objective time, since their "absence from temporal situation" or "timelessness" allows for their identical production in different times. This is how Husserl allows us to understand the supratemporality of the objectivities of the understanding as omnitemporality—that is, in the end, as a mode of temporality.[15] For the "supratemporal" unity is not "outside of time," but traverses temporal multiplicity. We thus pass from pre-predicative experience and the real objects that it constitutes in objective time to a predicative experience whose irreal *Leistung* can be repeated in every moment.

To pass from pre-predicative experience to predication and general judgment is the same as passing from passivity to activity, from "passive doxa" to "logical spontaneity." This opposition is also less clear-cut than its usual, ordinary meaning leads us to believe. This is why Husserl proposes "a more radical conception of passivity than that entertained by naïve consciousness,"[16] because in contemplating there is already an active moment—namely, that of explication. "Passivity" in the proper sense must therefore be named a "pure affective pre-givenness," the "passive belief in being," or the "mere 'stimulus'" that precedes attention.[17] But there is more: "the distinction between passivity and activity is not inflexible."[18] These terms are, after all, mere instruments of description, and Husserl recognizes the existence of a passivity in activity itself, a passivity built on the very activity of apprehension. There is thus an entangling of activity and passivity such that one cannot factually distinguish them,[19] but instead only oppose them in a genetic point of view. Receptivity certainly precedes predicative spontaneity, but it is not something autonomous that happens prior to any properly so-called cognitive activity: in fact, the predicative can occur directly on the level of the receptive. The degrees distinguished by Husserl, comprising the major divisions of the text *Experience and Judgment* (pre-predicative experience, predication, general judgment), are therefore abstractions: the genetic order does not constitute a hierarchy or real chronology, and in this regard, the difficulty is specifically to disentangle the passive from the active, or the doxical from the logical built over it.

Finally, we must address the massive distinction between the individual and the general, which refers us to the last section of the text. For prepredicative experience delivers only individual substrates (or individual pluralities), and both the judgments based on them and the objectivities of understanding obtained from them contain only individual nuclei. If the genetic order is abstract, however, then this means that perception already tends to grasp what is perceived through general concepts and that the appearance of an individual object always occurs in the horizon of a typical generality. There is therefore also an entanglement of the individual and the general.

On the basis of this general framework, we may return to the very theme of *Experience and Judgment* and "clarify the essence of predicative judgment by enquiring into its origin."[20] The partial character of the investigations undertaken there must once again be underlined, in contrast to those in the *Formal and Transcendental Logic*. It is a matter of a local investigation, whereas the programmatic text of 1929 promises the larger project of a phenomenological elucidation of the origin of logic—that is, the project of a transcendental logic. The concern in *Experience and Judgment* is only to bring to light the genesis of the hierarchized forms of judgment. But this will allow us to see that the domain of logic is more vast than what traditional logic has in view and that logical activity is already sedimented in layers unseen by the tradition.[21] Because delineating a phenomenological concept of logic and of *logos* in the large sense, encompassing all objectifying activities of the ego no matter what they might be, is the distant goal of every one of Husserl's "genealogical" enterprises, the investigation therefore takes on the sense of an *Auseinandersetzung*, of an "explication" with the whole of the logical tradition.

Proceeding to a phenomenological clarification of the judgment practiced in the genetic perspective implies relating the considered formation (*Leistung*), the judgment, back to its original intentionality. Now, a judgment presents itself as a formation that can surely be studied like any other object, but whose specificity resides in the fact that it is traversed by an intentional aim: judgment is presumed meaning, a relation to a possible filling-in, to a state-of-things. Judgment thus presents itself from the start as a claim or "pretention to knowledge," which, as Husserl emphasizes, the logician cannot ignore: "if the logician really aims at a logic in the comprehensive and serious sense of the word, then his interest is directed towards the laws of the formation of judgments—the principles and rules of formal logic—not towards the mere rules of the game, but the rules which the constitution of forms must satisfy if any knowledge whatsoever is possible."[22]

These rules constitute only negative conditions because they are only formal conditions of the truth. The supplementary and properly positive conditions of truth must be sought on the side of subjectivity: "these supplementary conditions lie on the subjective side and concern the subjective characteristics of intuitibility, of self-evidence, and the subjective conditions of its attainment."[23] The term "self-evidence" (*Evidenz*) is used somewhat precipitously here, and we must not see this as a simple appeal to a "subjective" feeling of obviousness. The term here means only the *givenness* of the thing itself insofar as it is required in principle in every claim of knowledge: "if the striving for knowledge is directed toward an existent being, if it is the effort to formulate in judgment what and how the existent being is, then that being must have been given beforehand."[24] We thus understand that the problematic of logic is divided into a question of laws and forms on the one hand and, on the other, into a question of the subjective conditions of access to self-evidence.[25] But as we have already underlined, it is not a matter of a psychological subjectivity.[26] For when the "subjective" activity of cognition enters into play, "objects must already be represented, either in a void or self-given in intuition."[27] There are different modes of the givenness of objects, but cognition is successful only to the extent that the objects' mode of givenness is self-evidence—that is, self-givenness (*Selbstgegebenheit*): "As 'self-evident,' then, we designate *consciousness of any kind which is characterized relative to its object as self-giving this object in itself*."[28] We must emphasize here that self-evidence is in no way the miracle solution to the problem of knowledge, but rather the opening of a field of research and the name of a problem, because there are different modes of self-evident givenness, depending on the objects.[29]

What is clear in any case is that the self-evident givenness of the object does not necessitate the predicative form and that properly predicative self-evidence is seen to be founded on a more originary pre-predicative evidence. But saying this merely expresses a truism insofar as judgments of experience are concerned. On the other hand, the necessity of this return to the pre-predicative takes on all of its weight and significance when we see that it proves equally necessary for the logician's judgments, which are not judgments of experience. The logical as a whole must necessarily be reattached to the pre-predicative, for it must be shown that judgments of logical self-evidence "do not have as a content any free-floating 'truths in themselves,' " but that they are "based on a 'world' of substrates" and presuppose the originary self-evidence of pre-predicative givenness as its condition of possibility.[30] This necessity of reattaching logic to a worldly foundation—we imagine here Kant's critique of the Platonic dove in the introduction to the *Critique of Pure Reason*[31]—recalls the motif that lies at the very basis of the elaboration of the notion of categorial intuition in the sixth *Investigation*—that is, the necessity of founding the categorial on the sensible and of having accounted for the absurdity represented by the idea of a thought not based in sensibility—that is, of pure and autonomous intellect.[32]

Yet the most "originary" objective self-evidence is that of the individual. This is Husserl's thesis with respect to *Selbstgegebenheit*, which seems to apply only to the individual: "Experience in the first and most pregnant sense," he claims, "is accordingly defined as a direct relation to the individual."[33] The individual constitutes what he calls the "ultimate substrate" on which the activity of judgment in the broad sense is based. We see here that the conception of the object as something-in-general is again potentially too dependent on the predicative structure to be able to designate the level of originary self-evidence: "formal logic can state nothing more about an ultimate substrate than that it is something still categorically completely unformed. . . . At the same time, however, this implies that such a substrate can only be an individual object."[34] Husserl thus establishes that all generality refers back at least to a primitive logical activity and that it cannot be encountered at the most originary level. We are thus in the presence of a reiteration of the "tiered" character of the categorial.

Section 7 of the "Introduction" is dedicated to the analysis of pregivenness, understood as the "simple certainty" whereby objects are always already there for us; this "always already there" refers to an absolute "transcendental" past, to a "before knowledge," which may appear as *dynamis* only in the entelechy of knowledge. Here, within *pollakhos*, within the multiplicity of the meaning of being about which Aristotle spoke, it is not the categorial sense of being, but rather the meaning of being as *energeia* that is invoked: "we can also say that before every movement of cognition, the object of cognition is already present as a *dynamis* that will turn into entelechy."[35] Affection, however, as more originary than a taking-hold-of, does not pertain to a singular, isolated object. For if the object as "pre-given in simple certainty" is indeed *Ansatz und Anreiz der Erkenntnisbetätigung*, "that which puts in motion and elicits the activity of cognition," then this activity detaches the object from its co-present surrounding domain of *Vorgegebenheit*, of pre-givenness.[36] This field, as pre-given in passive belief and the basis from which the object affects, is what Husserl calls "world" (world in general), which he defines as the "ground of universal passive belief in being."[37] The question consequently arises: what is the relation of the ultimate substrate, which is the individual pre-given in originary self-evidence, and this universal ground of belief in the world, which is discovered in the already-there of its *Selbstverständlichkeit*, its self-evident being? If Husserl's analysis is initially oriented in relation to singular beings—and here we could oppose him to Heidegger, who sees in originary experience not an "individual" but rather a *Zeugganzheit*, an ensemble of tools, and a structure of reference, the isolated tool becoming a "theme" only in its absence or insufficiency[38]—this does not mean that the problematic of the world is merely added on later. On the contrary, it is clear here that the relation to the individual can take place only on the foundation of the world. This is exactly what makes the activity of cognition, which is given as a verification, appear: "the activity of cognition, of judgment, aims at examining whether they [beings] are truly such as they give themselves to be, as they are presumed in advance to be; whether they are truly of such and such a nature."[39] The activity of cognition passes from *Vermeinung*, from presumptive and passive intention, to *Meinung*, to the active intention of the existent being as such—from *dynamis* to *energeia*—in a verifiable, active repetition of the originary passivity in which the existing being was previously given to me: "for example, in looking at a book resting on a table, then I grasp something which for me is an existing being, something which, as already existing in advance, was already 'there,' 'in my study,' even though my attention was not yet directed toward it."[40]

Husserl thus notes that consciousness of the world is not of the same kind as consciousness of objects and that it is not obtained by an express act that would insert itself into the continuity of lived experiences, since all doxical acts positing the being of an object already presuppose consciousness of the world, which is always already "pre-given" in passive certainty. Now, this implies that the grasping of objects only ever occurs on the basis of a fore-knowing. As Husserl explains in section 8, there is a horizonal structure of all experience, as well as a latent knowledge of the singular thing, which can be explained by its internal and external horizons—that is, beyond what is directly given in it and around it: "In this way *a transcendence of sense* clings to every singular apperception" as potentiality, continually anticipating new singular realities.[41] Husserl consequently proposes to make this universal ground of all singular experiences appear as the world of experience given prior to any and every logical operation. This world is the "lifeworld," the *Lebenswelt*, in which we always already find ourselves.

Let us skip abruptly from section 7 to section 12, which provides the starting point (*Ansatz*) for the particular analyses arising from the limited and local inquiry of *Experience and Judgment*. He considers the distinction between simple and founded experiences and the necessity of returning to the simplest experiences, those lying at the very foundation of the life-world, which, as the world of experience in the concrete sense, contains not only pre-given objects but also layers of meaning stemming from logical operations. Experience in the broad sense refers to practical axiological activity and to the theoretical activity of judgment and knowledge, with practical activity and theoretical activity each equally "founded" on experience, in the narrow sense of pre-givenness: "practical activity, the positing of values, the judgment of value is as such dependent *on* pre-given objects,"[42] which implies that the originary "substrate" in question is not only the substrate of *theoria*, but also of a possible *praxis*: "for something to be given as useable, beautiful, alarming, terrifying, attractive, or whatever, it must be given in immediate sensuous experience as something present and sensuously apprehensible."[43] Against such a claim, one could raise an objection of a Heideggerian sort, which would see in the purely sensuous experience of presence (*Vorhandenheit*) or in "natural" pre-givenness (*Vorgegebenheit*) not the *foundation*, but rather the *derivative* of originary experience, which would be the experience of an immediate apprehension of sense. And it is true that Husserl tells us that "every simple experience, that is, every experience that has as its meaning of being the experience of a simple substrate, is *sensuous* experience—the existing substrate is a body."[44] And he claims that nature is "the lowest level" of our experiences, "that which founds all the others," and he defines originary sense-giving experience as external perception.[45]

But we must also be attentive to the "abstract" meaning of this construction of the "cultural" (axiological, practical, theoretical) over the sensuous: Husserl will indeed continually insist on the "abstract" character of the genetic order, which can be disclosed only by de-construction, and which thus refers to no "real" genesis or chronology. We see this in particular in the example Husserl gives of the perception of the tool and the perception of another's body, which both have the particularity of necessarily including an understanding of what is not given "corporally": "both cases presuppose a sensuous perception of the corporal element which founds the expression, and from there, the transition to a reflection which thus, mediately or immediately, confers a final certainty to a being-with of the human *qua* person (of the ego-like)."[46] In order to perceive the alter ego or the tool, both sensuous perception and reflection are necessary; but as Husserl indicates in a footnote, the kind of reflection concerned is very curious, as it does not have the "objectifying" character of the look turning back toward lived experiences from objects, but is rather simply synonymous with "mediateness," since the "cultural" or the "subjective" is not perceptible. Because this reflection is not simply added on to sensuous perception, it is not a "subjective element," is not "simply or immediately experienceable or perceptible," but "it is experienceable only insofar as it is founded on what is simply and sensuously experienceable and only insofar as it is given in unity with [*in eins mit*] what is simply 'there' according to perception."[47] There is thus a unity of the perceived and the "reflected" that, as Husserl always maintained, implies that we initially perceive the body of the other as the *Leib* of an *Ich*, the living body of an ego, rather than as a *Körper*, a simple physical body, even though there is an invincible "mediateness" in this very immediateness. This reflection is not itself a perception, but is built on perception and diverges from a direct orientation to the sensuous. Husserl explains this divergence (*Ablenkung*) of the reflective look: the look is initially directed at the physical body (*Körper*), "but it does not *terminate* at the body; in the understanding of expression, it goes beyond [*geht weiter*], to the ego-subject."[48] Perception thus finds its telos here in the understanding of the expressive and not in the merely sensuous; this explains why we find the term *Ausdruck*, expression, constantly attached in these pages to the term *Verstehen*, understanding.

In order to come to simple sensuous experience, the expressive, whose sphere here seems to extend to everything (as was already the case for indication in the first *Investigation*),[49] has to be put out of play, and the simply perceived world and pure universal nature has to be held on to. By means of an abstraction similar to the one in the fifth *Meditation*—a reduction to the sphere of ownness[50]—we have to limit ourselves "to the domain of what is valid only for me."[51] This implies not only disregarding the other and all of the idealizations that constitute a common world, but also that first idealization, which is the givenness of general names to objects. In order to achieve an act of originary judgment, language itself has to be left aside, as Husserl had already specified in the famous section 7 of the *Logical Investigations*,[52] and we need to situate ourselves at the level of what in the *Cartesian Meditations* he calls the "pure, and so to speak, still mute . . . experience."[53] Husserl certainly recognizes that the putting out of play of this first idealization (language) is difficult and demands an always renewed effort. It is nevertheless the case that this putting out of play of nomination alone lets us arrive at "the most primitive building stones of logical activity"—that is, at "objects only for me," and at "a world only for me."[54]

In order to judge how Husserl pursues this project of a genealogy of logic, we would have to undertake a detailed reading of the whole first section of *Experience and Judgment*, entitled "Prepredicative (Receptive) Experience," which constitutes a new "transcendental aesthetic," or more precisely, a transcendental theory of receptivity in general, whose counterpart is the transcendental theory of spontaneity that Husserl develops in Part II, entitled "Predicative Thought and the Objectivities of Understanding." In this new "transcendental aesthetic," Husserl proceeds first to an analysis of the general structures of receptivity, whose point of departure is the external perception of individual objects. These objects emerge from the background of a field of passive pre-givenness, and the whole difficulty here lies in distinguishing what, in the ego's "awakening" of interest in the object, arises from passivity, from what already comes from activity.[55] In the next chapter, Husserl moves on to the analysis of the simple apprehension of an object and to what he calls "explicative contemplation,"[56] which involves orientating perceptual interest toward a penetration of the inner horizon of the object, whereby we gain access to a developed contemplation of the object, "articulating" the object as a substrate in relation to its "properties" or "determinations," and which is at the origin of what Husserl calls "perceptual syntaxes." Finally, in the last chapter of this first part dedicated to pre-predicative experience, Husserl treats the apprehension of relations and then moves on to the analysis of "relational contemplation"[57] that is the contemplative gaze's penetration into the external horizon of the object—that is, the co-present objective surroundings. This last analysis of the background of the object of originary evidence requires going beyond the domain of givenness in person, which had constituted the framework for the preceding analyses, because it is not only a part of the perceptual co-givenness of the objective background, but also of the typical horizon of pre-cognition in which every object is pre-given, which has its foundation in passive associative relations, and which make the non-present intervene.

What then remains "problematic" in such a conception of pre-predicative experience? Before responding to this question, we must specify what characterizes the Husserlian approach. The analysis of pre-predicative experience in Husserl's work remains centered on the individual object, even though this object is related back to a field of passive pre-givenness from which it emerges, and to an objective background with which it remains constantly in relation. Additionally, because "the activity of perception, the perceptual orientation toward particular objects, their contemplation and explication, are already active operations of an ego,"[58] the ego's welcoming of the pre-given, its receptivity, can be only viewed "as the lowest level of activity."[59] On this point, moreover, in one of the appendices to the *Analyses of Passive Synthesis* from 1923, Husserl invoked the general difficulty of the analysis of receptivity, given that all the concepts used to describe it belong to the doctrine of spontaneity. This is also true of the concepts of judgment, of the ego, of intention, and of motivation because "the same denominations of corresponding concepts do not at all cover the same essences," depending on whether one is situated in the receptive pre-predicative sphere or in the predicative sphere of spontaneity and positional awareness.[60] But could we conclude from this identity of names that Husserl insufficiently distinguishes the two levels? Is he not reluctantly led to conceive the originary layer of experience in light of the structures of the layers built on it?

This is what I would like to try to show with respect to the concept of passivity in order to conclude. Has Husserl not always fundamentally understood the passivity of affection as a weak activity and as a preliminary stage of objective intentionality? We might claim this precisely because he presupposes that affection can be localized in an object, so that the activity of consciousness always seems to be sustained in the domain where intentionality reigns, since these two concepts (object and intentionality) are inseparable. This would also let us understand that for Husserl, the term "intention" must have two meanings—the weak meaning of aperceptive intention and the strong sense of the ego's taking a stand or posit(ion)ing itself.[61] For in the apperceptive sphere, which is the sphere of receptivity, "everything is done by itself," whereas in the sphere of decisions, the ego "must" necessarily take a position. There is thus an intentionality that begins with the subject and another that works underground on the constitution of the subject.

But what is the origin of an affection that eludes every intentional apprehension? Can we really "situate" the affecting? Is it in the object or in consciousness? The origin cannot in fact be identified because it depends on the preliminary capacity to be affected, which Husserl calls "receptivity," and which is neither "in" the subject (because it comes in some way "prior to" the subject) nor "in" the object (since the encounter with the object presupposes it). As neither in the subject nor in the object, it can only be "between" them. Heidegger had understood that intentional consciousness is not able to "master" what the philosophical tradition has called *pathos*, affect, or *Stimmung*, and therefore he no longer thought of the human as intentional subject, but rather as this "between," this "place" where the encounter between subject and object can occur, a place of openness to the world.[62]

And in fact, one finds in Heidegger (already in *Being and Time*, but above all in his 1929–30 lectures on the problem of the world) an entirely different conception of the "pre-predicative" or "prelogical" level. For him, the concern is to take account of the origin of the *logos* and then to show that the *logos apophantikos*—that is, the predicative proposition—does not produce the relation to beings by itself but is instead based on beings, on a "manifestation of beings," which does not happen by itself. What he calls "pre-predicative manifestness" or "prelogical truth"[63] can be constituted only by originary openness to a world, on the basis of which alone the intentional relation to singular beings becomes practical and thinkable. This prelogical or pre-predicative manifestness of beings thus has the character of the "in totality" and can be revealed only by what Heidegger calls *Befindlichkeit*, disposition, or *Stimmung*, affective tonality, the "atmospheric" character of which must be underlined. We can say of tonalities that they are neither interior to a subject (since they specifically have the virtue of being immediately communicated to the other) nor exterior, as if they were objects. This is why neither a psychology of affects nor a philosophy of consciousness can take account of them. They are, as Heidegger emphasizes, "a fundamental manner and a fundamental way of being, indeed, of being-there [Da-sein]—and this always directly includes being with one another."[64] The true "pre-predicative experience" is therefore constituted for Heidegger, and in contrast to Husserl, not by the intentionality of an ego, but by the "transcendence" of Dasein, of an existence that is not closed in on itself but always originarily open to the world and to the other.

4

The Phenomenological Gaze and Speech
Husserl and Heidegger

"The mouth and the eye do not live on the same continent. Their sources are of opposed inspiration, their waters of different colors, their effects variable in their analogies." René Char's words, from his *Recherche de la base et du sommet*,[1] bring poetic confirmation to what at first sight seems like an antagonism between the orders of seeing and saying. The separate continents of the gaze and speech would therefore refer not only to the heterogeneity of the two forms of art, painting and poetry (whose dialogue René Char knew how to celebrate better than anyone else—consider just those texts he dedicated to Georges de la Tour, Braque, and Nicolas de Stael, among others), but also and more profoundly to the opposition of the two attitudes relating us to the world—one of pure receptivity with respect to what presents itself, the other of dialogue with what is addressed to us and demands response. The difference between these two attitudes is that one supposes an *accord* with the *logos* of the world, while the other is determined as the *desire* to *see* what is; in his 1955 lecture at Cérisy ("What Is Philosophy?"), Heidegger invites us to think this difference as what distinguishes Heraclitus from Plato, or even thought from philosophy. Thought comes to be philosophy, Heidegger explains,[2] only when the agreement with the *logos* of the world—that is, with the *hen kai pan*, with the unity of the whole—is broken, so that henceforth the thinker is refused every possibility of corresponding with this *logos*, of speaking as the *logos* speaks (*homologein*, as Heraclitus's fragment 50 put it).[3]

The loss of harmonic accord with *physis* (which from then on separates humans from the whole, making them nostalgic exiles) is at the origin of this inquisitive tension, determined by the Eros that philosophy is, as Plato forcefully emphasizes in the *Symposium.*[4] Instead and in place of an impossible homology, would we not have the regime of the question—the question that Heidegger calls the directing question, the *Leitfrage* of philosophy—*ti to on*, what is being? And would we also have, instead and in place of the harmonic accord with the whole, the reign of *orexis*—of a desire that the very first line of Aristotle's *Metaphysics* teaches us is essentially a desire to see. Aristotle demonstrates in the first book of the *Metaphysics* that "we prefer seeing to everything else" because it is the sense that "makes us know and brings to light many differences between things."[5] This privilege granted to sight over all the other senses leads him a little further on in the text to a first definition of philosophy as *epistēmē tōn prōtōn arkhōn kai aitiōn theorētikē*, as "theoretical science"—that is, as the science able to take account of first principles and first causes.[6] The opposition of seeing and doing, rather than of seeing and saying, is the essential opposition that leads Aristotle to the definition of philosophy as "theoretical" science; Aristotle's concern will be to determine a mode of the *logos* that can *say* what is *seen*, and this will be the *logos apophantikos*, which is specifically what logic treats. Philosophy is called a theoretical science in opposition to the poetic science, which proposes the realization of a *poiēsis*, of a work exterior to its author, whereas philosophy as an exercise of vision and thought pursues no utilitarian end and is itself its own end.[7]

The opposition of the "disinterested" character of *theōia* to the utilitarian character of *poiēsis* must not, however, lead us to cut pure seeing off from any relation to what Heidegger will call the "facticity" of existence; moreover, Aristotle himself underlines precisely this when he recalls, following Plato, that wonder, *thaumazein*, is what leads to philosophizing.[8] Here, then, is recognized the properly "pathic" dimension that accompanies every cognitive exercise and that inevitably makes every cognitive "activity," all understanding and all conception, into a "passivity," a sufferance, an endurance.[9] The pure noetic gaze is thus not born nowhere; it is not led solely by the will in order to catch things in the *flagrante delicto* of their presence; rather, it constitutes a response to their distancing and a means to come into an accord with their strangeness. This is why *thaumazein*, which characterizes a properly philosophical *pathos*, is *both* a recoil before what is (or the necessary distancing of vision) *and* the fascination by which the gaze is, so to speak, "held fast" to what it takes into view.[10] And Heidegger concludes his analysis in this way: "astonishment is the attunement within which the Greek philosophers were granted the correspondence to the Being of beings."[11] In this astonishment or admiration that *thaumazein* properly is (the root *thauma* refers to the same root *thea*, which means to contemplate), and that occurs only in the exiled "consciousness" that philosophy is, there still reigns a correspondence, an *Entsprechen*, a speech that replies to what Heidegger does not hesitate to call the "address" of the Being of beings: *Zuspruch des Seins des Seienden*.

We thus see that the primacy granted to seeing by the Greek philosophers—and in an exemplary way by the first philosopher, Plato, who defines philosophy as an *ideo-logy*, a saying of the *idea*—that is, of the aspect or the face through which things present themselves insofar as they *are*—is now placed under the higher obedience of the *logos* and of the *dialegesthai*, of the dialogue with Being that is not necessarily dialectical, but in which humans are always already essentially entirely engaged. This is why Heidegger refuses to see the Greeks as *Augenmenschen*—humans who, so to speak, are reduced to their eyes alone and who grant a directing role to the eye merely by the contingency of geographical "facts" about the power and luminosity of the Greek sky.[12] The Greeks certainly thought of the relation of humans to Being on the basis the eye, which is what led Plato and Aristotle to speak of "the eyes of the soul" (*omma tēs psychēs*) and to determine the being of what is, *ousia*, as susceptible to being taken into view, as *idea*; but they also defined thought as a dialogue that the soul has with itself, and they determined the essence of humans on the basis of the *logos*, defining human being as the animal possessing the *logos*, the *zoon logon ekhon*. Now, only a being who possesses the *logos* is able to respond to the address of Being, to its claim—*Anspruch*—and is therefore able to relate to beings and take them into view. For in the end, it is not the eye that sees, no more than it is the ear that hears, insofar as these are mere sense organs. All vision and hearing certainly work through the sense organs, but these organs are not what allow us to attain the seen or heard thing: the sense organ is a necessary but not a sufficient condition for the fact that we see and hear. It is *we* (that is, our soul, insofar as it is the *ability* to see and hear, or *to be related* to a being in general) who see, and not our eye, *we* who hear, and not our ear. We therefore do not see because we have eyes, but because we are *able* "to see": "If human sight were always limited to impressions received by the retina of the eye," Heidegger writes in the *Principle of Reason*, "the Greeks would have never been able to see Apollo in the statue of a young man, or to put this in a better way, they would never have been able to see the statue in and through Apollo."[13]

This example allows us to understand that for the Greeks, as for all other humans, there is not in fact a primacy of seeing: what the eye perceives is instead determined in advance by the meaning of what is presented to us, which is never reducible to a pure sensuous given. Perceiving is no longer the confrontation with the strangeness of the world, which is incommensurable in relation to us (and which, as Nietzsche hints in "On Truth and Lie in an Extra-moral Sense," would require the metaphoric leap from nervous excitation to the image and then from the image to the concept), but rather our manner of entering into dialogue with the world and with what we may call, as Merleau-Ponty does,[14] its *logos endiathetos*, its immanent *logos*, to which our *logos prophorikos*, our human speech, merely replies. This is why our perception is already in itself a response, *unser Vernehmen ist in sich ein Entsprechen*.[15]

This formula refers us back to what Heidegger had already clearly shown in 1927 when bringing to light the essential mode of the Being of Dasein, the "existential" structure that is *Verstehen*, understanding—namely, there is no pure and simple "face to face" between the ego and the thing, which is the determining reason Heidegger abandons the classical vocabulary opposing "subject" and "objects." There is no "pure sight" or "pure perception" constituting an originary mode of access to a being in its pure "subsistence"; the sight of a being is instead initially "comprehensive," and sight makes the being explicit *as* being this or that—that is, as inscribed in a horizon of meaning—on the basis of which every thing is announced and "appears" for us.[16] Something like a pure view could be possible only at the price of a privation of originarily comprehensive seeing—that is, of a change of attitude (*Umstellung*) whereby the look *fixates* on what now has but the "frontal" presence of a pure "something," which, as such, is no longer understood.[17] But if understanding, as existential, originarily articulates the apprehension of a being in the world, this implies that every explication of something *as* this or that refers to a preliminary intention, to a *Vorsicht* or a *Vorblick*, which allows any particular intention to be preceded, so to speak, by itself: the hermeneutic circle, according to which "every interpretation which is to contribute some understanding must already have understood that which is to be explained,"[18] is valid not just in the domain of philological interpretation or at the level of the science of texts, but also and above all, it is valid on the plane of existence, where it means that we *see* only what we have already *understood*.

The Platonic determination of *ousia* or essence as idea is therefore more decisively clarified. Essence is what we have in view every time we relate to something determinant. This preliminary view allows us to recognize all things as what they are and opens the space for their encounter. The Platonic idea is nothing but this preliminary intention, the *Vorblick* that decides our factual vision each time—the vision of this house *as* a house or of that tree *as* a tree. Most remarkable in the Platonic determination of *ousia*—that is, in Being as constant presence, is the reference it contains to *idein*, to seeing as a mode of understanding. Heidegger insists, however, that the perception of Being is a seeing only because Being is understood by the Greeks as what shows itself from out of itself.[19] The Platonic determination of *ousia* as *idea* is therefore not at all the mark of a privilege granted to vision whose being would no longer be anything except a simple correlate, but is rather the consequence of the understanding of Being as *phainesthai*, and thus as *idea*, as able to be taken into view. In Greece, the emphasis is placed not on seeing as such, but rather on the phenomenality of Being, on the determination of presence as *alētheia*—that is, as what emerges from hiding and opens itself to the light. It is thus uniquely on the basis of the essence of *alētheia*, and not in relation to a privileged seeing, that *theōria* must be understood as constituting the fundamental experience of Being for the Greeks.[20] With the loss of the Greek understanding of Being—a loss that for Heidegger refers to that capital event in the history of the West—namely, the translation of Greek into Latin[21]—the emphasis will unilaterally be placed on seeing as such, and *idea* will no longer be understood as having the character of a being itself, but instead as the result of a process of representation. The idea becomes a mere *perceptio*, and the intentional aim of the subject now determines the domain of what is.

It is nevertheless important that in Plato, Being and seeing are put into relation in a very particular manner: Being is not simply what is encountered by a seeing that merely scrutinizes, nor is it the fruit of mere observation; rather, it is as it were brought to light by this specific seeing—the vision of essence—of which it is in some way the *pro-duct*. The *pro-duction* of essence obviously must not be understood as anything other than the bringing of Being to visibility (which is the literal sense of *pro-ducere*, to bring before), but this implies that essence is not the object of a pure contemplation and that the means of its apprehension must somehow be "produced" (production being understood this time as a non-ontic activity [*faire*]). This is what Heidegger calls, in a way that is difficult to translate, *das Ersehen des Wesens*, the "production of essence through seeing."[22] It is uniquely in relation to this particular seeing, which is a "productive" seeing insofar as it is the necessary preliminary of all thought of essence, that one can define the philosopher as a seer. "The philosopher," Heidegger writes in his 1937–38 course, "is a thinker only if he is this kind of seer (*ein solcher Seher*) and not a gaper (*ein Gaffer*), a calculator, or mere babbler."[23]

In reading Heidegger's elegy to philosophical vision and rehabilitation of *theōria* understood as the highest form of *praxis*,[24] one cannot help but think of section 22 of Husserl's *Ideas I*, where he denounces "blindness to ideas" as a form of spiritual blindness and tries to defend himself against the charge of "Platonic realism" by affirming both the intuitive character of eidetic knowledge and the nonworldly character of its object. There is no doubt that with his theory of ideation, Husserl is no closer to the true Plato, whom Heidegger attempts to make comprehensible for us, than he is to the legendary Platonism, which situates the ideas in a *topos hyperouranios*, a supracelestial place where they are invested with an existence analogous to that of empirical objects.

Given that the "phenomenological gaze" is the central theme governing these reflections, we cannot underestimate the importance Heidegger attaches to what he calls (in the little biographical text of 1963, entitled, "My Way into Phenomenology") the practice of phenomenological seeing that he had learned beginning in 1916 through personal contact with Husserl.[25] Heidegger notes that starting in the year of Husserl's arrival in Freiburg, "Husserl's teaching took place in the form of a step-by-step training in phenomenological 'seeing' [*Sehen*] which at the same time demanded that one relinquish the untested use of philosophical knowledge. But it also demanded that one give up introducing the authority of the great thinkers into the conversation."[26]

The experience of learning the phenomenological method directly from Husserl led Heidegger not only to forge his own concept of phenomenology, as presented in section 7 of the "Introduction" to *Being and Time*, where he refers to the two fundamental words of Greek thought (*logos* and *phainesthai*), but also to designate his own mode of thinking as "phenomenology" until the end of his career—not in the sense that it characterizes a determinate philosophical position, as is the case for transcendental phenomenology in *Ideas I*, but rather insofar as it is the "normative method of philosophy"[27]—that is, the path that leads to what enters into presence and that lets itself be shown,[28] as Heidegger again confirms at the end of his last seminar at Zähringen in 1973 while paradoxically determining phenomenology as a "phenomenology of the inapparent," a seeing of what by essence does not show itself. Though this may remain enigmatic, it nevertheless confirms that the agency of seeing, the dimension of the gaze, is not necessarily devalued in being opposed to the "capturing" gesture of *Be-greifen*, *con-cipere*, whereas the Parmenidean tautology is revalued as the model of a speech that no longer belongs to the determinative dimension of the concept and that, as the "pure remark" about which Goethe speaks, would show nothing of beings, but rather only what is the most "inapparent" in beings—namely, their entry into presence itself, the *event* of presence.

We would thus be right to ask about what in Husserl's method could acquire such an exemplary value for Heidegger. Or, to express it differently, we could wonder if there is a moment in Husserl when seeing is in the service of *phainesthai* and not yet understood as the work of a constituting consciousness intending to appropriate the world (since constitution is, according to Merleau-Ponty's striking formulation, nothing but "the project of the intellectual possession of the world").[29] Does Husserl somewhere "become Greek" and think the phenomenon in the horizon of *Selbstbekundung*, self-manifestation, or of *Selbstgegebenheit*, self-givenness, without already referring this givenness back to self-givenness of consciousness, and in this way leading phenomenology (as does the Cartesian path of reduction) back to the determinate philosophical position of the Moderns, which took on the form of a transcendental egology with Descartes, Kant, and Fichte? In the autobiographical essay cited earlier, Heidegger acknowledges having incessantly read the *Logical Investigations* between 1909 and 1926—well before the publication of the most complete exposition of the Cartesian path of reduction in *Ideas I* of 1913—and thought he had discovered such a moment above all in the sixth *Investigation*. He writes in the same text:

> There I learned one thing—at first rather led by surmise than guided by founded insight: what occurs for the phenomenology of the acts of consciousness as the self-manifestation [*das sich-selbst Bekunden*] of phenomena is thought more originally by Aristotle and in all Greek thinking and existence as *alētheia*, as the unconcealedness of what is present, its being revealed, its showing itself. That which phenomenological investigation rediscovered as the supporting attitude of thought proves to be the fundamental trait of Greek thinking, if not indeed of philosophy as such.[30]

Yet by Husserl's own wish, the sixth *Logical Investigation* contains "the keystone of all phenomenology and all future theory of knowledge,"[31] as found in chapter VI, which is entitled, "Sensuous and Categorial Intuitions."

But what does the victory of the notion of categorial intuition represent in Heidegger's eyes? Not only the abolition of the Kantian difference between intuition and concept, but also and more profoundly "the liberation of Being from its fixity in judgment," as he declares in the Zähringen seminar.[32] Indeed, for the tradition, Being and its general categories are functions of the understanding, whereas the very expression "categorial *intuition*" suggests that there is a givenness of the category just as there is a givenness of sensuous intuition and whereas the categorial in Kant is only "deduced" from the table of judgments. Yet what Husserl shows in chapter VI of the sixth *Investigation* is that "Being" has no objective correlative in the sphere of sensuous perception, but that it also does not have one in judgment, of which it is not a "real object" because it intervenes in judgment only as a "meaning-intention"—that is, as an incomplete or "unfilled-in" sign in the form of the little word "is." It is given in itself only in the intuition that makes the judgment true and therefore *outside of* judgment, when the judgment's correlative state-of-things proves true. We are therefore led to the view that, analogous to the sensuous perception of given data (which Husserl will later call "hyletic"), there is a categorial perception of the state-of-things of the type "gold-is-yellow" (Husserl's example) that remains "in excess" of the sensuous perception of gold or yellow.[33]

The analysis of such an example teaches that an articulated expression appears to be the exact reply [*réplique*] of a perception—it would seem that I can only express what I see—as if meaning resided in perception itself, whereas in reality there is not an enunciation of a simple vision, but rather a linking-together of complex acts of meaning and vision. For these categorial acts are not only "analogous" to sensuous intuitions, but are also "founded" on them. This categorial is arranged in a tier-like fashion over the sensuous (Husserl speaks of *gestufte Akte*), which is why it is in position to limit the "excess" of meaning and pure thought, which in turn is consequently no longer able to soar freely (in the image of Kant's Platonic dove) or to be without anchorage in the sensuous. Heidegger emphasizes precisely this point in 1925, when he speaks of categorial intuition in his course on the *Prolegomena to the History of the Concept of Time* (published in 1979). For we must first understand that extending the domain of intuition has the consequence of transforming the idea of truth, which from one can then no longer find its adopted place solely in the proposition or in the *logos* (in the restricted sense of *logos apophantikos*), but which is instead now defined more broadly as the identity of the intended and the intuited—that is, as a truth not only of *logos* but also of *nous*, if by *nous* or *noēsis* we mean the broader meaning granted to intuition insofar as it brings the category to light. Truth is thus found in the vision (*noēsis*) of the categorial and not only in the predicative statement.

The theory of categorial intuition therefore allows us to take account of the "excess" of intention that we discover in every perceptual statement: the "idealist" solution to this problem since Locke has been to attribute to the subject and its internal perception all the categorial forms that have no correspondence in the real. We are thus led to identify the ideal purely and simply with the conscious, the subjective, the immanent. It is possible to triumph over this old "prejudice" only through the discovery of an intentionality that snatches the "contents of consciousness" away from immanence. For if categorial forms are not something psychical or subjective, they could only be objective—but then they would be "objectivities" of a new type that, while not legitimated through sensuous perception, are nevertheless susceptible to an originary givenness. But in order to conceptualize the nature of these new objects, the character of the act that gives them has to be questioned. The activity of sensuous perception has the character of simplicity, as Husserl explains in section 47, in the sense that "the 'exterior' thing appears 'in one blow' (*in einem Schlage*) as soon as our glance falls on it,"[34] which implies that through the continuous flow whereby different aspects of an object are given to us, the unity of perception is not a result of synthetic acts but rather of an "immediate fusion of part-intentions."[35] The categorial acts (insofar as they are founded acts) can be arranged [*s'étager*] on this foundation of simple perception, which has the sensuous or the object as its correlate. Founded acts are characterized by the fact that they give access to the objectivity on which they are founded as a new mode of the same object: the level of *expression* is not simply the reply to perception, but also that which makes the sensuous object appear in a new way, and which corresponds to a modification of the intentionality that intends it. The act of ideation necessitates a basis that serves as an example for it, even though it is in itself "indifferent" to the quality of the foundational act: the concept of red, for example, is indifferent to this or that red given by the senses, but the presence of this particular red nevertheless founds the act of abstraction permitting the realization of the species "red," thanks to which this particular red can be recognized as red.

We are situated here at the level of the general object, the correlate of general intuition, of the idea insofar as it is "given" and not "constructed," and we may say that, on many points, Husserl's analysis of the ideational act rejoins the production of essence through seeing (*Das Er-sehen des Wesens*) that Heidegger saw in Plato. Husserl's idea, however, is that categorial acts have categorial forms as correlates and so in the final analysis rest on sensuous intuition, which means that a thought that is not founded on sensibility would be an absurdity. The idea of a "pure intellect," which Husserl says can be conceived only "before there had been an elementary analysis of knowledge in the irrefragable evidence of its being," is thus invalidated.[36] But because Husserl continues to oppose the two species of sensuous and categorial intuition, there is the constant risk of reinterpreting the categorial in terms of the *spontaneity* of an understanding that would impose its forms on inert matter. This risk exists as long as we misconstrue the intentional structure of thought and consequently every time that we neglect to achieve the phenomenological conversion of the gaze.

What Heidegger sees in 1925 in the Husserlian theory of categorial intuition is thus the sobriety of a thought that never entirely leaves the ground because its "freedom" remains "founded" ultimately on the sensuous: thought must have a "given" in order to begin thinking, which implies that it can never rise up as a pure thought of itself, into *noēsis noēseōs*. Broadening the concept of intuition and enlarging the amplitude granted to seeing do not consist in overcoming the sphere of finitude toward an absolute that would give itself the form of the ego (in contrast with post-Kantianism, which invokes intellectual intuition, both against Kant and in his name, by contending that it has meaning only at the "practical" level and not at the theoretical level, which alone is what Kant allowed). Because all concepts are always concepts of the object and thus have validity only in the objective sphere, Schelling could claim that the absolute I, which is not opposed to any object and is not itself an object, is grasped only in intellectual intuition.[37] In contrast, Husserl does not at all try to leave the objective sphere with his theory of categorial intuition; instead, he proposes (also in opposition to Kant, but differently from the post-Kantians) to stop opposing the two modes of intuition (one originary, the other derived) and to generalize the *intuitus derivativus* itself, seeing it as the only possible mode of intuition that humans share identically with God. For Husserl, God "does not naturally [possess] what to us finite being is denied, the perception of things in themselves,"[38] because that would imply that our human perception does not attain the thing itself, but only its appearance or image, which would contradict the very essence of perception, which gives the object "in the flesh" (*leibhaft*). Husserl's broadening of the intuitive field, far from liberating the subject from its attachment to the sensuous, instead aims at anchoring the subject more firmly in it than the "intellectualist" tradition had done.

It is nevertheless the case that the deepening of finitude, insofar as it is coextensive with the broadening of the field of givenness, is a Husserlian motif that Heidegger could have taken up. But what prevents him from doing so is the foundational status granted to the sensuous and the idea that there is a pure gaze, an *intuitus*, that would be grasped from "hyletic" data alone. We have already seen that in section 32 of *Being and Time*, which treats the development of the understanding in the concrete explication of the world, Heidegger denounces the Husserlian idea of pure perception as an originary mode of access to a being that would give the being "in person," "in the flesh," "in the original," and that itself would not already be an articulation and interpretation of the world.

The names of Husserl and Heidegger are juxtaposed in the subtitle of this chapter because we have tried to reflect on the fact that Heidegger—whose itinerary leads him always more decisively toward the question of the essence of language and the thought of a correspondence between humans and Being that must be thought on the model of *Gespräch*—

nonetheless always includes himself in the phenomenological project, which thinks the relation of humans to the world on the basis of a seeing and in the mode of intuition, and which, by raising up originary intuition as the de jure source of knowledge,[39] brings to term the intuitionism characterizing Western thought since its inception with the platonic Idea. But should not the project of "overcoming" metaphysics have to lead Heidegger to abandon the phenomenological attitude and the primacy of seeing that it claims? For does not all seeing presuppose both an exteriority of what sees in relation to what it is seen (is sight not the sense of distance, and is vision not always a tele-vision, as Merleau-Ponty notes?)[40] as well as a "subsistence" of what is taken into view, insofar as it sees itself fixated in the "face" offered to the gaze? And can we think a primacy of seeing outside the space of what the tradition calls representation? This is exactly what Merleau-Ponty was trying to do in his incomplete last work.[41] But what Heidegger proposes is to think a relation that is not an exteriority of Being and humans, and that makes the human not a subject closed in on itself and threatened by solipsism, but rather an ek-sistence—that is, a being essentially outside of itself, an ecstatic being that can no longer be thought on the basis of the categories of thing or substance. To think human being-in-the-world requires that the human *Umwelt* no longer be understood as the sum of objects, but rather as the structure of meaningfulness or significance that essentially unites the objects of use, objects that cannot be offered to the pure theoretical gaze that humans might cast on them, but only to their "preoccupation," on the basis of the "commerce" undertaken with them. A philosophy of the pure gaze like Husserl's, on the other hand, encounters the world as an enigma from the beginning and inevitably collides with the experience of its incomprehensibility. This is the skeptical moment that transcendental phenomenology necessarily passes through (whence the importance of Hume for Husserl); transcendental phenomenology can be constituted only by the confrontation with what in section 49 of *Ideas I* Husserl calls the hypothesis of the "destruction of the world": it could be the case that the experience that the subject has of the world is so fundamentally discordant that it lacks regularity and coherent order. All phenomenology, insofar as it is a phenomenology of the perception of objects foreign to the subject, is always exposed to the risk of discovering a radical discordance in experience. Heidegger, in contrast, starts from the meaningfulness of the world, whereby the world loses all intrinsic strangeness, since it is first of all the milieu of our existence. No constituting consciousness has to appropriate it or give meaning to it, and there is therefore no need to determine the act of "consciousness" as a *Sinngebung*, a giving of meaning; instead, it is a matter of thinking the hermeneutic relation to a meaning that is always already there before me even though it also requires my participation. If Heidegger takes care to join, rather than oppose, the terms "phenomenology" and "hermeneutic," it is because he is less concerned with invalidating the order of seeing than he is with subordinating it to the order of saying.

The recognition that meaningfulness or significance (*Bedeutsamkeit*) constitutes the structure of the world goes together with the affirmation of the fundamental hermeneutic structure of human existence.[42] This leads Heidegger in section 7 to define the phenomenology of Dasein as hermeneutic.[43] But what exactly must we understand by this term, and in what way is phenomenology itself hermeneutic? How can the intuitionism on which it rests be joined with the fundamental character of the existential structure of understanding? Heidegger tries to respond to these questions only much later, in the dialogue with the Japanese friend, found in *On the Way to Language* from 1953–54. Contrary to what Heidegger claims there, we know today that he began to use the term "hermeneutic" before 1923,[44] since we find it already in the 1919 course in the form of the expression, itself singular, "hermeneutic intuition,"[45] which Heidegger still places in relation to the Husserlian dimension of living (*das Erleben*), since at that point the "concept" of Dasein had not yet been forged, and which he understands as subtending the foundation of every theoretical objectivating position. In this conversation, Heidegger claims that under the rubric "hermeneutic phenomenology" he tries to "think the nature of phenomenology in a more originary manner, so as to fit it in this way back into the place that is properly its own within Western philosophy."[46] In this regard, Heidegger's project in the 1920s is clear: his concern is to demonstrate more decisively than Husserl that phenomenology is not a new "orientation" in philosophy, but that it merges with the initial Greek philosophical project of Plato and Aristotle. And although Heidegger himself recalls that he had first heard the term "hermeneutic" in a theological context, and then in Schleiermacher and Dilthey,[47] we can nonetheless wonder if it instead came to his attention from a reading of Aristotle, who was, through the intermediary of Brentano's *Dissertation*, his very first philosophical reading. Further on in the interview, Heidegger attempts to elucidate the term "hermeneutic," and in accordance with his enjoyment of the practice of popular etymology, he places it directly in relation with the name of the god Hermes, messenger of the gods, adding that Hermes is also god of speech and eloquence. By bringing Hermes and *hermēneia* closer together, Heidegger pursues the goal of making the original meaning of *hermēneuein* appear, which for him is not interpreting but rather bringing to knowledge, *Kunde bringen*, delivering a message, *Botschft bringen*.[48]

Considered in light of the original meaning of hermeneutics, the human is human only to the extent that he is able to be attentive to and hear this message, this announcement, and he can do so only by taking them up and in turn becoming their messenger and herald.

With the reference to the idea of an announcement or a call or a message, which the human would bear and to which he would respond, Heidegger wants to indicate that even before the least word has been said, an originary alliance between Being and the meaning to which we have always already acquiesced has already taken place. This is what explains why, in a passage from *On the Way to Language*, he returns to an old claim according to which questioning would constitute the proper gesture of thought, in order to state at the end that instead what constitutes thought as thought is listening to what in speech addresses itself to us.[49] Questioning is thus not what determines thought *as such*: because every question is already a response, even in its statement, to the address of Being, then no question, as Merleau-Ponty says well, *goes* to Being, but rather *returns* from it.[50]

That thought is fundamentally more a listening than a questioning implies that we are already and since always engaged in a dialogue or in a colloquium that unites us with Being. This means that all speech, all saying, is a saying-in-reply, a way of responding to the address made to us and that makes us be what we are. As soon as we begin to speak, we already find ourselves engaged in this *repetition* or *resaying* [*cette* redite] by which we celebrate that immemorial event, the so-called absolute past, which makes there be meaning for us. We cannot go further back or beyond, we cannot denounce or betray this originary alliance, or erase the horizon of meaning where the emergence of all speech plays out. This engagement of our speech with the inaudible speech of Being and of the world is played out in every "act of language" and gives to the order of saying its unsurpassable character. What Heidegger teaches us in the end, by calling the relation of the human to Being "hermeneutic," is to listen to the speech that orders all saying and all seeing, which have meaning and efficacy only in relation to the originary engagement in which we have always already staked our being.

PART II

The Self and the Other

5

Reduction and Intersubjectivity

Husserl

In the 1930 preface to the English edition of *Ideas I*, Husserl defines phenomenology as "the science of beginnings"—that is, as the resumption of the original idea of philosophy, found in Plato, as a "universal science."[1] The idea of philosophy for Husserl is, and will be to the end, the idea of a rigorous science, as indicated by the title of the famous 1911 article "Philosophie als strenge Wissenschaft" (Philosophy as Rigorous Science).[2] As a "universal science" and a "rigorous science," philosophy is radically distinct from every positive science and, as Husserl already said in *The Idea of Phenomenology* in 1907, is situated "in a totally new dimension," which is why "it needs *fundamentally new starting points* and a fundamentally new method, which is to be contrasted with the 'natural' method" of the natural sciences.[3] The method of the positive sciences is essentially one of verification that seeks to confirm a hypothesis by returning to "data," to "phenomena"—that is, to what is given to every positive science in advance as its "object" and, indeed, must necessarily be presupposed for "science" to be realized as such. Philosophy, on the other hand, can presuppose nothing, cannot depend on any preliminary data that had not already been submitted to examination. This is what Husserl underlines in the "Preface" to the translation that we just cited: "Philosophy is a science of the first foundation. . . . There lies embedded in its meaning as philosophy a radicalism in the matter of foundations, an absolute freedom from all presuppositions, a securing for itself an absolute basis: the totality of presuppositions that can be 'taken for granted.' But that too must itself be first clarified through corresponding reflections, and the absolutely binding quality of its requirements laid bare."[4]

The "method" of philosophy is therefore akin neither to the method of verification appropriate to the natural sciences nor to the demonstrative method appropriate to mathematics,[5] because Husserl's concern is not to *make* philosophy *become* scientific by modeling it on the already constituted sciences (in the sense of the Kantian project of a "Copernican revolution"), but instead to understand clearly that by itself philosophy constitutes the idea of science; that it *is* science *par excellence*. Philosophy therefore demands "a fundamentally new method"[6] by which it provides for itself its own terrain and its own premises.[7] This method is the reductive method, which we have already seen sketched out in the *Logical Investigations* in 1901 and which is systematically presented as the "phenomenological reduction" in *The Idea of Phenomenology* in 1907.

But before explaining what this reduction is, it is important to highlight the fact that, for Husserl, method and phenomenology constitute an identity without which the reduction might appear to be a mere procedure or simple technique for gaining access to the phenomena that Husserl calls pure and that, once attained, would no longer need the reductive method to become the objects of the new science of phenomenology. In contrast, we will see that Husserl's *epokhē* is distinct from the Cartesian method it takes as a model in that, unlike methodical and hyperbolic doubt, it is definitive. Descartes doubts in order to overcome doubt, discovering what alone resists doubt—namely, the indubitability of the cogito. Husserl also practices the *epokhē*—the suspension of the positing of the world, the abstention from belief in the existence of the world—in order to establish a veritable science of the world; but unlike in Descartes, this science is not established *against* doubt and in order to refute skepticism, which for Descartes requires the guarantee of divine veracity, indissolubly linking metaphysics and theology. Phenomenology is, in contrast, established *within* the *epokhē*, as the science of the true essence of consciousness, which remains closed to the natural attitude of belief in the existence of the world—leading Husserl to look for the solution to the problem of knowledge not in theology, but only in egology.[8]

The concern is thus to maintain philosophy *within* the *epokhē* because philosophy is not possible without it. This is why phenomenology is for Husserl essentially a concept of method rather than a science characterized by its content: "Phenomenology . . . designates above all a method and an attitude of thought: the specifically *philosophical attitude of thought*, and the specifically *philosophical method*," he declares in *The Idea of Phenomenology*.[9] Phenomenology is decidedly not the science of some new object (the phenomena) pre-given to it, for which an adequate mode of access has to be furnished, but is rather the search for what a phenomenon truly is. A phenomenon is not to be understood in the current sense (that is, as a thing of the world as it presents itself to consciousness), nor in the traditional philosophical sense (that is, the appearance that the thing offers to the look and that is distinct from its hidden essence), but rather as the "pure absolute given" of the thing, which can appear only if we stop being interested in the thing's being, stop giving or refusing it our assent, therefore only if we practice the *epokhē* (the skeptical suspension of judgment) with respect to it, and only if, by breaking with our participatory relation with the world, we adopt the position of the "disinterested onlooker."[10]

Defined in this way as the science of what Husserl calls in *The Idea of Phenomenology* the "pure phenomenon" understood in the phenomenological sense,[11] phenomenology thus not only necessarily proceeds by way of the reduction, but also has meaning only within the *Umstellung* that the reduction is, a *conversion* that leads us from the "natural" attitude of belief in the world to the philosophical attitude as such.

But if all authentic phenomenology occurs by means of the reduction, must we still consider the *Logical Investigations* as relevant to phenomenology? Husserl speaks explicitly of the "phenomenological reduction" beginning only in 1907, in *The Idea of Phenomenology*.[12] But since the appearance of Rudolf Boehm's 1966 edited volume of unpublished manuscripts from 1905 to 1920 concerning the phenomenology of internal time-consciousness, we know that Husserl used the expression "phenomenological reduction" for the first time in 1905. And he later noted himself (at an unspecified date) on an envelope containing a manuscript from 1905, "Historical note: I had already found the concept and the correct use of the phenomenological reduction in the *Seefeld manuscript* of 1905."[13] Could we therefore say that, prior to 1905 and in the guise of a "descriptive psychology" borrowed from Brentano, there was a phenomenology without reduction? Husserl writes in 1901, in the first edition of the *Logical Investigations*, "Phenomenology is descriptive psychology. As a result, the critique of knowledge is essentially psychology, or at least must be constructed on the ground of psychology." And though he added that, in order to distinguish the purely descriptive study of lived experiences from the properly psychological investigations oriented to empirical and genetic explanation, it is better to employ the term "phenomenology" than the term "descriptive philosophy," it is nevertheless the case that his project is defined as that of a psychological foundation of pure logic.[14] In contrast, from the moment when he develops the problematic of reduction, and as he explicitly says in

The Idea of Phenomenology, Husserl proposes "*to abandon once and for all the basis of psychology, even descriptive psychology,*"[15] in order to found what will be designated in *Ideas I* in 1913 as "transcendental phenomenology," so named because it poses "transcendental" problems (that is, problems that come from what is *beyond* [*trans*] consciousness) on the basis of the immanence of consciousness alone, since every type of transcendence is put out of play by the reduction.[16]

The transcendental turn undoubtedly coincides with the exposition of the phenomenological reduction that takes place in *The Idea of Phenomenology.* But is there no trace of the reductive method in the *Investigations*? Do we not already find the idea of this method, even at the level of phenomenology defined as descriptive psychology, in what Husserl calls "the principle of presuppositionlessness" in section 7 of the introduction to the *Investigations*? The question there is to exclude all hypotheses not arising from the phenomenological procedure in principle, insofar as this method is one of auto-foundation. This is why a phenomenology of knowledge *explains* nothing (for one explains only facts, only what is already-given), but instead *elucidates* the idea of knowledge. This *Aufklärung*, in contrast to any *Erklärung*, requires returning to the "adequate filling intuition"—that is, giving itself the task of a "descriptive analysis of lived experiences into their real components."[17]

We find the same idea in the fifth *Investigation*: Husserl speaks of the "phenomenologically reduced ego,"[18] even of the purely psychical ego limited to its phenomenological content, to the real complex of lived experiences that it finds in itself, lived experiences that, as what is adequately perceived, constitute the first and absolutely certain domain of the theory of knowledge.[19] The "reduction" in question here therefore has the sense of a limitation on the real components of lived experiences insofar as they constitute a sphere of absolute evidence. The domain of phenomenology is limited to lived experiences, to *cogitationes*, and thus excludes their intentional content, their *cogitatum*. Therefore, according to the conception of phenomenology seen in the *Logical Investigations*, what is phenomenologically given is only the real content of lived experience, which Husserl will call in *Ideas I* the hyletic and noetic moments of lived experience, and not the intentional contents or the noematic moments, which are "transcendent" to the real meaning—that is, they do not constitute an integral part of the *cogitationes*. The phenomenological sphere is thus "reduced" or limited (*beschränkt*) precisely because at that time, Husserl did not think that "intentional" content could be a phenomenological given. Only the domain of lived experience in their real contents could be a phenomenological given. This explains why phenomenology merges with descriptive psychology: subjectivity is not knowable in its totality, but rather only as *psychological* subjectivity—that is, as a subjectivity still understood as mundane or worldly—which the readers (and in particular, the neo-Kantians readers) of the *Logical Investigations* will not fail to do when they see the work's second volume as merely a relapse into psychologism.

What will change in the years 1905–7, and what will be at the origin of the transcendental turn, is the idea that the *cogitatum* also participates in the phenomenological sphere, that it too is also an absolute given. This is what Husserl clearly indicates in *The Idea of Phenomenology*. We initially find there the resumption of the point of view of the *Investigations*: insofar as it really is immanent to consciousness, the *cogitatio* seems to be the only absolute given, which Descartes had shown in his *Meditations* through the method of doubt. This is why, to the extent that the Cartesian method is taken as a guiding thread, the reduction can have the meaning only of exclusion and limitation: an exclusion of all the transcendent in the real sense, and a limitation of phenomenology to only the *cogitationes*. But next Husserl shows that the *cogitatio* must not be understood as Descartes understood it, as a "psychological" *cogitatio* inherent in a mundane and thus transcendent mind,[20] and he shows that psychological phenomenon must be distinguished from pure phenomenon, since the transcendent in the real sense also belongs not only to the domain of singular *cogitationes*, but also to the domain of the absolute given—that is, to the domain that Husserl calls pure immanence, even the domain of general objects or general essences. These generalities are not parts of lived experience, but are nevertheless "immanent in the intentional sense,"[21] as are intentional objects, the *cogitata* as *cogitata*.

The overturning to which the simple opposition of immanence and transcendence submits, both from within and from without, has the consequence of deepening, even changing, the meaning of the reduction. What *The Idea of Phenomenology* teaches us is that immanence in the phenomenological sense—what Husserl calls pure immanence—is not only reduced to the real contents of lived experience—to sensations insofar as they are "animated" by a form—that is, to the *hyle-noesis* couple of *Ideas I*—but that it also includes intentional immanence, the noematic moment, the *cogitatum* that takes part in transcendence in the real sense. Like a Leibnizian monad, phenomenological consciousness thus finds access to the outside, to the transcendent, from *within* itself: it is both "self-contained," "closed in on itself," or "without windows or doors,"[22] and yet, in virtue of its own immanent essence, open to transcendence, to the other. Reduction consequently no longer means the exclusion of the transcendent in the real sense, but the exclusion of the transcendent only in the presumptive sense of existence, of what is not absolutely given in full evidence.[23]

What, then, is the phenomenological sphere as a "reduced" sphere? It includes the transcendent, and, as such, it can no longer be considered as a limited sphere or as one "region" of being among others, but is instead the sphere of absolute being, the proto-region where all objectivity is constituted. Phenomenological consciousness can no longer be thought of as a representational consciousness where a preexistent being would appear as an image, but must rather be thought as a "constituting" consciousness—that is, as the source of all being. The reduction therefore no longer has the restricted meaning that it previously had, but now has an affirmative sense—not a sense of limitation but rather of liberation: the liberation of consciousness from its subjection to the in-itself, to the preexistent given. The reduction consists in an act of liberation whereby we lose nothing, but as Husserl says in *Ideas I*, we "gain the whole of Absolute Being, which, properly understood, conceals in itself all transcendences [of the world], 'constituting' them within itself."[24]

Understood in this way, the reduction is no longer a limitation, but rather the destruction of the limits of natural objective knowledge, which is always unilateral and abstract. The transcendental phenomenological reduction in its authentic sense is nothing but the passage or transition *from* the inherent limitation of the natural attitude insofar as it is receptive (that is, passive) with respect to things of the world that have the value of being in itself, *to* the philosophical thought that sees the "production" of consciousness in the world. When Husserl explicitly thinks the reduction as "conversion" or change of attitude (as he does in the "Author's Preface," for example),[25] he is simply thematizing what Plato had explained in the Allegory of the Cave when he identified the natural attitude with a state of incarceration or alienation in a world of shadows, and what Hegel, repeating Plato, had explicated as the state of a natural consciousness unable to see what is going on "behind its back" because it is fascinated by the presence of an object that it posits as an in-itself without apperceiving that this in-itself is only for-itself or that it is the origin of this posited object rather than "receiving" it as an always new object.[26] This "authentic" liberating, rather than limiting, sense of the reduction is already present in *The Idea of Phenomenology*, since Husserl speaks there of a constitution of the object in knowledge and of a "miraculous correlation" between knowledge and its object,[27] a correlation that the traditional (and Cartesian) theory of the idea-image—and thus of the representational character of knowledge—cannot at all take account of, precisely because it supposes the absolute exteriority of things in relation to a consciousness thought as absolute interiority.

But what exactly does Husserl understand by "constitution"? Should we follow here Fink's interpretation given in the famous article he co-signed with Husserl himself, where *Konstitution* is equivalent to *Kreation*?[28] Must we then recognize in human knowledge something that we ordinarily grant only to divine thought—namely, a creative power, and not simply a power of discovery? In reality, the alternative of creation and discovery, which refers to the opposition defined clearly by Kant between *intuitus originarius* (divine) and an *intuitus derivativus* (human), is exactly what the Husserlian concept of constitution wants to thwart. Just as, for Husserl, God does not perceive things better than we do and does not by nature have a perception of the thing itself that is denied to us finite beings (which would imply that our human perception does not attain the thing itself but only its appearance or image, which in turn would violate the proper meaning of perception as grasping the thing itself in its corporeal presence, its *Leibhaftigkeit*),[29] likewise the being of a thing does not refer to an in-itself that consciousness would have to receive passively, but only to a possibility of experiences concordant with infinity. Being, therefore, is and can only be for us a *being-interpreted*[30]—that is, a correlate of the concept that we ourselves form of it, inseparable from the experience we have of it. To speak of constitution thus refers to everything's becoming-object for us: it is as an *ob-ject*, as a correlate of consciousness, that any thing is constituted for us in knowledge. In the first edition of the *Logical Investigations*, Husserl understands constitution as interpretation, in the sense that all perception of objects is reduced to the interpretation of the sensory content,[31] and to understand constitution in this way is to see it neither as a discovery (because the object does not preexist but is the "result" of the interpretation) nor as a creation (because constitution does not make the object arise *ex nihilo* but only gives it a meaning).

The transcendental turn whereby consciousness, as constituting, recognizes itself as origin of the world—as an integrating part of the world, and no longer as mundane consciousness—thus takes place in *The Idea of Phenomenology* in 1907. In this text, as well as in the text where he delivers the most articulated exposition of the transcendental phenomenological reduction (specifically, the first chapter of the second section of the *Ideas* of 1913, which bears the significant title "Fundamental Phenomenological Meditation"),[32] Husserl takes Cartesian doubt as a starting point. It is certainly not a matter of repeating the Cartesian method, but rather of utilizing it as *methodischer Behalf*, a methodical auxiliary, in order to bring to light what properly constitutes the *epokhē*,[33] which as universal *epokhē* is radically distinct from doubt. In section 31, which explains the meaning of the *epokhē* as the "putting out of play" (*Ausschaltung*) of the thesis of the world, Husserl shows that the *epokhē* is compatible with the certainty of the existence of the world, contrary to doubt, which is the negation of it. At no point is there "a transformation of the thesis into its antithesis, of the positive into the negative," writes Husserl, nor is it "a transformation into presumption, suggestion, indecision, doubt (in any sense of the word); such shifting indeed is not at our free pleasure. *Rather is it something quite unique. We do not abandon the thesis we have adopted; we make no change in our conviction*, which remains in itself what it is. . . . And yet the thesis undergoes a modification: while remaining in itself what it is, we set it as it were 'out of action,' 'disconnect' it, 'bracket' it," or place it in parentheses."[34]

Although Husserl sees the prototype of the meditations that give birth to philosophy in Descartes's *Meditations*,[35] it would be erroneous to consider transcendental phenomenology as a mere resumption of Cartesianism because Husserl's problem is in no way the same as Descartes's. Husserl does not wonder if things exterior to him truly exist because at no time does he doubt the exterior world; rather, he wonders *how* in immanence we can know the transcendent. For Husserl, the existence of the world is not uncertain, as it is for Descartes, but rather incomprehensible. This is why his concern is not at all to *guarantee* the certainty of the existence of the world against skepticism, but rather simply to *understand* the meaning of being of the world. Husserl's effort to reconcile his own method of reduction with Cartesian doubt is therefore unfortunate in every way because it gives the impression that pure consciousness (the cogito) is what escapes from the *epokhē*, or is the "residue" of it (according to the significant title of section 33 of the *Ideas*: "Intimation Concerning 'Pure' or 'Transcendental Consciousness' as Phenomenological Residuum"), and that the reduction is therefore limited to the world in order to make consciousness appear as an "absolute ontological region."

Thought in this way, the reduction, insofar as it makes a remainder or a residue appear, has only a restrictive or limiting character and therefore cannot claim universality, since it is limited, excluding the region of nature and leaving the region of consciousness untouched: absolute consciousness appears, then, as what remains of us after the annihilation of the world. This is exactly what is expressed in the title of the famous section 49: "Absolute Consciousness as Residuum after the Nullifying of the World." Though Husserl has claimed that "we have lost literally nothing, but have won the whole of Absolute Being,"[36] it is nevertheless difficult to see the *whole* of absolute Being in what is merely a residue, a region, or a part of Being. The fundamental defect of what Husserl will subsequently call (in section 43 of the *Crisis*)[37] the Cartesian path of reduction is that it makes the reduction appear as the loss of the world and consciousness as its residue and therefore as the fundamental axiom on whose basis we can regain all that had been lost, seemingly making of the *epokhē* a *provisional* episode, of the same type as methodical doubt. But as we have seen, Husserl understands the reductive method in a completely different sense. The authentic meaning of the reduction refers us to the literal meaning of the word itself: *reducere* is *to lead back to,* to bring consciousness back to its truth, which is to be a constituting consciousness rather than a consciousness delimited with respect to what it is not.[38] As Husserl specifies in section 43 of the *Crisis,* the Cartesian path as the shortest path to the transcendental *epokhē* leads "as if in a leap" to the transcendental ego, "brings it into view as apparently empty of content,"—which corresponds to the "abstract" character of consciousness considered as "residuum"—"so one is at a loss, at first, to know what has been gained by it." Husserl concludes that this is why, "as the reception of my *Ideas* showed, it is all too easy right at the very beginning to fall back into the naïve-natural attitude—something that is very tempting in any case."[39]

But the fundamental defect of the Cartesian path—the defect that requires Husserl to seek other paths to the transcendental reduction in the 1920s[40]—is that it does not allow one to gain access to what for Husserl constitutes the full meaning of subjectivity—namely, *intersubjectivity.* Other subjects are given, according to Husserl, only in a non-originary manner, by an "appresentation" on the basis of their living bodies,[41] which are necessarily a part of the things of the world, of *realen Dingen*: "I can have the experience of a foreign subjectivity, which on its side exists only by directly being experienced itself, only on the mediate mode of indication, which thus makes me aware of the other subject only by the intermediary of presentification (*Vergegenwärtigung*) of self-perception, of self-memory, etc."[42] To begin, as Husserl does in *Ideas I,* by putting the world "out of play," or by hypothesizing its annihilation, therefore does not allow the discovery in transcendental consciousness (which is the "residue" of it) of the least trace of a foreign subjectivity. The other sees itself instead tossed to the side of pure phenomenality along with all that constitutes the totality of the world. Yet in the courses from 1923–24 on *Erste Philosophie,* Husserl himself stigmatizes this fundamental defect of the Cartesian path and explicitly proposes an "extension" (*Erweiterung*) of the *epokhē,* which makes it truly universal (without remainder), and which leads to "a reduction of still greater significance . . . than that to which we had initially come via the Cartesian path . . . by also including in its method a foreign subjectivity, transcendental *intersubjectivity*."[43]

Husserl wonders whether he, as a phenomenologist, is necessarily a solipsistic thinker and whether philosophy would be possible only as a *transcendental egology*.[44] Understanding the reduction to my own transcendental ego—that is, to what effects the reduction and to its own life—can only lead to considering the *epokhē* as *provisional*, to thinking that "there will nevertheless be a moment when it will be necessary to leave the phenomenological *epokhē*" and return to natural experience where a foreign subjectivity will be reestablished in all its rights.[45] This is what the beginner will inevitably think, Husserl says, "unless he has already experienced these 'winged' sensations that incite him to seek all true exteriority in interiority."[46] Descartes, who did not manage to rise above mundane subjectivity, had apparently lacked these wings, but this "beginner," who Husserl himself claims to be,[47] has never been deprived of them. For if it is only in the last years of Husserl's life that the Cartesian path is revealed to be truly impractical—he takes his distance from it only in the *Crisis*[48]—, it was, in contrast, during the period when he was elaborating his theory of the phenomenological reduction that he begins to be interested in the problem of intersubjectivity. The very first text in the first of the three volumes of manuscripts edited by Iso Kern on the *Phänomenologie der Intersubjektivität* indeed dates from the summer of 1905 and belongs to the famous *Seefelder Manuskripte* that treat individuation and the difference of individuals and that also explain the concept of the phenomenological reduction for the first time.[49] The problematics of the reduction and of intersubjectivity, far from being irreconcilable, instead form one and the same problematic.

But in his course during the Winter Semester of 1910–11, called *Basic Problems of Phenomenology* (also edited by Iso Kern in 1973 as volume XIII of the *Husserliana* and then in 1977 as a separate volume), Husserl already proposes—well before the 1920s and the courses on "first philosophy"—an "extension of the phenomenological reduction to intersubjectivity"—that is, the introduction of intersubjectivity in the "thematic" field of pure phenomenology.[50] The concern then was already to "seek all true exteriority in interiority," but on the condition of understanding interiority differently from the Cartesian mode of it as an absolute given.[51] The question that Husserl posed was, "may one admit those modes of phenomenological experience that do not have an absolute character?"[52] He responded to it in the most affirmative manner. It is possible, after we have put out of play the mundane empirical subject, that we are not dealing with just one sole absolute given. It is obvious, in contrast, that we find ourselves facing "an infinite fullness of phenomenological givenness,"[53] not all of which is given absolutely—that is, actually. There is, for example, the lived experience of remembering, which is accessible by reflection and which is an absolute given, and the lived experience that we remember, which is contained (in the intentional sense) in the remembering and which itself does not constitute an absolute given. Could we then say that it is not a phenomenological given? The concern with this extension of phenomenological experience to non-absolute givens is not about falling back into the natural attitude—that is, into empirical psychology, but rather about constituting "transcendental psychology" or "a science of lived experience in the phenomenological reduction" in the guise of phenomenology.[54] When we accomplish this reduction to the "pure subjective," which alone is taken as a theme, what appears as "most remarkable" is that each experience allows for a *double* phenomenological reduction: one from the actual lived experience itself and another from its content and intentional object.[55] The field of phenomenological experience includes not only actual lived experience accessible to reflection, but also presentifications (*Vergegenwärtigungen*), among which are included those lived experiences linked to actual lived experience by a relation of motivation: "If a perception motivates other perceptions, and if in the connection of consciousness itself a consciousness (and not the thing posited by it) gives rise to the expectation of a new consciousness, itself not given, then that is my domain"—that is, my field of phenomenological experience.[56] The perceptual lived experience of the other living body (*des fremden Leibes*) is thereby linked by a relation of motivation to the position of a consciousness and of a life of an other consciousness that is not part of my own consciousness's life, but that is posited in it by empathy (*Einfühlung*), effectively extending the field of phenomenological experience to the dimension of the "sphere of a plurality of self-enclosed streams of consciousness, which are joined together with my stream of consciousness through relations of motivation of empathy."[57] What had thus become necessary, already in 1910, in order to replace solipsistic Cartesian subjectivity,

> was the Leibnizian model of a *monadology*, that is, a transcendental theory of the communication of separated consciousnesses.[58]

The concern now would be to show, by means of an attentive reading of the second part of the 1923–24 course on *Erste Philosophie* concerning the "theory of phenomenological reduction," how the "second path" to the transcendental reduction that Husserl there proposes (and that is the path of intentional psychology)[59] takes up the same method of thought. The reduction will see itself extended to intersubjectivity by means of the same critique of the limitation of phenomenological experience of indubitable, real data. For it is "precisely because a foreign subjectivity does not enter into the sphere of my possibilities of original perception [that] it is not dissolved into intentional correlates of my own life."[60] Because the other is not and can never be absolutely or originarily given, it never becomes an objective correlate, but it is *also* because of this that a transcendental community is possible. The *universal* phenomenological reduction thus delivers not only a second transcendental life, in community with my own life with which it will never be confused, but also a multiplicity of transcendental lives. "Thus," Husserl concludes, "phenomenology leads to the *Monadology* anticipated by Leibniz in a stroke of genius."[61]

The paths of the reduction will thus have done nothing other than lead Husserl from abstract solipsist subjectivity to the concrete community of monads—that is, from Descartes to Leibniz.

6

Time and the Other
Husserl, Heidegger, Levinas

Time and the Other is the title of a short but famous work published in 1948, reproducing the stenographic record of four lectures given in 1946 and 1947 by Emmanuel Levinas at the Collège Philosophique founded by Jean Wahl in the Latin Quarter. In this text, for the first time, Levinas accomplished what we could call, borrowing from the title of an essay he had published in 1935, an "evasion"[1] of the thought of being by trying to understand the relation to the other, not in accordance with the Heideggerian horizon of *Mitsein*, being-with, but rather as time—that is, as "non-coincidence," "in-adequation," and "dia-chrony."[2] Levinas sees in time the paradox of a relation to the infinity of the absolutely other and finds in it the model of a distance that is at the same time a proximity. He thus lets himself be guided in this essay by the analogy between temporal transcendence and distance in relation to the alterity of the other. In this undertaking, it seems clear that Levinas wants to distance himself from the Heideggerian question of being and instead try to radicalize the question of the other as posited by Husserl in the fifth *Cartesian Meditation* in such a way that the dimension of the "Otherwise than being" or of the "beyond essence" can appear,[3] making it possible to attribute the role of first philosophy no longer to ontology but rather to ethics.[4]

But we may wonder whether the alternative of being *or* the other constitutes a true alternative that would lead us to emphasize the opposition between Husserlian thought (which sees the foundation of objectivity in intersubjectivity), and Heideggerian thought (which sees the ground of being-with within the understanding of being). Can we so easily oppose Husserl's thought as the thought of alterity to Heidegger's thought as the thought of the same? Ought we not instead question how each of these two thoughts encountered and posited the question of the other? This question is not at all absent from Heidegger's thought, which could be characterized as the thought of the synchrony of being only at the price of a vulgar oversimplification, precisely because it gives itself the tasks of showing that being must be understood on the basis of time and that being has a temporality that definitively tears it away from the horizon of the present.

Because the question of the alterity of the other cannot be separated from the question of the alterity of time itself, as Levinas rightly claims, I would like to try to show that these two questions remain narrowly intertwined in both Heidegger and Husserl. For it seems to me that this intertwining has to be thought when one poses the question of the other, precisely because what Husserl calls the experience of the foreign (*die Fremderfahrung*) can never be understood as full synchrony, but must instead always be understood as the experience of an absence in presence—of an absence that, in the final analysis, refers to that total absence that death is. If the other can only ever be presented as a mortal other, then it is not possible to understand the relation to the other as a fusion; rather, as Levinas rightly emphasizes, the relation must be understood as an absence in the horizon of the absolute future, which is death. We are here at the level of the plurality of existences about which Levinas speaks[5] and that Heidegger understands as the "dispersion of Dasein as such, that is, being-with."[6] Pluralism requires mortality—that is, the finitude of time—and this is why the question of time is revealed as decisive for the question of the other. But can we find a thought of death and of the finitude of time in Husserlian transcendental phenomenology? If we cannot, then would this mean, paradoxically, that Husserl had not truly posed the question of the other and had thus been unable to escape from the solipsism of his Cartesian starting point? Does the Husserlian transcendental ego constitute a sphere that is absolutely closed off to time and to the other? This will be my first question.

We can view time and the other as the limit-problems of a philosophy of the subject to the extent that the subject has been modeled on the identity and autarchy of substance. In *Ideas I*, Husserl himself defines the immanent being of consciousness as the absolute Being that in principle needs nothing else to exist (*nulla "re" indiget ad existendum*) and thus uses the Cartesian determination of substance as the definition of the subject.[7] As absolute Being, Husserl again claims in a 1924 manuscript,[8] the transcendental ego has no outside, which is why Heidegger will often characterize it in *Being and Time* as a "subject without world." But this does not mean that the transcendental ego is pure interiority or that we identify it with its lived experiences. Husserl already underlines in *Ideas I* that "although it is interlaced with all of 'its' lived experiences, the experiencing Ego is still nothing that might be taken *for itself* and made into an object of inquiry of its *own* account."[9] As Husserl explains in the *Cartesian Meditations*, Descartes missed the transcendental turn (and became the father of the philosophical absurdity that is transcendental realism) precisely because he saw a reality, a *substantia cogitans*, in the ego.[10] Husserl will subsequently abandon the model of substantiality completely and will instead understand the pure ego as the center of the current of lived experiences or as the pole of affections and actions. Because it has neither psychical nor worldly reality, the pure ego can be constituted only *in* time and *as* time.

Now, Husserl posed this question of the constitution of the ego—which he calls *Urkonstitution*, primordial constitution—at the very beginning of his transcendental turn, starting in the *Lectures on Internal Time-Consciousness* in 1905. We must emphasize that 1905 is not only the year of the discovery of the transcendental reduction, but also the year of the first investigations on time and intersubjectivity. In *Ideas I*, Husserl opposed the transcendental absolute—that is, the immanent being of consciousness, which is the result of the reduction, qualified as "ultimately and truly absolute"[11]—to nothing other than what he will later call "the living present as absolute and final soil"[12] and the "place of origin for all being."[13] The living present of the ego is the original phenomenon in that what Husserl calls in the 1905 *Lectures* "longitudinal intentionality" is constituted in it. While consciousness constitutes the temporal unity of the immanent object by means of a transversal intentionality, which effects the constant retention of the original impression, the flow of consciousness constitutes its own unity by means of a longitudinal intentionality, which allows for the retention of retention, such that the intentional regard goes off in two directions at once, as if by an originally divergent strabism. To speak of self-constitution seems "initially shocking, if not even absurd" to Husserl himself,[14] because it implies the total covering over of the difference between constituting and the constituted, which would in turn mean the immediate annihilation of time and the total petrifaction of the flow of consciousness. As we have already learned from Levinas, time is nothing other than the noncoincidence of the constituting and the constituted, of the subject and the object, the self and the world, the seeing and the seen. This is why Husserl also must recognize the nonidentity of the constituting and the constituted, which does not mean, however, that he ends up in a *regressus in infinitum* or that he is obliged to require a second flow in which the first may appear. If there were a self-appearing of the flow, and if the unity of the flow were ungraspable in its flowing—that is, in multiplicity—then the constituting would consequently always be temporally ahead of the constituted, such that the flow would only ever appear as past and would have to remain invisible as actual. The original constitution of the flow can become graspable and visible only in the dimension of the always already constituted, of the always already happened. What truly appears in self-constitution is thus the *finitude* of consciousness, which cannot be contemporaneous with itself, which cannot assist in its own birth, and which consequently can constitute time only because it is already in itself temporal. It seems, therefore, that time is paradoxically required to constitute the ego while, at the same time, the ego is required to constitute time. Husserl thus discovers the internal limit of the constitutive power of consciousness in the depths of "the definitive and true absolute" of the living present. The "subject" somehow always arrives too late, always preceded by the alterity of time or the pure flowing in its original passivity, such that the subject necessarily has the experience of what Heidegger once characterized as the "ek-static, i.e., *excentric*' " essence of existence.[15]

Even if, as we will see later on, the thought of transcendence and of the ecstatic is not absent from the last phase of Husserl's phenomenology, the emphasis in the 1905 *Lectures*, where only a small paragraph is devoted to protention, is still on the past rather than the future. The primacy of retention is put into relation with the *reflexive* character of phenomenological analysis: reflection means a backward flexion or bending, a looking back on lived experiences and an objectification of acts of consciousness. The immanent time of the ego is objectified by reflection so that the flow is, so to speak, frozen. This is why the reflexive ego can be considered as intemporal or supratemporal, as not being in time.[16] Just as Kant remarked in the first analogy of experience, which posits the principle of the permanence of substance,[17] so too does Husserl note in the 1905 lectures on internal time-consciousness that time is immobile yet flows, and in the flow of time, a time that does not flow—a time that is absolute, fixed, identical, objective—is constituted.[18] What Kant and Husserl mean is simply that time and the ego are not "in time" or "intratemporal." This "beyond" of the time of the transcendental ego must not be understood as its eternal and perpetual being, but instead as its "omnitemporality," to use the term that Husserl himself employs in an appendix to *Erste Philosophie*.[19] It would thus be a question of thinking the permanence of absolute subjectivity as that of temporalization itself, with the absolute ego being graspable only in the retrospective gaze that it casts on its temporalized being, because, as Husserl claims in a manuscript from the 1930s, "the absolute is nothing other than absolute temporalization."[20]

There is consequently an exteriority of transcendental life with respect to itself that allows its self-constitution. In this way, the pure immanence of the ego proves to be manifestly unthinkable and, as he says in a manuscript from 1930, transcendental life constitutes immanent time (that is, the current of lived experiences with its past and its future) as "a first transcendence."[21] The noncoincidence of the self-constitution of the transcendental ego is now understood as the "operation" (*Leistung*) of the continual self-transcendence of the flow and as the constant metamorphosis of transcendence into immanence, whereby the ego comes to itself from the future.[22]

If the transcendental ego is open to time in such a way that it can be understood as ekstatic and as advent, and therefore seems very close to Heideggerian Dasein, could we also say that it is open to the other in the same way? And does the strange experience of the other have anything in common with temporal experience? Husserl affirmed the resemblance of these two experiences several times, or, more exactly, he affirmed the analogy that links empathy to remembering,[23] in the sense that temporal noncoincidence with myself can be thought as analogous to my relation with the other *as* other. There is assuredly a radical difference between one's own experience, which is absolutely immediate, and the experience of the foreign, which is always mediated. A foreign subjectivity (which, on its side, directly experiences only itself) can be given to me only in the mediate mode of indication, whereas I have direct access to my own experience as self-perception, self-remembering, or self-anticipation. But in the immediacy of self-relation, there are also relative degrees of immediacy and mediacy, degrees of intentional implication, because I am given absolutely and immediately only in the present of my life.[24] Because as a past ego I am absent from myself, I must make the past-ego present again—that is, bring it back to life. In the case of experience of the foreign, just as in the experience of the self in memory, an absence becomes *present as absence.* In these two cases, I have the experience of nonnegatable distance in proximity to myself or in proximity to the other as *alter* ego, an other me.

Subjectivity can be understood as neither instantaneous being [*être*] nor as an objective being [*étant*] precisely because the nonoriginary givens are intentionally implied in it, and because the pure ego conceals hidden mediations within itself.[25] This is why Husserl can speak in his 1923–24 course on *Erste Philosophie* (as he had already in his 1910–11 courses on *The Basic Problems of Phenomenology*) of an intersubjective reduction. In the 1910–11 course, Husserl requires "going beyond the domain of the absolute given"—or, in other words, overcoming Cartesianism—as a necessary stage.[26] The phenomenological field contains not only indubitable givens, but also presentifications that are never absolutely given—that is, the field also includes absences. Yet the possibility exists of a double reduction of presentifications: they can be reduced not only as actual presentifying lived experiences, but also as presentified intentional contents. It is therefore possible to introduce into the phenomenological field "the remembering consciousness, and to no less a degree, one's own consciousness as it is indirectly assumed within the ongoing flow of the events of consciousness, and . . . *the other consciousness as it is posited in empathy*."[27] Intentional implications that open infinite horizons of absolute subjectivity lead us to the idea of a universal *epokhē*—that is, an *epokhē* "without residue." What is therefore revealed is the infinity of transcendental life, as Husserl claims in *Erste Philosophie*: "in truth, we are involved in *the monadic universe of a system of life without end*, in the infinity of our own life and of historical intersubjective life which, as such, constitutes a monadic universe of validities engendering themselves *in infinitum*, but revealing themselves *in infinitum* when one penetrates further into the horizons of the present, past, and future."[28]

It becomes clear here that subjectivity is essentially intersubjectivity in virtue of its flowing—that is, temporal—character. Empathy, by means of which the other is appresented to me in absence, presupposes an originary co-presence of the other—just as remembering, by which the ego makes present its past ego to itself, presupposes a community of consciousness with the past ego.[29] Because the true absolute is temporalization, it is also "intersubjectivity in flow," as is said in a manuscript from March 1931. In this text, we can even find the term *Mitsein*, and with it, the idea of a reciprocal relation between the self and other, rather than the dissymmetrical relation of the face-to-face which, according to Levinas, describes the original relation with the other:[30] "Being-with others is inseparable from the ego in its living self-presentation of itself, and the co-presence of others is foundational for the mundane present, which itself is the presupposition for the meaning of all temporality of the world, including mundane co-existence (space) and temporal sequence."[31] This being-with is therefore foundational with respect to the world, in the sense that, as claimed in the fifth *Meditation,* the other, in the neutral sense of an object, must be founded by intersubjectivity, such that "the intrinsically first other, the first non-Ego, is the other Ego."[32]

There is therefore an intersubjective temporality that allows for the co-remembrance of the other in analogy with the remembering of the ego's own life, such that a *Selbst-er-innern*,[33] a self-remembering of the other (which is at the same time its "interiorization"), is thereby made possible. The other is not an absolute outside: it is "present in me," and its living presence is linked to mine, just as mine is to its. But does this infinite intersubjective life find a limit somewhere in its incessant constitution? And can the mortality of the transcendental ego be represented without absurdity? The recognition of the "extraordinary" character of the Cartesian discovery of the cogito's apodicticity incites Husserl to refute the absurd hypothesis of the death of the transcendental subject in *Ideas II*: "Every cogito, along with its constituents, arises and vanishes in the flow of lived experiences. But the pure subject neither lives nor dies."[34] Because neither the birth nor death of the transcendental ego is intuitively provable, there is no sense in saying that the ego lives or dies. As he says in the *Analyses of Passive Synthesis*, "the process of living on and the ego that lives on are immortal," and, Husserl adds, "*Nota bene*: the pure transcendental ego, not the empirical world-ego, that can very well die."[35] What is in fact immortal is immanent time itself: "Enduring is 'immortal.' When the tone ceases, precisely something else is there in its stead as the enduring present. It could be the case that the world does not exist—as we have shown, it is a possibility. In contrast, it is absurd to say that immanent being, this present being constituted in the enduring, ceases: it is inconceivable that everything would come to a halt or that there would be nothing."[36] Whatever has no relation, whatever is pure temporalization, cannot be destroyed: Husserl already said in *Ideas I* that the tree could burn, but that its noematic meaning could not.[37] Every real mortal self contains within itself an immortal transcendental self; there is therefore an eternal being within becoming. But as we have already seen, this "eternity" is "in" time—it is only the infinite length of time, the becoming eternal itself within which "real" birth and death take place. Nothing is further from Husserl's thinking than the idea of a "becoming in perishing," or the Heideggerian thesis according to which time is in itself finite.

If we turn now to Heidegger, we find the finitude of time as a first point of departure. The thesis of the finitude of original time is formulated only at the end of section 65 of *Being and Time* (that is, after the famous analysis of being-toward-death), where temporality is presented as the ontological meaning of "care." But it is less the result of these analyses than it is the presupposition in principle of the concept of Dasein as such. To consider the human as something other than a subject, the model of substantiality must be abandoned. This means that it is not sufficient to define the being [*être*] of consciousness *negatively* as nonsubsistent, nonintratemporal, non-being [*non étant*], as is still the case with Husserl; instead, the being of the human must also be understood *positively* in relation to time. This is why we should no longer understand time on the basis of eternity, but rather, as Heidegger says very clearly to the Marburg theologians in his lecture on "The Concept of Time" in July 1924, on the basis of time itself.[38] When we have resolved to "speak temporally of time" rather than situating it in another place as if it were a being whose identity would betray its temporal character,[39] we discover that the question of the essence of time is transformed into another question, which asks *who* (and not *what*) time is. The question of time leads to the question of the being that every time I am. The being "every time" of a self that characterizes Dasein has the sense of a "participation" in Being of the being that is not indifferent to its Being, but on the contrary has "to be it," as Heidegger explains in one of his courses prior to the publication of *Being and Time*.[40] This distributive structure of *Jeweiligkeit*[41]—Heidegger will no longer speak of *Jeweiligkeit* in *Being and Time* but rather of *Jemeinigkeit*, the "mineness" of a being that is "each time my own"[42]—is what defines not the *quid* of Dasein, but rather its *quomodo*, its modality of being: in the dimension of "participation" in being that has yet to be, Dasein is at every instant—*jeweils*—a self; and to say "I" is the way in which a Dasein is returned to its own being.[43] There is therefore not a Dasein in general that we could say *is* after having put its particular instances "in parentheses." The question "who is time?," the question of Dasein, does not concern any physical or psychical reality, precisely because it is what Dasein is each time: Dasein is its being and not just any determined *quid* that would have its own manner of being among others.[44] There is therefore no sense in wondering if Dasein has a body or a soul because these characteristics would "have placed me in a completely different dimension of being, really extraneous to Dasein."[45] Heidegger wants to think singularity rather than generality, but he does not understand singularity as something empirical, as is still the case with Husserl, who remains captive to the thought of essence to the extent that he continues to oppose the empirical psycho-physical ego to the transcendental ego.[46] But abandoning the thought of essence means at the same time that we apperceive the finitude of time and the plural structure of existence. For Dasein's being each time its own—*Jeweiligkeit* or *Jemeinigkeit*—has the sense of a distributive structure that implies the plurality of Dasein in advance.

This plurality is nothing other than what Heidegger calls in his 1928 course on *The Metaphysical Foundations of Logic* "the [metaphysical or transcendental] dissemination of Dasein as such, that is, being-with in general."[47] Being-with has—and Heidegger always insists on this—an existential-ontological meaning. This means that it is not something that takes place simply by virtue of the fact of the actual presence of others. This is why the fact of being alone is, for Heidegger, also a being-with others. Solitude simply means the factual deficiency of being-with: it is the experience of the lack of others, and precisely by this lack, the existential meaning of being-with is indicated. Being-in-the-world and being-with are cooriginal existentials, and we cannot have one without the other.[48]

We consequently see that "mineness" is not at all incompatible with being-with-others; rather, the contrary is true. The most extreme isolation is, in fact, the presupposition for being-with in general.[49] Because this isolation—in the extreme form of being-alone-with-death—means nothing but the assignment of taking itself in charge—that is, of factual existing.[50] Heidegger had already clearly said this at the end of his July 1924 lecture: the anticipation of death is what gives Dasein its ipseity or selfhood, but this individuation is not "the fantastical emergence of exceptional existences"; on the contrary, "it individuates in such a way that it makes everyone equal."[51] What each has in common with all others is precisely "the unique 'this-time' of its unique destiny in the possibility of its unique being-past."[52] The incomparable difference between myself and the other is what makes me equal to the other, and what separates me from the other is precisely what I share with the other. Being-alone and community are thus not exclusive: "We would have to show," Heidegger writes in the 1925 course, "how facticity and individuation are grounded in temporality, which, as temporalization, unites itself in itself and individuates in the metaphysical sense, as *principium individuationis*. But this isolation is the presupposition of the primordial commerce between Dasein and Dasein."[53]

The term "Dasein" simply cannot be taken as a new name for consciousness or the subject, as if Heidegger were starting from the "isolated" human in order subsequently to attribute to it the relation to the other and to being. This is why being-with is not the name of the factual relation with the other, but rather is an "attribute of one's own Dasein" in the existential-ontological sense.[54] The being of Dasein is being-with rather than the individual egoity of the isolated subject, so that every time Heidegger uses the term "Dasein," being-with is coimplied. *It is therefore not at all a paradox to claim that in* Being and Time, *the question of the other is posed everywhere.* We can even go as far as to say that this work would become rigorously *unreadable* if we did not take account of the fact that "Dasein in itself is essentially being-with."[55] Heidegger recognizes, however, that the analysis of the worldliness of the world is initially restricted to the being that is not of the order of Dasein, and in this regard, he even speaks of "a violent constriction of the analysis of the world."[56] This restriction or constriction is nevertheless necessary because being-with-others in the everydayness is at first blush unseen and seems to be self-evident. For others are not simply there in the environing world and in the things with which they are concerned, but they are also those beings from whom one has not yet distinguished oneself. Could we then say—with help from Eugen Fink's proposed distinction between the operational and the thematic[57]—that the others to whom I myself partially belong are operationally coimplied when the analysis of worldliness thematizes the *Zuhandenheit* and the *Vorhandenheit* of the being that is not of the order of Dasein? This is why the "who" of being-in-the-world is at first entirely indeterminate. Because the world is always also a common world, we do not find others "on the side" of intraworldly things, but rather *on the same side* that "I" too am on. But at the level of worldliness, Dasein does not simply encounter the being of things in the world, but also being-with-others and even its own being, which "come against" Dasein [*lui font encontre*] from the world. That Dasein always behaves in a triple fashion—in relation to the being that is not of the order of Dasein, in relation to the being that is of the order of Dasein, and in relation to the being that it itself is—comes from the fact that the understanding of Being is its fundamental determination, so that whenever it is a question *for* itself, it is *also* always a question *of* the other—that is, the other thing or the other person.

If Dasein is essentially being-with, then it is not possible to understand Dasein's characteristic as existing "by its own design" (*um seiner selbst willen*),[58] in an individualist-egoist sense. The ontological must also be strictly separated from the ontic here. The egoicity of Dasein in the ontological sense is the presupposition of every factual-ontic I-Thou relation. For when Heidegger speaks of mineness and of egoicity, it is not in the sense of an individualist subjectivism, but rather, what is in question is the essence of egoicity and of ipseity in general.[59] Consequently, this metaphysical or ontological egoicity is not what is distinguished from the Thou (namely, de facto egoicity), but is rather what is also at the basis of the Thou. Heidegger names this latter "ipseity" and understands by it the fundamental characteristic of existence.[60] Dasein's being-itself is not a solipsistic retreat into self, but is on the contrary *existing*, the free choice of self, as being-with the other Dasein and the being-near of the being that is not of the order of Dasein.

For the same reason, we find in *Being and Time* a critique of the theme of empathy, in which Heidegger sees the response to the absurd question of knowing how an initially isolated subject can exit from itself and gain access to the other subject. We have already seen that for the later Husserl, empathy (that is, the appresentation of absence and the invisibility of the other) presupposed a co-presence. Heidegger shows in the same way that "'empathy' does not first constitute being-with, but is first possible only on its basis."[61] Because just as knowledge as a founded mode of being-in-the-world does not create of its own initiative the subject's *commercium* with the world,[62] so too is empathy not the origin of Dasein's relation to Dasein. Empathy, similarly to knowledge whose enigmatic character Husserl underlined several times,[63] presupposes the closing-off and encapsulating of a subject that must exit itself in order to encounter the object or be introduced by empathy to an other subject. And this is possible only if one "projects" the self-relation into the other, or, in other words, only if we understand community with the other in analogy with community with oneself, as is the case for Husserl. The other is thus considered as an "alter ego"—that is, a "double of the self."[64] According to Heidegger, the Husserlian solution would consist in understanding Dasein's being in relation to itself as a being in relation to an other, so that alterity would, so to speak, be interiorized. In contrast, Heidegger underlines that being in relation to others is "an irreducible and autonomous relation of being," analogous neither to the relation to self nor to the relation to a being that is not of the order of Dasein. This relation is, like the other two, as original as Dasein itself, which is "nothing" outside of these relations. Moreover, for Heidegger, self-knowledge is not reflexive in nature—I cannot be known to myself by introspection, but always on the basis of the world alone; this is equally true for knowledge of others—I do not need to introject myself by empathy into an other subject, but rather, I can understand the other subject only on the basis of the world. Empathy is not an original, existential phenomenon, but is merely the apparent solution to the problem posed by the existential encounter with the other, which already presupposes being-for-each-other on the existential level.

But is not this distinction of two planes—one ontic-existentiell, the other existential-ontological—a new form of the Husserlian distinction of the empirical and the transcendental and thus a repetition of the metaphysical thought of essence? And is not the factual self alone a real singularity and Dasein something general and unreal? Could we not pose the same questions to Heidegger that he had posed to Husserl in October of 1927: "What is the meaning of the absolute ego as distinct from the purely psychical ego? What is the mode of being for this absolute ego? In what sense is it *the same as* the ego that is factual each time, and in what sense is it *not the same*?"[65] Heidegger's concern is clearly not for an ego, but rather for a self that does not refer to the identity of an always already subsisting being and that must be understood as existentiality—that is, as thrownness and care. But the question nevertheless remains the same: how must the distinction between the ontological and the ontic be understood? And is the ontological-existential *expressly* thought in relation to time and its finitude?

The temporal analytic of Dasein is characterized by the fact that it cannot rest on the ontological plane alone: the "possible" existential being-towards-death remains "a phantasmagoric pretention" as long as "the ontic potentiality-for-being has not been shown in terms of Dasein itself": the ontological possibility of overcoming death therefore requires an existential attestation.[66] The question of the authenticity and wholeness of Dasein is a factual-existential question that requires the resoluteness of Dasein as an existential response.[67] For the existential analytic can be only a "hermeneutic of facticity": this means that the ontological cannot be separated from the ontic and that without existential understanding and participation, the analysis of existentiality remains deprived of ground.[68] "Ontological" Dasein is *the same* as factual Dasein, which always has a preontological understanding of itself, even when this everyday self-explication tends to dissimulate its authentic being. This is why the ontological interpretation of existence produced in *Being and Time* is not guided by an arbitrary idea forged from random tidbits, but is instead based on a factual ideal. The circular process of the analysis does not, however, constitute a logical vice, but is instead the necessary method for Dasein's self-explication, whose existence is temporal; this means that it is a being that has *to become* what it is. Between ontological and ontic Dasein, just as between authentic-resolute Dasein and inauthentic-fallen Dasein, there is only a "temporal" difference, a difference in the mode of the temporalization of temporality—and not, as in Husserl, a difference between a factual mortal ego and an immortal transcendental ego.

Because Dasein is both near to and distant from itself, because Dasein is time itself, it is also being-with—not in the sense of a "philosophy of communion,"[69] but rather in the sense of a philosophy of the originary dispersion of Dasein.[70] As we have already seen, this original dispersion demonstrates that Dasein is always simultaneously related to itself, to the being that is of the order of Dasein, and to being that is not of the order of Dasein; and we have seen that to each of these manners of being-related, there belongs a multiplicity proper to it—many objects, many others, and even many "selves" according to the structure of historicity. This transcendental dispersion is founded on being-thrown and constitutes the structure of an ek-static being that lacks a substantial center and that is therefore essentially "ex-centric." Being-thrown means nothing but the projection or *élan* of the ek-static temporalization.[71] This free *élan* of temporality is the ground of the plurality of existing that attests to the essential "diachrony" or multiplicity of being.[72] Heidegger relates this diachrony to an essential finitude of time, whereas Levinas saw in time the "mode of the beyond of being" and the "relation of the Wholly Other, the Transcendent, the Infinite."[73] Like Husserl, Levinas still seeks a "victory over death,"[74] and he finds it in the relation to the other—that is, in Eros and in the pluralist existing of Paternity.[75] In contrast, because Heidegger thought *the finitude of being itself* and not only of the human Dasein, he was able to understand death as the possibility of existing in general, as a *capacity*,[76] and he could therefore see the basis for being-with and for the historiality of Dasein in mortality.

7

Phenomenology and Therapy

The Question of the Other in the Zollikon Seminars Heidegger and Boss

In a book published one year after Heidegger's death, gathering the recollections of those who were close to and knew Heidegger,[1] Medard Boss spoke of the seminars that Heidegger gave several times each year over a ten-year period (1959–69) in Boss's home at Zollikon in front of an audience of fifty to seventy medical students and young psychiatrists.[2] Perhaps because it is entirely dedicated to the memory of a friend who had just died, this text is more explicit than the preface to the *Zollikoner Seminare* about why Boss wrote to Heidegger in 1946,[3] a few years after he had discovered *Being and Time*, and the reasons that prompted Heidegger to respond to Boss's first letter. Boss recounts that it was only much later, during their tête-à-tête interviews in Zollikon, that Heidegger explained the motivations for what can seem an unusual behavior of a famous philosopher who received hundreds of letters every year:

> He then revealed to me that he had hoped that his thought could leave its philosophical ivory tower and, by my intermediary as doctor and psychotherapist, be beneficial to larger circles, notably to many sick people. What had considerably impressed him was that in the first letter I had sent, I had specifically mentioned page 122 of his book *Being and Time*, drawing his attention to the fact that in the phrase "concern that leaps ahead" [*vorspringende Fürsorge*], we find the exact description of the ideal relation of the psychoanalyst to his patients. Moreover, the contrast noted by Heidegger of this "anticipa-

> tory concern," which alone is worthy of the human [*einzig menschenwürdig*] with a "concern that leaps in" place of the other doing violence to it [*eine den Anderen stets vergewaltigende "einspringende Fürsorge"*] allows the analytic therapist to bring out explicitly what is new and unique in his particular method of treatment with respect to all other medical behaviors, which are for the most part behaviors of "substitution," and to delimit what is appropriate to it.[4]

Rather than any particular anthropological determination of Dasein (ZS, 190), Boss had thus initially situated the therapeutic relation with respect to what in Heidegger is "the name for the whole unfolding essence of Dasein" (ZS, 227)—that is, *die Sorge*, care, as the Latin *cura* also suggests.[5] If Heidegger was "considerably impressed" by this and was led to engage in a dialogue with Medard Boss for nearly thirty years, it is probably because he saw in it the possibility of a passage from the ontological to the ontic plane—from a *Daseinsanalytik* to a *Daseinsanalyse* (ZS, 124)—which would not be "a complete misunderstanding of [his] thinking" (ZS, 277), as is represented by Binswanger's psychiatric analysis of Dasein. Binswanger does not see the ontological difference (ZS, 204) and thus confuses ontological views with ontic things (ZS, 227)—that is, he confuses the phenomenon of phenomenology, which is not perceptible in itself (for example, the existence of something) with the phenomenon in the ordinary sense (this thing itself), or the most knowable in-itself with the most knowable for-us, according to the distinction already made by Plato and Aristotle (ZS, 7 and 187). Binswanger proposes moreover "to complete Heidegger's gloomy care" (*Heideggers düstere Sorge*) by taking into account, in his "lengthy book" *Grundformen und Erkenntnis des menschlichen Daseins*, of the phenomenon of love, which Heidegger had "neglected."

Heidegger explains in a seminar from November 1965 that what Binswanger had not understood was that the analytic of Dasein has absolutely nothing to do with solipsism or subjectivism because Dasein is determined as an originary *Miteinandersein*—a being-with-one-another—which is why what is true for Dasein in its very Dasein is also always true for others (ZS, 116). As Heidegger will later say to a seminar participant, this means that "you exist and I exist . . . we are both related to each other existentially" (ZS, 123). We could therefore oppose *Fürsorge* to *Sorge* itself and think them (as Binswanger does) as a "dual mode of being" (*ein dualer Seinsmodus*) only by misunderstanding care as an ontic modality of behavior, whereas it is properly thought in an ontological or existential sense as what fundamentally constitutes Dasein, and as such, is never accessible to ontic description (ZS 116). What Binswanger had retained from *Being and*

Time is only *In-der-Welt-sein*, being-in-the-world, without seeing that it is itself grounded on *Seinsverständnis*, the understanding of being, which constitutes the "sole concern of *Being and Time*" (ZS, 118). He thus did not understand that being-in-the-world is not the condition of Dasein; rather, the contrary is true (ZS, 192). His *Daseinsanalyse* is therefore not truly an analysis of Dasein (ZS, 188), remaining an ontic and *existentiell* interpretation of factual Dasein.

But if Binswanger's effort to make the *existentials* of *Being and Time* into an *application* for psychiatry without taking into account their true ontological meaning only ends up confusing the ontic and the ontological, how then can the necessary correlation of the two planes be guaranteed? And is there truly a possibility of constituting a "doctrine of human illness in accordance with the philosophy of Dasein," as Boss already proposes in his *Einführung in die psychosomatische Medizin*, written in 1954 and dedicated to Heidegger? Is it truly possible to practice what Boss calls in his *Grundriss der Medizin und der Psychologie* in 1971 "eine daseinsgemässe Therapie und eine daseinsgemässe Präventiv-Medizin," a therapy and preventive medicine in accordance with Dasein?[6] In an interview with Boss from September 1968 (that is, from the period when Boss was elaborating the book just cited, with Heidegger's help), Heidegger states that "the method of investigation appropriate to Dasein is not in itself phenomenological, but depends on and is guided by phenomenology in the sense of the hermeneutic of Dasein."[7] Describing ontic phenomena such as factual pathological behaviors is possible only in light of ontological phenomena—that is, the existentials of Dasein: the "mediation" (this is Heidegger's word: *vermittelt*) of the ontological is therefore needed in order to gain access to the ontic, and "mediating" is something altogether different from "applying" the ontological to the ontic. Yet this mediation can occur only through the personal conversion of the investigator: "the most difficult task is demanded of the investigator, that is, to make the transition from the projection of the human being as rational animal to the projection of being-human as Dasein" (ZS, 223). The doctor must initially experience himself as Da-sein, as ek-sistent, in order then to be capable of determining all human reality on this basis, which implies the suspension of inadequate representations that one has of the human. Yet this requires the exercise or the "training of the experience of being human as Dasein" (die Einübung in die Erfahrung des Menschseins als Da-seins). The concern is therefore nothing less than training doctors in "phenomenological seeing," which for Heidegger means *beim Selben verweilen*, lingering with the same, the self, and *den Sinn für das Einfache wecken*, awakening the sense for what is simple (ZS, 263). But as Heidegger explains while addressing those who are not just members of the audience but also participants, this requires one "to engage [*sich einlassen*] in the way of existing in which you always already exist, of performing it" (ZS, 109), which is altogether different from a simple intellectual understanding of this manner of being.

This is what the method that alone gives access to human phenomena consists in, whereas the scientific method of the natural sciences, reducing these phenomena to pure calculable data, leads only to the "destruction of man" (*Zerstörung des Menschens*) when it produces a cybernetic representation of man (ZS, 123). It must be forcefully emphasized that this method is not merely a becoming aware of the relation that we have with what confronts us, but also consists in properly engaging in and *performing* this relation.[8] The method opposed to the Cartesian method of the sciences of nature is Greek,[9] insofar as it shelters and "saves" the phenomena (ZS, 110): *sōzein ta phainomena.* In his Summer 1943 course on Heraclitus,[10] Heidegger understands this phrase used by Greek thinkers to characterize their thought in light of the Heraclitean *logos*—that is, as a *legein ta alēthea*—as the gathering together of what shows itself, which is why Heidegger insists on the fact that the German word *retten* does not mean "save" but rather "keep in guard, liberate, shelter."[11]

Apprenticeship in such a method in no way consists in turning doctors into philosophers, but rather in simply making them more attentive to what inescapably concerns the human (ZS, 113) and therefore in forming doctors who think (*denkende Ärzte*) (ZS, 103). As Boss emphasizes, such apprenticeship requires not that Heidegger's teaching be followed as a series of magisterial courses, but rather that it resemble a kind of group therapy, and even a *Heideggersche Kur*, a "Heideggerian cure," which would, moreover, give rise to the same resistances as those encountered in Freudian analysis. In his personal letters to Boss, Heidegger himself expressed from the start his desire to engage in a dialogue, *ein Gespräch*, rather than giving lectures that risk remaining "mere spectacle" (eine Sache der blossen Repräsentation) (ZS, 301). This is why he will prefer the brief encounters with a small group that will take place in the 1960s at Boss's home because "nothing can replace the living word and discussion" (ZS, 247). He enjoys these meetings and asks Boss to invite the younger generation, less in order to teach them than to learn himself: "Real thinking cannot be learned from books. It also cannot be taught unless the teacher remains an apprentice, even in his old age," he writes in 1948 to Boss (ZS, 239). And in March 1965, he declares to the participants that in the preceding seminar (dedicated to time), he had learned more from them than they from him, and that this is completely normal (ZS, 67). As he had already written in *What Is Called Thinking?* "the teacher is ahead of his apprentices in this alone, that he has still far more to learn than they—he has to learn how to let them learn. The teacher must be capable of being more teachable than the apprentices are. The teacher is far less assured of his own ground than those who learn are of theirs."[12]

His concern is thus for a mutual relation of teaching between teacher and students, which has nothing to do with dispensing information, but which instead is a *Mitteilung*, a communication that is also a sharing, *ein Mit-einander-teilen*—and moreover this sharing is what initially makes communication possible (ZS, 161). It is not by chance that Heidegger evokes Socrates several times in the seminars because "Socrates knew better than anyone else up to the present about the things above, but we hardly know anything of what he knew" (ZS, 240). Socrates is not only the greatest thinker of the West because he wrote nothing, but also because unlike the Sophists, he knew how to do what was most difficult: to say the same of the same and (like Parmenides!) to speak in tautologies (ZS, 24). Socrates did not have a "philosophy," any more than Heidegger did.[13] His whole art is in his practice: this is what gives birth to minds—that is, sets them free. Rather than being dedicated to the critical discussion of theories, one ought to practice the art of questioning as Socrates did, which consists in endlessly debating the same phenomena and in showing that what is taken as a theme had already been ontologically understood in habitual behaviors and representations. It thus appears that the relation called "pedagogical" and the therapeutic relation are of the same nature, essentially consisting not in a violent behavior of "substitution," which would lead the teacher or the therapist to exert dominance over the student or patient and to act in the student's or patient's place, but rather in a practice of "deliverance," which may not be exempt from violence—as "resistance" to the cure testifies—but which aims merely at allowing the other to complete by himself the task incumbent upon him.

Boss had been struck by how Heidegger speaks in section 26 of *Being and Time* about "anticipatory concern" to the point that he sees the description of the ideal therapeutic relation in it because his own theory of transference coincides exactly with such a practice of deliverance in the framework of an analysis that must be conceived as eminently "terminable," unlike Freudian analysis. Here is the explicatory parable, borrowed from a "venerable Arab legend," that he gives in his *Einführung in die psychosomatische Medizin:*

> An old father on his deathbed summons his three sons, and leaves all of his worldly goods, seventeen camels, to them. He declares that the oldest son will receive half, the second son a third, and the youn-

gest a ninth, and after having said these words, he dies. The children are confused. They end up finding a sage, as wise as he is poor, who owns but one camel. The three sons call on him to help resolve the apparently unsolvable problem of the inheritance. The sage is happy to add his own camel to the seventeen others. The division of goods in accordance with the last will of the deceased is now child's play. The oldest son receives half of eighteen camels, that is, nine; the second son, a third, which is six camels; and the youngest gets two camels, a ninth. As foreseen by the father, the numbers nine, six, and two add up to only seventeen. And so, the remaining eighteenth camel is returned to the sage. They no longer need it, though at a given moment, it had been necessary.[14]

And Boss concludes: "Contrary to all the popular talk about transference, this is how the role of the analyst ordinarily ends." The merely "momentary" necessity of the presence of the therapist defines the essential character of the therapeutic relation: the doctor is not the cause of healing, but is only the occasion (*Anlass*) for it, which is why the therapeutic situation is a "human" situation characterized by the being-together, the *Mitsein*, of the doctor and the patient, which in no way can be reduced to the production of an objective process analogous to natural processes (ZS, 210–11).

One of the points on which Heidegger insists in the seminars concerns the distinction of motivation and causality, thus taking up again a fundamental theme of Husserlian phenomenology.[15] If causality is acting (*bewirkende*) and constraining (*zwingende*), motivation is by contrast determining (*bestimmende*) and free (*freie*) (ZS, 22). What characterizes the motive, says Heidegger, is that "it moves me" (*mich bewegt*), that "it addresses humans" (*dem Menschen anspricht*), or rather, it "tries" to do so, since *ansprechen* has not only the sense of addressing speech in German, but also of pleasing, or tempting; it belongs to the motive of being determined (*bestimmend*)—that is, of making a voice (*Stimme*) heard, to which it is possible to respond (ZS, 23). The motive can thus act by itself, as does the cause, and it can be a motivation (*Beweggrund*) only insofar as it is understood; as such, it is never independent of the understanding that one has of it (ZS, 200). The same goes for the doctor: he must not be understood as the efficient cause of the healing lest he remove the human and "communitarian" dimension from the therapeutic relation. He must instead be understood and behave as the occasion (*Anlass*) for the cure: being-in-common, *Mitsein*, in therapy is, for the doctor, a letting-be of the other, in letting the other heal itself (ZS, 210). We here find an idea that Aristotle had very strongly expressed in the first chapter of Book II of the *Physics* (1.192b23–27), on which Heidegger comments in 1939: it is the example of the doctor who heals himself, but who, as a doctor, is not the *archē* of his healing, but he is this as human—that is, as a living being endowed with a body and belonging as such to the order of *physis*. Heidegger comments on the passage in the following manner:

> Even then the art of medicine has only better supported and guided *physis*. *Technē* can merely cooperate with *physis*, can more or less expedite the cure; but as *technē* it can never replace *physis* and in its stead become the *archē* of *health* as such. This could happen only if life as such were to become a "technically" producible artifact. However, at that very moment there would also no longer be such a thing as health, any more than there would be birth and death.[16]

The doctor, insofar as he is the motive for and not the cause of the healing of the sick, adheres very exactly to the positive possibility of concern that Heidegger calls *vorausspringende Fürsorge*: a concerns that leaps out ahead of the other "not in order to take care away from him, but on the contrary to restitute it," as Heidegger says in section 26 of *Being and Time*. This is a care for the other, not for the thing about which it is concerned, and is the true aid that allows the other to "become free for his care." This extreme positive possibility of concern is therefore a "letting the other be" as "authentic care"—that is, in its own Dasein—and it is in this letting-be that Heidegger sees the highest form of the relation to the other.[17] There is, however, another *positive* possibility opposed to this one, which must not be included among deficient modes of concern such as indifference or socially organized assistance (which are the relations to the other that reduce the other to the mode of being manipulable [*Zuhandenheit*] like an everyday tool). This other positive possibility is the concern that leaps in for the other (*die einspringende Fürsorge*), a "substitutive" concern that is also a relation to the other as Dasein, but that, instead of being liberating, is dominating (*beherrschend*). It consists in putting the other in its place, taking charge of its care, completing its task for it, and it therefore runs the risk of putting the other in a situation of dependency and subjection that, as Heidegger notes, can remain veiled as such. With this second positive modality of concern, we are dealing less with a specialized model of somatic medicine that, when not accompanied by an account of the patient's overall human situation, would constitute a deficient mode of concern (the patient is not considered as a Dasein but as a collection of objective natural processes), than with a model of the perversions of the therapeutic (or pedagogical) relation, which slow rather than favor the patient's healing (or the student's process of apprenticeship) and which are therefore not forms of true aid, because they foreground not care for the other's existence but a preoccupation characterized by a use of tools.

Fürsorge is thus the modality of *Sorge* that concerns being-with, *Mitsein*, just as *Besorgen*, preoccupation, is the modality that concerns beings in the mode of a useable tool. *Sorge*, in the double sense of concern and care, characterizes all relations to beings as such (the relation of Dasein to the being that it itself is, the relation of Dasein to the being that is not itself and that is not of the order of Dasein, and the relation of Dasein to the being that is not itself but is of the order of Dasein). It is therefore not at all astonishing that the *same* form of the relation prevails everywhere. Heidegger understands what he calls *Verhalten*, comportment or the manner of being related, as what constitutes what is appropriate to the human who, in virtue of understanding being, is related to himself and to the being that is not himself (ZS, 153). This comportment or manner of carrying oneself is what constitutes Dasein, and is not at all the support for a relation that would merely be an ontic determination of its being. For comportment in the Heideggerian sense must not be understood as a relation uniting one pole to another but rather as an "engaging oneself in and with something, sustaining the manifestness of beings" (Sich-halten in und bei etwas, Aushalten der Offenbarkeit des Seienden, Aushalten der Offenständigkeit) (ZS, 198). But it is important to emphasize that what becomes manifest is *always* a being in the *triple* sense indicated. We could therefore reproach Heidegger for having been deaf to the voice of the other and for having listened only to being, if and only if being and other constitute a true alternative.[18]

Now, what characterizes Dasein, what constitutes its *Grundbestimmung* (not only its fundamental determination, but also its fundamental being-in-accord and destination), is to be open to the call, the claim, the address of presence: "*Grundbestimmung des Daseins: Offen für den Anspruch der Anwesenheit*" (ZS, 217). Such an opening, *Offenheit*, characterizes this domain where no proof prevails, the domain of a freedom that has to be understood as "being-free and being-open to an address" (*Freiheit ist Frei- und Offen-sein fur einem Anspruch*), and that is confused with *humanitas*, itself understood as the "free relation of the human to what encounters it such that he appropriates these relationships and lets himself be claimed by them" (Humanitas: Freier Bezug des Menschen zu dem, was ihm begegnet, dass er sich diese Bezüge aneignet und dass er sich dafür in Anspruch nehmen lässt) (ZS, 154). Human-being, *Menschsein*, is always presupposed in the grasping of any ontic phenomenon, even in the seizing of the preexistence of the earth *before* humans, because insofar as the human stands in the clearing of being, he can thus let be (*zulassen*) the particular mode of presence that is having-already-been. But if the human is thus the true a priori (*Das Früher-sein gehört zum Menschen*) (ZS, 181), then this implies that so too is *Miteinandersein*, being-with-one-another: "is being-with-one-another an encounter or does the potentiality for encounter presuppose being-with-one-another? The latter is the case" (ist das Miteinandersein ein Begegnen oder setzt das Begegen-können das Miteinandersein voraus? Dies letztere ist der Fall) (ZS, 216). Only in everyday being-with-and-for-one-another (im alltäglichen Mit-und Füreinandersein) can tears or blushing be perceived, and these are neither somatic nor psychical phenomena, but rather phenomena-of-the-flesh (*Leib-Phänomene*), which, as such, presuppose the relation to the similar (*den Bezüg zum Mitmenschen*) (ZS, 81, 114). If there is a common being within what confronts it (ZS, 112), this implies the mutuality of *Mitsein*, of a being-with that prompts us to speak of a relation between you and you, of a *Du-Du Beziehung* (ZS, 210), rather than a relation of I to you, or even of a we.

What finally unites the human with the world, with itself, and with the other is a relation of speech and the unity of a *Gespräch*, which, as Hölderlin says in "*Friedensfeier*," we are (ZS, 140). The universality of such a conversation makes possible the address and the response, the correspondence and the relation, taking in charge and assistance: "in his essential receptive-perceptive relatedness to what addresses him from his world-openness, the human is also already called upon to respond to it by his comportment. This means that he must first respond to it in such a way that he takes what he encounters into his care and that he aids it in unfolding its own essence as far as possible" (In seinem wesensmässigen vernehmenden Bezogen-sein auf das sich ihm aus seiner Weltoffenheit Zusprechende ist der Mensch aber auch immer schon aufgefordert, diesem mit seinem Verhalten zu ihm zu entsprechen, d.h. zu antworten, und zwar so, dass er das Begegnende in seine Hut nimmt, ihm nach Möglichkeit zu dessen Wesensentfaltung verhilft) (ZS, 231).

Because the human is "the guardian of this clearing and of *Ereignis*" (ZS, 178), he stands in a relation of assistance with respect to an opening that is not outside of him. Every thought that posits the being of the clearing in and for itself thereby refuses to be limited to what can be immediately experienced (*das unmittelbare Erfahrbare*)—that is, to the human as human, which is nothing other than the very standing of this relation. Such a thought—and Heidegger refers here to Indian thought[19]—can propose as a goal only the transformation of Dasein into pure clarity—that is, in the end, the idea of a dehumanization (*Entmenschlichung*). Heidegger remains within [*s'en tient à*] the thought of abiding [*se tenir*] in the clearing of Being, which elsewhere he calls *Inständigkeit*,[20] as constituting the very essence of the human, which can no longer be interpreted as a form of manifestation of the clearing itself. Such a thought implies not only what he had already named the "finitude of being" in "What Is Metaphysics?,"[21] but also the "finitude of the human," which must now be thought as a richness rather than a limitation: it is a richness (*Reichtum*) that is not to be submitted merely to the presence of the present (*die blosse gegenwärtige Anwesenheit*) but is to be equally open to the presence of the having-been and the yet-to-come (ZS, 177–80). Such a finitude does not, however, imply merely the mortality of humans, but also the death of humanity itself, that one could not conceive as existing indefinitely (ZS, 289).

To speak of the "therapeutic" relation is therefore something of a pleonasm similar to what made us speak of "human Dasein" (ZS, 120). The singular name of *Verhältnis* is *Sorge*, concern and the care of being, which alone can allow a being, in its triple sense, to have an encounter. We must therefore not be astonished, much less scandalized, by seeing in this a simplification of his thought, of what Heidegger gives an ontological interpretation of *stress* on the basis of what determines the *Verhältnis* as such—that is, the tension between *Beanspruchung* and *Entsprechen*, between the fact of being claimed by being and the necessity of responding to it or corresponding to it (ZS, 139–40). Without this being-claimed, the human would not be able to exist, Heidegger claims, and this is why stress, understood (like *Belastung*) as the fact of bearing a responsibility [*porter une charge*] is what maintains life. Stress must therefore be considered as an ontological phenomenon: it is an existential that has to do with *Verfallen*, fallenness, because it refers to the factual situation of everyday being-in-the-world (ZS, 137). It constitutes the inauthentic modality of the relation to the world that Heidegger called *Gelassenheit*, which should not be understood only as being freed of the charge—*Entlastung* remains a privative modality of *Belastung*—but as the "capacity" to be assigned the highest of tasks: the ontological task of the letting-be of beings.

For if "human illness" consists essentially in disturbances of adaptation and freedom (ZS, 155), then the issue in the therapeutic relation in the strict sense—that is, in the relation of doctor to patient—simply puts to work a modality of the relation that anticipates the freedom to be discovered by the patient. It is therefore only by witnessing her own freedom that the doctor or the teacher can give the other, the patient, or the student, his freedom. And this is the meaning of what Heidegger calls *vorausspringende Fürsorge*. For "the human is only an administrator of freedom," a being who has the possibility of liberating freedom and who, by letting freedom be, is "the being through which being in its totality and as such speaks and where it expresses itself [*hindurschspricht und ausspricht*]."[22]

8

Conscience: The Most Intimate Alterity

Ricoeur, Heidegger, Levinas

Must we say, as Levinas does, that in the Western tradition there is a primacy of ontology that does not allow for taking the alterity of the Other into account? We know Levinas's argument: the Other is neither "Being" [*être*] nor a "being" [*étant*] easily grasped by a concept, and understanding the Other within the ontological dimension would therefore be to objectify and do violence to the Other. What Levinas calls "the face" is the signification of the Other that does not come from me and that invokes my responsibility to the Other. This ethical address of the Other fundamentally puts the privilege granted to Being into question and authorizes Levinas, in *Totality and Infinity,* to attribute the role of first philosophy to ethics rather than to the science of Being. And at the end of this book, he haughtily declares that "morality is not a branch of philosophy, but first philosophy."[1]

But is there truly an incompatibility between ontology and ethics, and must Being and the Other be irreconcilably opposed? Does ontology not already have a practical and ethical dimension within itself that fundamentally determines it? Heidegger tells us in the "Letter on Humanism" that the thought of Being is in itself an "original ethics,"[2] because, in conformity with the fundamental meaning of the word *ēthos*, which means place of habitation, thought thinks Being as the original element of the existence of the human. And so for Heidegger, ethics is merged with ontology itself.

But what kind of ontology is in question here? Certainly not the Greek or classic ontology that posits Being outside of or "in front of" the human, which for Heidegger is an ontology of substance, of the preliminarily given, of *Vorhandenheit*, and which in principle excludes the properly human dimension; rather, the ontology concerned is the kind that, in *Being and Time*, Heidegger calls "fundamental ontology." Such an ontology places the relation of the human to Being at the very foundation of every statement of "being" and thinks the human as the particular kind of being that is not indifferent to being and that questions (at first, practically, then theoretically in the framework of philosophy) the being that it is and the being that it is not, which it does precisely because it is not "given" to itself, and instead has to realize its own being, has "to become what it is"—or in other words, because it exists and can only exist as a self-project. As we see here, ontology for Heidegger is not deprived of a practical dimension: it does not give primacy to pure seeing, to *theōria*, but instead to the "practical" freedom of an existence unfolding itself in the dimension of history, which is nothing but the realization of the relation to self and to other that the human is.

For Heidegger, "ontology" thus understood is always "practical," always "engaged," and therefore always includes an intrinsically ethical dimension. This is no doubt why Heidegger did not write an ethics: it is not at all necessary to "add" it on to an ontology, which would then become nothing but a simple part of philosophy. This implies that he thinks Being otherwise than does the tradition, which identifies Being and substance, and it also implies that, like Levinas, he critically situates his thought with respect to the Western tradition, unfolding it "outside" of philosophy or at the "end" of it, as he clearly suggests after the "turn."

Must we necessarily choose between Levinas, who invites us to think "otherwise than being," and Heidegger, who leads us to another thought of being? Could there instead be the possibility of thinking Being and the Other without opposing them? It seems to me that this is the question that Ricoeur takes up afresh in the last pages of *Oneself as Another*, pages that seem to bear witness to the culmination of the dialectic of alterity and ipseity that constitutes the most fundamental level of his hermeneutics of the self, which wants "to hold itself at equal distance from the cogito exalted by Descartes and from the cogito declared dead by Nietzsche."[3]

This dialectic of alterity and ipseity, whose "principal virtue" is "to keep the self from occupying the place of foundation,"[4] cannot be elevated to the properly speculative level of the meta-categories of the Same and the Other without preserving in a principled manner the aletheic (veritative) dimension, which is the dimension of a hermeneutics that can never be thought as anything other than reciprocal implication (and decidedly not as the exteriority) of the interpreting and the interpreted. This is no doubt what profoundly impedes considering the tenth study of *Oneself as Another* as constituting a truly superior degree of interpretation, which would have acquired an autonomy with respect to the preceding analyses. Such an autonomization of the speculative-ontological level would in principle fail to take account of an alterity that is only ever given in the dimension of attestation and that is therefore essentially disparate and broken. In this regard, the ironic tone of the last page of *Oneself as Another* in no way seems to be a mere evasion.[5] Ricoeur invokes Socratic irony there and plagiarizes Plato's *Parmenides* while alleging that only a discourse that leaves the modalities of alterity in a state of dispersion suits the very idea of alterity, "lest alterity be suppressed by becoming itself." The refusal to make alterity into an all-encompassing super-category, or, in a word, a genre, does not come simply from what we imagine to be Ricoeur's own decision to leave the three envisaged modalities of alterity (which refer to three great experiences of passivity of the proper body, the Other, and consciousness) in a state of dispersion,[6] or to put a question mark after ontology, as he does in the tenth study, entitled, "What Ontology in View?" The refusal is, in contrast, implied by the very type of ontology proposed there, the essential dimension of which is "engagement." This engagement places the finitude of the interpreting gaze at the heart of an enterprise that can be defined only as an ontological *approach* and never as a systematic construction. We understand why, in opposition to the short way of the Heideggerian analytic of Dasein, Ricoeur imposes what he subsequently calls the long way of the interpretation of existence, making a detour through the epistemological question; and we also understand why in this perspective, ontology remains "a promised land" only glimpsed, which he already emphasizes in *The Conflict of Interpretations*: "thus ontology is indeed the promised land for a philosophy that begins with language and reflection; but, like Moses, the speaking and reflecting subject can only glimpse this land before dying."[7]

The reference to another hermeneutics of the self, whose confirmation is the essential dimension (that is, the Heideggerian hermeneutics) of care, seems to impose itself here. Perhaps we should first briefly recall that, for Heidegger, ontology is something completely different from a promised land, not because finitude would be overcome in it, but rather because, as he clearly says in Davos, it is the "index or clue of our finitude."[8] For "only a finite creature needs ontology,"[9] and that which attests in us specifically to the necessity of interpretation and to the projection of a horizon of comprehensibility is the fact that we have to "welcome" the simultaneously frightening and marvelous alterity of a being that does not originate with us, but that is also ourselves, among others.

The entire Heideggerian undertaking is concentrated on a task that had already been Kant's—namely, the elaboration of an analytic of *Gemüt*—that is, of the self determined as a "structure to welcome" the other-than-self.[10] It is in this perspective that he is linked to Aristotle, the author of both the *Nichomachean Ethics* and *On The Soul*, who says that the soul is a being in its entirety, a phrase that Heidegger cites at the beginning of *Being and Time* as a confirmation of the ontico-ontological privilege of Dasein, which makes Dasein the condition for the possibility of all regional ontologies.[11]

An attentive rereading of *Kant and the Problem of Metaphysics* could show that it is the Kantian theory of pure sensibility, of a sensibility that preforms what it is prepared to receive, that leads to seeing the very structure of the ipseity of a finite subject in time understood as autoaffection,[12] a subject that subsequently can no longer be understood on the model of the substantiality of an ego, but must instead be defined essentially as care. Because care is above all the capacity of self-solicitation or self-address, of *Sich-selbst-angehen*, which permits its dependency on receptivity: "*angewiesen auf Hinnahme*," as the German text of the *Kantbuch* says.[13] It is the implication of the *Sich-selbst-angehen* and of the *Angewiesenheit*, of self-care and dependency, that then defines what Heidegger calls existence: "Existence means to be dependent upon the being as such in the submittance to the being as such which is dependent in this way."[14]

We clearly see here that if care is always self-care, "care for the self"—Heidegger explicitly says that "care for oneself . . . would be a tautology"[15]—then we cannot in any way understand it as a closing in of the self: "care cannot mean a special attitude towards the self, because the self is already characterized ontologically as being-ahead-of-self; but in this determination are already included the other two structural moments of care—the being-already-in and the being-together-with."[16]

We would therefore risk misconstruing the existential meaning of care, which implies the reference to the Other, if we were to replace autoaffection by the "hyperbole" (Ricoeur's word) of a heteroaffection, which would have the "exteriority" of the Other of which Levinas spoke as a presupposition. Ricoeur specifies: "By hyperbole, it must be strongly underscored that we are not to understand a figure of style, a literary trope, but the systematic practice of *excess* in philosophical argumentation."[17] And after having analyzed how in Levinas the Other is absolved of the relation and is absolutized, both in continuity and in rupture with Kantian ethics, Ricoeur concludes, "in truth, what the hyperbole of separation makes unthinkable is the distinction between self and I, and the formation of a concept of selfhood defined by its openness and its capacity for discovery."[18]

A pure heteroaffection is as unthinkable as a pure autoaffection. We can certainly reproach Heidegger for having unilaterally put too much emphasis on autoaffection until 1929, and for then defining Being only as the self-projection of Dasein. But thinking finitude still more profoundly, and being open to the "event" of the coppropriation of Being and of the human (that is, being open to a thought of the encounter as the simultaneity of call and response), is precisely the meaning of the "turn" (to which, unfortunately, Levinas gives little attention).

But to go back to the period preceding the turn, we would even have to say that if finitude—that is, receptivity—is what *makes itself* into existence, as Heidegger declares in the *Kantbuch*,[19] then *autoaffection never occurs except in view of this eminent capacity of heteroaffection* that characterizes the human in distinction from the animal, which is not open to Being as such because it is not open to itself as a nonsubstitutable singularity. The animal does not say "I," but if the human does—and if existence is at every moment my own in the distributive sense of *Jemeinigkeit*—it is because the human being is the kind of being that is not indifferent to its being,[20] and this nonindifference is concern for what is Dasein's ownmost—that is, death—from which no one can escape. The *same* of the self-same happens only in death, which explains why Heidegger could write "*sum moribundus*," the I is always in the midst of death, dying. He declares in his Summer Semester 1925 course that "if such pointed formulations mean anything at all . . . it is the *moribundus* that first gives meaning to the *sum*."[21]

But we must add that this hermeneutic of care as a hermeneutic of finitude and mortality is a hermeneutic of attestation. In these hermeneutics of the self, the self is understood not as an instance of representation in the dimension of a purely theoretical reason (to speak like Kant), but rather as essentially acting and responsible. In this respect, there is no doubt that the concept of *Sorge*, which itself has a noble heritage (and we would have to revisit its genealogy, before Seneca and the Stoics, all the way back to the preoccupation with death (*meletē thanatou*), which is philosophizing for Plato in the *Phaedo*),[22] must be reconciled with Aristotelian *praxis*, as Ricoeur underlines, drawing from the work of Franco Volpi and Jacques Taminiaux.[23] For the essentially temporal structure of autoaffection necessarily has a teleological sense: all behavior presupposes a "for-the-sake-of-which," an *Umwillen* that "always concerns the being of Dasein"[24] and that also equally refers to both the Aristotelian *hou heneka* and to the Kantian *Endzweck*.

But in the same breath, this implies that responsibility is understood as a constitutive structure of a being that understands itself only by responding to itself, only by assuming responsibility, since its facticity, far from being assimilable to the *factum brutum* of natural being, must instead be understood as what constrains existing being from taking charge of its own being: it is a matter of a *Faktizität der Überantwortung*,[25] a facticity of the reduction of Dasein to itself, as Heidegger specifies. Patočka often insisted in his reading of Heidegger on this ontologization of responsibility, which would later allow Heidegger to see original ethics in ontology itself, as he says in his "Letter on Humanism." But he sees there not an "elision of ethics" (which is the expression Ricoeur employs with respect to Heidegger in a 1988 interview),[26] but rather the abolition of a modern distinction between the representing subject and the acting subject, "a useless distinction partly responsible for those false moralisms of modern times that motivated Nietzsche's attack against morality."[27] This ontologization of responsibility requires, in any case, that fundamental ontology pass through attestation, *Bezeugung*.

We cannot be content to rest at the ontological-existential level, the level of the second degree of philosophical speculation (or meta-level, Ricoeur says), without raising the suspicion of a purely artificial construction. We must therefore go back down to the level that had preliminarily been placed in parentheses, the level of the ontic-existentiell. We must do this certainly not in order to appeal to the facts and the experience of it, as these would be considered natural facts given to description, modeled on what Heidegger calls *Vorhandenheit*. We must do this in order to appeal to another sort of fact, which in the second *Critique* Kant calls a "fact of reason" (*Faktum der Vernunft*),[28] and which is for him nothing other than consciousness of the moral law imposed on us by reason itself. This "fact of reason" as a metaphysical fact puts every description in check because it includes in itself the constitutive dimension of the affirmation of *Gewissen*, of moral conscience.

In the same manner, Heidegger seeks the affirmation of the being-able-to-be a self in a "*Faktum*," a fact recognized by common consciousness since it comes from Dasein's everyday self-explanation: the voice of conscience (*die Stimme des Gewissens*). But this fact is not a natural *Tatsache*, a fact of nature, since its reality is subject to controversy—essentially subject to suspicion, Ricoeur will say. And like him, Heidegger sees in the "ambiguity" of this fact the proof that it is in the original phenomenon of Dasein. For only what needs to be affirmed and is not presented as a fact of nature can be contested, according to that rigorous logic wherein the dimension of belief, of faith, is inseparable from the dimension of doubt. Ricoeur underlines that this vulnerability of affirmation goes together with its practical (not theoretical) essence—that is, with the fact that the discourse of affirmation is not a discourse of foundation,[29] and that it consequently *always demands once again* new "practical" confirmations.

For, we must insist—and this is why I was led to use the superlative in the title of this essay (the *most* intimate alterity), taking as a model Ricoeur's statement about conscience as "the most deeply hidden passivity" in contrast to other passivities that belong to the experience of the proper body and the relation to the Other[30]—that what in my view makes the character of moral conscience paradigmatic as the experience of alterity and passivity is that the dimension of affirmation originally constitutes it and is inscribed directly on it. What is moral conscience? The noun *conscience*, *cum scientia* (to which in French it is sometimes, but not always, necessary to add the adjective "moral" in order to distinguish it from psychological consciousness), is in a sense more precise than the German noun *Gewissen*, which refers to the idea of certainty, because it copies exactly the Greek *syneidesis*, and above all because it bears the mark of *cum-*, of *syn-*, of *with*, thus implying a relation to alterity. *Synoida* in Greek has the meaning of "knowing with another," "being complicit with," and also "being witness to," as well as knowing in itself, of knowing "internally." This inner knowledge thus somehow supposes that it testifies to itself, which we might in German call *Mitwissen* rather than *Gewissen*. But to become witness to oneself requires that this being-with-self be experienced precisely in dissymmetry, which manifests the character of the address of the voice of conscience. We cite Ricoeur here: "In this intimate conversation, the self appears to be called upon and, in this sense, to be *affected* in a unique way. Unlike the dialogue of the soul with itself, of which Plato speaks, this affection by another voice presents a remarkable dissymmetry, one that can be called vertical, between the agency that calls and the self called upon. It is the vertical nature of the call, equal to its interiority, that creates the enigma of the phenomenon of conscience."[31] And earlier, it was a question of "this passivity without equal," of which "the metaphor of the voice, at once inside me and above me, is the symptom or clue."[32]

Essential here is that the verticality of the call is what constitutes the self as self, as if within the autoaffection by which ipseity comes forth, and as if within the immanence of the self, the refraction of transcendence, the dimension of heteroaffection, was necessary. Yet this union of incompossibles, of autoaffection and heteroaffection, occurs as voice, as call, as address: "here is found the feature that distinguishes the phenomenon of consciousness, namely, the sort of cry (*Ruf*) or call (*Anruf*) that is indicated by the metaphor of the voice."[33] And Ricoeur immediately specifies that it would be necessary here to think the disclosing capacity of metaphoricity by referring to the analyses of the seventh study in *The Rule of Metaphor* that ends up at the idea of "metaphorical truth."

A little further on, after the ordeal of suspicion called for by the metaphorical character of conscience itself, which denounces conscience as "bad" in Hegel and Nietzsche, Ricoeur comes back to Heidegger and underlines that he has the merit of tearing conscience away from the false alternative of good and bad by not referring it to a capacity to distinguish good and evil "in itself." He declares, "We are all the more attentive to Heidegger's analysis as we owe to him the starting point of this entire discussion of the metaphor of the voice."[34] We thus find in Heidegger a truth of the "metaphor" of the voice that has to be placed in relation to the fact that the voice "says" nothing and that, against the neo-Kantianism of values and Schelerian material ethics, conscience is placed in a perfectly Kantian manner "beyond good and evil." Because for Kant, as well (and this is what explains the formal character of the imperative), good and evil cannot be determined prior to the moral law. Kant declares in the second *Critique* that "the concept of good and evil must not be determined prior to the moral law (which . . . should however serve as ground), but only after this law and because of this law."[35] This "paradox" (Kant's own term) is at the very foundation of the notion of autonomy, since heteronomy is characterized precisely by dissociating the good and the will, by making the good into an object of the will rather than the very form of the will. It consequently seems to me that the Heideggerian position depriving the silent call of conscience of all content is in line with Kantianism.

The phenomenon of conscience in Heidegger thus refers to the idea of autonomy: "Dasein calls itself in conscience."[36] There is the same identity of the calling and the called, of the agent and the patient that already characterized the phenomenon of angst. We find here in the structure of the call the triplicity of the temporal structure of care: (a) what is called is fallen Dasein captivated by the world; (b) what at present calls is Dasein in its pure facticity, Dasein as thrownness, which is in the past; and (c) what is called to is authentic Dasein projected into the future as authentic being-toward-death. The call does not call for doing this or that, but rather only *to be in another mode* or *to want to be otherwise*, and therefore the call, like the Kantian imperative, has a formal character.

This identity of autoaffection as autonomy has to be conjoined with the strangeness of the call, which makes us leave behind the simple dialogue with oneself: "The call without a doubt does not come from someone else who is with me in the world. The call comes *from* me and yet *over* me."[37] This strangeness is precisely the strangeness of a self not originally at home with itself, but instead always thrown into the world. As Ricoeur underlines, it arises from the radical passivity of a being that is not at the origin of itself and is therefore in the position of receptivity with respect to itself. *This implies that facticity itself flows from the superiority of the call that inscribes alterity in the very heart of the self, and that therefore makes all autonomy also a heteronomy.* We must mention in this regard that at Davos, Heidegger recalls to Cassirer (who seems to have forgotten it) that the Kantian imperative has meaning only for a finite being and that it is therefore intrinsically inscribed in the constitution of a finite being. To Cassirer, who sees an overcoming of finitude in Kantian ethics, Heidegger declares that "we proceed mistakenly in the interpretation of Kantian ethics if we first orient ourselves to that to which ethical action conforms and if we see too little of the inner function of the law itself for Dasein."[38] In his interpretation of the *Critique of Pure Reason*, Heidegger wanted to show precisely that in Kant, the infinity of the ontological understanding of a being remains principally linked to ontic experience.

Yet this strange union of the ontic and the ontological, of infinity and finitude, of immanence and transcendence, occurs *in* the voice and *as* voice. I would like to underline this last characteristic. Heidegger insists on the fact that everyday discourse must be taken literally: "what is characteristic about conscience as a call is by no means only an 'image,' like the Kantian representation of conscience as a tribunal."[39] This is not a metaphor for Heidegger, but instead a true experience of what the voice is. For it is not essential to discourse (*Rede*) to have to be stated phonetically, to be language (*Sprache*) and voice (*Stimme*), and in German, it does not have the purely vocal meaning of the Greek *phōnè*, but instead the juridical meaning of giving one's opinion by a vote. This is why Heidegger underlines that the "voice is understood as giving to understand."[40] There may therefore be a silent voice, one that does not "speak," as a pure phenomenon of "understanding," a pure phenomenon of sense, just as there can be a listening that is not reduced to simple acoustic perception.

We may, moreover, wonder whether or not what we understand by "meaning" always supposes this dissymmetry or temporal inadequacy with oneself, which is experienced in the call, and whether or not "meaning" must be put in relation to temporality. This is what obliges Merleau-Ponty to say in *The Prose of the World* that "in any language, there is nothing but *under*standings" and that "the very idea of a complete expression [is] inconsistent," since "meaning is beyond the literal, meaning is always ironic."[41] For voice here does not at all mean immediate self-presence, but instead reveals that the self has no intimacy with itself, since it is only in the inadequation, the lag between the two voices of everydayness and of conscience, that it knows (to speak in terms borrowed from Merleau-Ponty referring to the experience of another passivity and alterity—namely, that of the flesh) "a proximity in distance" or a "partial coincidence" with itself. Both the silence of the call and its formal (and not phonetic character) are therefore yet to be inscribed in the dimension of an ipseity that always exists in the mode of the promise of the self-same—that is, in the mode of a maintenance of self, a *Selbständigkeit* that has nothing to do with the substantiality of an ego.

Can we therefore speak of a "de-moralization of conscience," as Ricoeur does concerning Heidegger?[42] It seems to me (or at least this is what I have tried to show by drawing a parallel between Kant and Heidegger) that we can do so only from a Hegelian point of view, which indeed has its pertinence—that is, from the point of view of a suspicion cast on the *moralische Weltanschauung*, on the "moral vision of the world." Hegel likewise insists on the fact that abstract Kantian morality is the very principle of immorality in that all immoral or unjust behavior can be justified by the definition of duty as simple formal agreement with the self.[43] In this respect, the critique of resoluteness as "resoluteness to nothing" addressed to Heidegger curiously recalls the critique of the beautiful soul, the Kantian *schöne Seele*, Peguy's formulation of which is often cited, and gives an arresting summary: "Kant would have pure hands, but he doesn't have hands."

But on the other hand, this critique must be taken seriously, since it has the merit of bringing to light in both Heidegger and Kant that moral realization is a problem—and no doubt more of a problem in Heidegger than in Kant, precisely because the practical is no longer distinguished from the theoretical, and because thinking seems to constitute all morality. Does Heidegger not claim at the beginning of the "Letter on Humanism" that "thinking acts insofar as it thinks" and that "action is presumably the simplest and at the same time the highest because it concerns the relation of Being to humans"?[44] What finally allows us to distinguish the Kantian interpretation of conscience from the Heideggerian is the status of the call in the second person, the "Thou Shalt" of the imperative, which is not marked out *as such* in Heidegger. This is why the gesture whereby Ricoeur asks that the phenomenon of affirmation and of injunction be narrowly associated seems to me to constitute the passage to a true ontology of action.[45] For in this way, the passivity of being called is decisively related to another alterity, the alterity of the Other (of the *aliud*) announced in the constitutive alterity of the self (the alterity of the *alter*), which is, according to Heidegger, of a temporal essence.[46]

That the *alterity* of the Other sketches itself out in the *alterity* of conscience does not mean, however, that they are merged. And it is precisely on this point that Ricoeur takes his distance from Levinas, whose reductive gesture is now called into question.[47] Ricoeur sees in Levinas a reduction of the alterity of consciousness to the exteriority of the Other, which constitutes for Ricoeur the symmetrical gesture of the Heideggerian reduction of being-in-debt to the foreignness linked to the facticity of being in the world. Ricoeur's concern is to oppose to this alternative (either foreignness for Heidegger, or exteriority for Levinas) a third solution that would see the very structure of ipseity in being-joined. This is why he severely criticizes the Levinasian "phenomenology of separation," in which he sees rather a "phenomenology of egoism" marked with the seal of hyperbole that leads Levinas to statements of the type "in separation . . . the I is ignorant of the Other."[48] Ricoeur underlines that the hyperbole of the absolute exteriority of the Other takes a paroxysistic turn in *Otherwise than Being*, when, in order to affirm the boundless assignment of responsibility, Levinas goes so far as to claim that "ipseity, in its passivity without the archē of identity, is hostage."[49] What this hyperbole of absolute heteronomy makes unthinkable by filling in the abyss between identity and alterity is exactly what Ricoeur wants to bring to light—that is, ipseity as the structure of welcome for the Other, an other who is no longer "scandalously" identified with an offender or a persecutor.

The double response that Ricoeur thus gives—to Levinas, on the one hand, he responds that injunction is originarily affirmation, and to Heidegger, on the other hand, he responds that affirmation is originarily injunction—seems to me to constitute a rigorous fidelity to a hermeneutics of the self, which is also authentically a hermeneutics of finitude. He therefore refuses the speculative facility that always consists in generalizing—that is, erecting alterity as a homogenous genre. Ricoeur's concern is "to maintain a certain equivocity on the purely philosophical plane of the status of the Other." This is why *Oneself as Another* ends with this phrase: "On this aporia of the Other, philosophical discourse comes to an end."[50] That there is an aporia of the Other is perhaps eminently what the philosopher has to think because his discourse "comes to an end": mortal like him, it could not be totalized—that is, it could neither know absolutely in what way it is of the Other nor be understood absolutely with the help of those meta-categories that are the great genres of speculation.

Remaining in resonance with this final remark by Ricoeur, as well as with Heidegger's original ethics, I would like to conclude by saying that the philosopher must also be able *to be silent* on the subject of ethics, for such a silence alone is perhaps what makes the opening to ethical *practice* possible.

PART III

Temporality and History

9

Temporality and Existence
Merleau-Ponty between Husserl and Heidegger

In the chapter "Temporality," found in the third part of *Phenomenology of Perception*, Merleau-Ponty recalls that starting in his first book, *The Structure of Behavior*, his concern is specifically to understand the relation between consciousness and nature and to link together the realist and idealist perspectives—that is, to link the point of view of a consciousness *constituting* the object to the point of view of a consciousness *constituted* by the objective world and inserted into it.[1] Consciousness and the world, the inside and the outside, sense and non-sense, had for him never been separate beings that required an external philosophical reflection to be reunited, but instead are interdependent beings. This interdependence became legible in the phenomenon of embodiment and of perception, wherein the paradoxical relation of spontaneity to receptivity, of activity to passivity, is announced. But as Merleau-Ponty emphasizes, the analysis of time is not only an occasion to repeat what had already been discovered at other levels, but also to clarify the total project of a phenomenology of perception "by making the subject and object appear as two abstract moments of the unique structure that is presence."[2]

For Merleau-Ponty, the problem of time is the problem of the subject's *relation* to time; that is, it is not derived from the principal problem, that of subjectivity (the analysis of which would require "drawing out the consequences of a pre-established conception of subjectivity"), but is instead the problem of the *tension* between the subject's presence to itself and its transcendence beyond itself toward the world. Like corporeity, sexuality, and spatiality, temporality is not a contingent attribute of existence. If, according to Merleau-Ponty, "there are no principal and subordinate problems," but rather "all problems are concentric"[3]—that is because, for him, there is only one unique problem, which includes within itself all other problems (of the body, the other, space, and time)—namely, the problem of subjectivity, of the subject's transcendence—a subject that by virtue of living *in* the world is consequently unable to reduce the world to the status of a mere object. All problems of transcendence (whether it be the problem of the body, the other, space, or time) pose the same question of knowing "how I can be open to phenomena which transcend me and which exist only to the extent that I take them up and live them, *how the presence to myself (Urpräsenz) which establishes my own limits and conditions all alien presence is at the same time depresentation (Entgegenwärtigung) and throws me outside of myself*."[4] For Merleau-Ponty, the subject's relation to time is even more intimate than the relation described by Kant, for whom time is the form of inner sense and the most general character of mental facts. Now, the analysis of time comes after the analyses of the body and the perceived world (which constitute the first two parts of *Phenomenology of Perception*), and after the analysis of the cogito (the first chapter of the third part, "Being-for-self and Being-in-the-world"), and will subsequently serve as the ground of freedom in the very last chapter of the book. This is because time alone provides us access to the "concrete" structure of the subject; for Merleau-Ponty, the subject is neither "in" time in the manner that spatial things and mental events are, nor is it eternal, nor can it be identified in any way with the absolute spirit, whose gaze is born from out of nowhere and dominates and embraces the totality of all objects. The subject's temporality comes from an "inner necessity" of the human condition that makes the subject and time "communicate from within": it is ultimately *time* that is "the meaning of life," as Claudel claims in *Art poétique* in a turn of phrase that Merleau-Ponty borrows as an exergue for the chapter on temporality, adding to it a complementary sentence from Heidegger.[5] Neither is Time *in* the subject, nor the subject *outside* of time; we must instead say that "we *are* temporality"[6]—that is, that existence is the dialectic of past and future, which alone makes us *present* to the world and allows us to inhabit it.

For Merleau-Ponty, the object of the analysis of time is thus the embodied subject's simultaneous self-presence and presence to the world. This new conception of the subject allowed him to leave behind the abstract intellectualism of a cogito or a subject without world;[7] instead, he identifies the subject with engagement in the world, as Sartre had already done.[8] Merleau-Ponty abandons an analysis of subjectivity's pure form in favor of showing the function assigned to time in every intellectual act, a path in inquiry initially opened but not pursued by Kant in his theory of the schematism.[9] This consequently requires a descent into the "hyletic" depths of consciousness, as Husserl had done in his *Phenomenology of Internal Time-Consciousness*; or, put differently, starting from time itself, we must proceed to concrete subjectivity. "To analyze time," Merleau-Ponty thus states, "is not to follow out the consequences of a pre-established conception of subjectivity, it is to gain access, through time, to its concrete structure. If we succeed in understanding the subject, it will not be in its pure form, but by seeking it at the intersection of its dimensions. We must therefore consider time in itself, and by following its internal dialectic, we will be led to reform our idea of the subject."[10]

As John Sallis shows in a close interpretation of the chapter on temporality in *Phenomenology of Perception*,[11] it becomes clear that we will have to work through three successive stages in order to resolve the question. For what characterizes the development of a thought as it merges with experience is that it first passes through realism (first stage) and then through idealism (second stage) before finally coming to phenomenology (third stage), which alone is capable of thinking passivity *as* activity and of seeing a "passive synthesis" in time, according to one of Husserl's expressions borrowed by Merleau-Ponty.[12] This triadic structure of the process of thought, a reflection [*reflet*] of the dialectic of experience, comprises first the realist response to the problem of time (the subject is *in* time), then the idealist response (the subject is *outside* of time), and finally Merleau-Ponty's phenomenological response (the subject *is* time).

The realist position is that the subject is *in* time, and like any thing is "subject" to time, which implies a "factuality" or an "objectivity" of time. This is what we mean when we speak of time as a flow, according to a metaphor as old as philosophy—namely, that of time as a river, into which one can never step twice, as we've known since Heraclitus.[13] Merleau-Ponty clearly demonstrates the confused character of this famous metaphor, which claims to situate successivity (the before and the after) within objective events themselves, which a subjectivity would then merely record even as it participates in them. But because time is not a thing or a dimension of things, but rather a relation, "it arises from *my* relation to things."[14] The future and the past do not exist in the objective world, which is "too full for there to be time," since the non-being of yesterday and tomorrow is missing from it; this non-being can be unfolded only by a subjectivity who is the "witness" of the flow and for whom what is upstream and downstream, though not actually given, is nevertheless present—whereas we find only "nows" everywhere in the objective world, detached from the finite perspectives opening on it and from the gaze of the finite observer who carves events out of it.[15]

But putting time "in" subjectivity does not let us escape the realist point of view, which views time as a real process. The Bergsonian critique of physiological theories of memory discredits the idea of a bodily preservation of the past in cerebral traces, but does not break with the idea of memories preserved in the unconscious.[16] The thesis of psychological preservation continues to assume the being-present of the past in the form of contents of consciousness. Yet no present bodily or mental trace *by itself* could ever refer to the past or the future unless these two dimensions have already been unfolded *in advance* by a being who has a sense of the past and the future and that is *itself* always situated in the dimension of successivity. We cannot make the past or the future out of the present; the present must instead become a *sign* of what was or what will be, which is possible only if the *passage* of time (from the present to the past and from the future to the present) already constitutes our originary experience. Only on this basis can we then delimit events within time and give them autonomous existence by objectifying them. This is why Merleau-Ponty states that "time is thought by us before the parts of time, the temporal relations make possible events in time. The subject must thus correlatively not be situated itself so that it may be present in intention to the past and the future. We no longer say that time is a 'given of consciousness,' but rather more precisely we say that 'consciousness deploys or constitutes time.' "[17]

Saying that consciousness deploys or unfolds time thus leads us from the realist to the idealist point of view. But the idealist refutation of the subject's being-in-time leads to the claim of the subject's nontemporality. The subject must be outside of time if we want it to be able to synthesize all the parts of time. Time is thus subjected to the subject, and the subject is no longer subject to time. A consciousness constituting time must be outside of the moments of time and not imprisoned in any one of them, precisely in order to be able to freely place them in relation. Merleau-Ponty wonders whether consciousness's liberation from time is nothing more than an illusion of freedom that closes off rather than opening up consciousness's access to temporality, in the sense that being free *of* time is not equivalent to being free *for* time. For time constituted wholly by consciousness is a "leveled" time, a succession of nows similar to real time, which is *for* no one, since the subject is entirely disengaged from it. Yet the very "essence" of time is such that it can never be completely deployed beneath the disengaged spectator's gaze, and it can never be completely constituted and "completed" precisely because it "is" not of the order of being, but rather of the order of *process*, of coming-forth or passage: "it is essential to time to become and not to be," as Merleau-Ponty says, translating the Heideggerian discourse on time that "*is* not, but rather temporalizes itself."[18]

Realism immerses the subject in time to the point of destroying every possibility of the consciousness of time as a unitary phenomenon because consciousness is enclosed exclusively in the dimension of its present. But idealism, which wants to free consciousness from its imprisonment in the "objective" present and open it to the totality of time, only manages to make incomprehensible what it wants to "make explicit" (namely, consciousness's *intrinsic* relation to time) because the time constituted or deployed by idealism is not "true" time (that is, "the passage or transit itself") but only its derivative result ("this setting distinct from me where nothing either elapses or happens").[19] In the two cases, what remains beyond reach for objective thought (in both its realist and idealist modes) is *passage* itself, which this thought can grasp only in its result—precisely because objective thought remains incapable of truly relating time to consciousness or consciousness to time, making them into distinct and separate "beings" that have to be reunited from the outside, instead of joining "from within" this non-being that "is" consciousness with this other non-being that "is" time. As John Sallis says, "it is prescribed in the framework of these alternatives that the subject must be wholly in time or wholly outside time, and each possibility leads, in the end, to a sacrifice of time-consciousness."[20]

Another "alternative" must therefore be considered, one that does not end with the "sacrifice" of time-consciousness, an expression that must now be written with hyphens in order to show that we are dealing with a unitary structure expressing the non-scission between "a real that unfolds and a consciousness that watches" (or in other words, expressing the reciprocal "immanence" of consciousness in relation to time and time in relation to consciousness, which is exactly what constitutes Husserl's problem in the 1905 *Lectures*, as Gérard Granel has shown).[21] Time-consciousness is always sacrificed when the connection of the different parts of time (that is, the synthesis of time) is thought as *already* accomplished, either in the object or in the subject. The synthesis of time itself must instead be understood as temporal, or in other words, as always in the midst of being accomplished rather than as always already completed, which is how the "hyperdialectic" that Merleau-Ponty develops in *The Visible and the Invisible* allows one to conceive it.[22] The hyperdialectic is a dialectic without *Aufhebung*, or a dialectic whose synthesis remains always incomplete, because it is always "inchoate" and in a "nascent state" in that it is a dialectic of experience and not the coming-to-self of an absolute subjectivity. Indeed, for Merleau-Ponty, this absolute subjectivity remains the "philosophers' dream"—the dream of an eternity beyond the permanent and the changing, hindering them from accessing the eternity encountered "at the heart of the experience of time," which is the point from which we must begin but from which it is in no way a question of escaping because, as Merleau-Ponty states, "the problem is how to explicate time in its nascent state and while it is appearing, and how it is always subtended by the notion of time, which is not an object of our knowledge, but a dimension of our being."[23]

Merleau-Ponty's interest is therefore to pursue this third way, the phenomenological path, in order to think consciousness's engagement in time and the structural identity of temporality and subjectivity. This implies accomplishing the dialectical "sublation" [*la relève*] of the positive content of realism and idealism,[24] rather than opening an entirely new path and abandoning the well-worn traditional paths. But concretely, this means that we have to bring Husserl and Heidegger, whose different phenomenological styles are normally opposed, into dialogue, which in turn leads Merleau-Ponty to claim (in his original interpretation of Husserl's famous diagram of time in the 1905 *Lectures*) that operant intentionality [*die fungierende Intentionalität*] "which Husserl is led to place in evidence under the intentionality of act that is the thetic consciousness of an object is nothing less than what Heidegger calls transcendence."[25] The discovery in the 1905 *Lectures* of this "anonymous" intentionality, which makes consciousness into a unitary flow and thereby makes objectifying intentionality possible, may well constitute an advance over the "transcendental voluntarism" on which the *Logical Investigations* still depended (wherein intentionality is too one-sidedly conceived as the subject's activity),[26] but the consequence of this for Husserl is neither the destabilization nor the shattering of the subject. Instead, it lets Husserl bring to light what one might call the "passivity of its activity." Husserl's last word—at least in the 1905 lectures on internal time-consciousness, the only one of Husserl's texts on time cited by Merleau-Ponty in *Phenomenology of Perception*—is the affirmation of the absolute temporal flux's self-constitution and its identity with subjectivity.[27]

The bringing to light of consciousness's double intentionality—which we could call its originally divergent strabism, which directs the intentional gaze both through temporal profiles to the object constituted by them and to the flux of constituting consciousness itself as a flux of profiles or phases of the temporal flow—does not in any way lead Husserl to the subject's "deconstruction," but instead leads him to the affirmation of the flow's self-constituting phenomenality, which implies the possibility for the flow itself to appear in its flowing, and for the One to make itself appear in the multiple. Merleau-Ponty seems to rejoin Husserl's position when he understands ek-stasis as a subject's ek-stasis, whereas Heidegger understands it as the ek-stasis of an existence that is, so to speak, always "thrown." This is what emerges from this passage from *Phenomenology of Perception*:

> This *ek-stasis*, this indivisible projection of an outcome that is already present to it, is subjectivity. The originary flow, says Husserl, not only *is*, but must also necessarily give itself as a "manifestation of itself" (*Selbsterscheinung*), without our needing to place behind it another flow which is conscious of it. . . . It is essential to time to be not only actual time or time which flows, but time which is aware of itself, for the explosion or dehiscence of the present towards a future is the archetype of *the relation of self to self* and traces out an interiority or an ipseity.[28]

Heidegger appeals to the transcendence of an *existence* rather than a subject to show the *derivative* character of intentionality (objectifying or operant, transversal or longitudinal)[29] and of every intentional *gaze* with respect to a being always already thrown in the world and attuned to it. For Heidegger, affective disposition (*Befindlichkeit*), in the sense that it is attunement (*Stimmung*) with the whole of the being, is what originally opens us to the world—not the gaze by which we intend the phenomenal, whether the latter be understood as manifest being or as a self-manifesting subjectivity. Moreover, Heidegger openly makes this claim in "On the Essence of Ground," a 1928 text dedicated to Husserl for his seventieth birthday, by underlining that transcendence allows for an understanding of intentionality rather than the reverse.[30] Heidegger rejects the classical opposition of transcendence and immanence (which still orders Husserlian thought despite the complication to which phenomenology submits it)[31] and claims that it is not the thing that is transcendent (that is, exterior to consciousness), but rather that what is transcendent—that is, what authentically transcends—is on the contrary what modern thought conceived of as an immanent subject. For we are not dealing with a subject that initially and originally remains in itself in order then to transcend itself intentionally toward objects, but rather with an existence that is always already outside of itself and ek-statically open to the world. Insofar as such an existence merges with the very movement of transcendence that originally takes it outside of itself, it cannot be understood on the model of *hypokeimenon*, the substrate that was translated into Latin as *subiectum*. All intentional relations occur only on the ground of such a transcendence because intentionality puts into play not only the subject's *intentio* and the object as *intentum*, but also, as Heidegger shows in *The Basic Problems of*

Phenomenology,[32] the understanding of the object's mode of being—that is, the preliminary opening of being that alone makes the disclosure of beings possible or, put in more concrete terms, the preliminary opening of the world that alone makes the discovery of the singular thing possible. Now, this opening precedes every objectifying grasp effected by transcendence insofar as it is merged with an existence that is always in the midst of completing itself and that is able to "see" itself only as always already completed, according to the finitude inherent to thrownness.

When Merleau-Ponty joins the terms "subject" and "transcendence" together in the same sentence, we could say from a strictly Heideggerian point of view that he in some way mixes fire and water and tries to identify subjectivity with existence, intentionality with transcendence, by making the subject inseparable from the world and by making activity into a mere consequence of a passivity of intentionality. In doing so, *he enlarges subjectivity instead of deconstructing it*. I would like to try to think of Merleau-Ponty's position in *Phenomenology of Perception* as the intermediary position between, on the one hand, the completion [*achèvement*] of the tradition and the fulfillment [*accomplissement*] of modernity represented by Husserl's transcendental phenomenology and, on the other hand, the "new beginning for thought" that Heidegger wants to promote, insofar as he attempts not so much to "overcome" (*überwinden*) but rather to assume or take on (*verwinden*) metaphysics—that is, to restore the tradition to its truth without, however, taking up once again its fundamental concepts, but rather by returning to the original experiences from which those concepts are derived.[33]

In such a perspective, Merleau-Ponty appears as the figure of the phenomenological movement situated "between" Husserl and Heidegger. Now it is precisely with respect to the problem of time, whose capital importance for both Husserl and Heidegger is well known, that Merleau-Ponty's mediating position appears in all its fullness. We must recall that in 1905, Husserl sees in the question of time "the secular cross of the problem of knowledge"[34] and, later in 1913, the place of "the definitive and true absolute" with respect to which the transcendental absolute brought about by the reduction is only secondary.[35] Heidegger's fundamental question, in contrast, concerns the explication of time as the horizon of the understanding of Being on the basis of the kind of being that understands Being, which he calls "Dasein" rather than "subject." I would like to try briefly to highlight Merleau-Ponty's situation "between" Husserl and Heidegger by following the movement of the entire chapter on "Temporality" in *Phenomenology of Perception*. For the moment, I will have to leave aside the perspectives opened in *The Visible and the Invisible*, a book in which, despite its incompleteness, it is clearly suggested that the "reformation of consciousness" will more decisively take the form of a *destruction* of the classical subject and in which transcendental phenomenology is definitively dismissed, precisely because consciousness is thought in it (against the Husserlian project of bringing mute experience to speech)[36] as operant intentionality and because the emphasis is placed on the irreducible divergence between Being and meaning, the silence of experience and philosophical speech.[37]

Merleau-Ponty's third way carries out the sublation of realism and idealism and so retains their positive content. What it preserves of realism is the privileged character of the dimension of the present that comes from the immersion of the subject "in" time: "there is time for me because I have a present. . . . None of the dimensions of time can be deduced from the others. But the present (in the broad sense, with its originary horizons of past and future) has a privilege because it is the zone where Being and consciousness coincide."[38] Does Merleau-Ponty here simply renew the privilege granted to self-presence (which Derrida sees in Husserl's work)[39] by invoking the necessity of avoiding an infinite regress by arriving at an ultimate consciousness that has nothing else behind it and in which Being and being-conscious are one and the same? It seems that the present to which Merleau-Ponty refers here is the Husserlian "living" present, which is not reduced to the punctuality of the now, but rather as an "enlarged" presence, includes retentional and protentional horizons within it. There may therefore be a primacy of the present, but it is *not* the present in which realism sees the dimension appropriate to objective being, which Heidegger calls *Vorhandenheit*—that is, being's always already complete presence conceived as substance. For Merleau-Ponty, however, this primacy of the present does not refer only to this "life" of consciousness, which, because it is able to retain all of the past, guarantees its own continuity and thus leaves behind the instantaneity that Bergson had confused with unconsciousness itself.[40] For Merleau-Ponty, consciousness of the present is not the result of a subject absolutely transparent to itself, for which Being is reduced to the knowledge that the subject has of it, but rather of a subject "complicit" with the world; and because it is "in-the-world," its "being conscious" is merged with "ex-sistence" itself,[41] implying that its self-presence is also self-absence and likewise exists "in" the world.[42] By seeing the experience of a self-presence (which is at the same time presence to other) in the consciousness of the present, Merleau-Ponty paradoxically rejoins the Heideggerian existential analysis. This is in effect what he states: "It is by communicating with the world that we indubitably communicate with ourselves. We take time in its entirety and we are present to ourselves because we are present to the world."[43] Heidegger does not define Dasein any differently when he sees it as the kind of being that is itself concerned with its own being, the kind of being that is not indifferent to its being, precisely because it is open to Being and because it is concerned by the Being of beings.[44] This ontico-ontological privilege of Dasein—by which (as Aristotle says of the *psyche*) it is "in a certain way beings"—is what, by making its being the site of presence,[45] prevents thinking the human's being as a subject closed in on itself and deserted by the truth.

But the subject's situation in the present must allow it to originarily open itself to other dimensions of time (the past and the future) if it is to have consciousness of time as a whole—and as we have seen, this is what constitutes idealism's "positivity," which frees consciousness from its realist incarnation in the present alone. This liberation guarantees the Husserlian enlarged present because it opens it to the immediate past and future by showing the abstract character of the punctual now and of the linear representation of time in contrast to the effectivity of the "field of presence" where the "network of intentionalities" comprising time is unfolded. As Merleau-Ponty says, "Everything therefore refers me back to the field of presence as the originary experience where time and its dimensions appear 'in person,' with no intervening distance and with absolute self-evidence."[46] The impressional, retentional, and protentional intentionalities "anchor me in an entourage" that is not explicitly perceived in its totality: these intentionalities therefore cannot be correlated to a "central ego" that would dominate them, but rather only to the perceptual field of a being situated in time—which "again takes in hand" its immediate past, which already "bites into" its future, and for which the "thick" present is not in any way the present of an instantiated consciousness. This is why there is no need for the synthetic *activity* of a "central ego" that would connect the past to the present and reattach them to a life's discrete events in order to constitute a cohesion; there is instead a need for a *passive* synthesis or, to borrow again a term from Husserl, a synthesis not of identification but of *transition*,[47] a synthesis effected not by the intervention of an intellectual act of gathering, but rather by its flight outside of self or in the total dehiscence that time is. Merleau-Ponty vigorously underscores this: "Once again, time's 'synthesis' is a transition-synthesis, the movement of a life which unfolds, and there is no way to bring it about other than by living that life, there is no seat of time, time bears itself and launches itself afresh."[48] The emphasis is therefore placed on the continuity of time and on the unity of the temporal process, which means that time is not a series of instants juxtaposed to one another but rather a continuous passage wherein "each present reasserts the presence of the whole past which it supplants, and anticipates that of all that is to come."[49] Time's presence "in person" in experience constitutes the truth of the river metaphors and of the mythical personifications of time because the metaphor and the mythology are the only means to speak justly of "that for which we lack names"[50]—namely, the absolute flow, the "undivided thrust" of time,[51] which alone is able to take account of time in its proper unity as successive multiplicity, or of what Heidegger calls intratemporality.[52]

By placing the emphasis on the subject's ek-static rather than synthetic character, Merleau-Ponty is led to discover "in the hollow of the subject itself . . . the presence of the world."[53] Temporality therefore tears the subject away from its substantial or formal being: with time, it is radical exteriority, the "outside of self in itself and for itself" that bursts into the very heart of the for-itself.[54] This is why Merleau-Ponty can see the "archetype" of ipseity in time itself and thus conjoin the philosophy of the subject and the thought of existence. This conjugation of Husserl and Heidegger constitutes the proper singularity of Merleau-Ponty's work, which manages to give an eminent sense to the unity of what we have rightly called not the "school" but the "movement" of phenomenology. Phenomenology as "movement" goes in the direction of Merleau-Ponty's work, which remains inchoate after having been abruptly interrupted by his death. This is to say that he goes from Husserl to Heidegger, from "concrete" subjectivity to the deconstruction of subjectivity, from a phenomenology of the auto-appearing of the absolute flow to the "phenomenology of the inapparent,"[55] about which the later Heidegger spoke, and which, it seems to me, we could show constitutes the horizon of *The Visible and the Invisible.*

10

Phenomenology of the Event

Expectation and Surprise
Husserl and Heidegger

Is philosophy ready to take account of the sudden emergence and factuality of the event, which since Plato has been defined as a thought of the generality and invariance of essence? Such is the very general question with which I would like to begin. As Husserl recalls at the very beginning of his lectures on the phenomenology of internal time-consciousness, the question of time and its contingency has always constituted the most crucial challenge for philosophy, marking the limits of its enterprise to intellectually possess the world because, as the very stuff of things, time seems to escape radically from the grasp of concepts. As Merleau-Ponty shows in *Phenomenology of Perception*, philosophy can no longer give a realist or an idealist solution to the problem of time and can neither place time only in the things nor assign its residence exclusively to consciousness. For if one makes time into a simple dimension of things (which then could no longer be explained), then time is just the relation of the before and the after (that is, of succession) that itself, if it is to have a view of the whole of time, can be posited only by a consciousness that cannot be completely immersed in time. But if *a contrario* we make time into a simple dimension posited by a consciousness that embraces it in the gaze (which we could then no longer account for), then time is the very temporality of time—which can never be completely unfolded before the gaze or completely constituted, precisely because it does not belong to the order of being, but rather to the order of process, advent, occurrence, or passage. Thus, neither the realism that immerses the subject in time to the point of destroying any possibility of consciousness of time nor the idealism that lets consciousness survey the whole of time (which then no longer passes) allows us to understand what each nevertheless claims to "make explicit"—namely, consciousness's relation to time. In these two cases, philosophical thought wants to make time into either a reality or an idea, but what remains out of reach for both is the nonessence of time (which *is* not, but which *becomes* [*se* fait]) and its properly processual and transitory character. Philosophy fails to take account of the passage of time when it becomes too one-sidedly realist or idealist; such one-sidedness inevitably leads the realist or idealist to think the connection of the different parts of time as already realized, either in the object or in the subject. But time's "synthesis" is, on the contrary, a problem rather than a solution, and the task for "true philosophy" is to take account of the discontinuity of time that makes events possible for us.

Such a philosophy should be able to take account of the very passage of time and of what we could call its *eventality* or its structural "eventuality."[1] To speak here of the *eventuality* of time obviously does not mean that time might not be, but on the contrary, that time's eventuality is in itself what introduces contingency, unforeseeability, and chance into the world. I would like to show that this "true" philosophy is phenomenology. What is phenomenology? Nothing other, Husserl says, than the restitution of philosophy's most original idea, which finds its first coherent expression in Plato and Aristotle and is the basis for European philosophy and science. Unlike Hegel, phenomenology for Husserl is not to be seen as a propaedeutic to philosophy properly so-called, but should instead be viewed as the true name of a philosophy that no longer places the truth beyond phenomena. Identifying with Husserl and radicalizing his movement of thought, Heidegger is then able to state, "There is not an ontology next to phenomenology, but on the contrary *scientific ontology is nothing other than phenomenology*."[2] Putting what separates them aside, what unites Husserl and Heidegger is the idea that there is nothing to look for behind the phenomena or what shows itself from out of itself, and that philosophy's object is only phenomenality itself and not some distant "beyond" of a "being-in-itself" hidden and separated from us. This is why Heidegger takes up the catchphrase "return to the things themselves" that Husserl had always used to define the task of phenomenology. Phenomenology requires going directly to the phenomena themselves (because they themselves are the doctrine, as Goethe said)[3] and abstaining from all speculation (that is, from all metaphysical construction that would elaborate an abstract ontology) and from any psychologistic reduction that would identify phenomena with subjective experience.

But this does not mean that phenomenology merges with a pure phenomenalism or that its practice is limited to the pure and simple description of what is given in experience. When Heidegger claims in section 7 of *Being and Time* that it is "precisely because phenomena are initially and for the most part *not* given that phenomenology is needed,"[4] he is amplifying Husserl's idea (articulated as early as 1907) that phenomenology's task is not simply to open the eyes and look, "as if the things were simply there and need only be seen";[5] quite the contrary, its task is to show how the things are constituted for a consciousness that is no longer viewed in the classical manner as the passive receptacle of images. Bringing to light the constituting operation at the origin of the fully constituted object as it arises before our eyes requires that the existence of the object be placed in parentheses or put out of play, as Husserl says. According to Husserl, this *epokhē* or "suspension" of the value that things have for us in daily life decisively gives us access to the philosophical attitude, properly speaking. The philosophical gaze is not turned away from the real world and cast on the heavenly place of eternal essences, but instead makes the things given in the natural attitude of our everyday life appear as pure phenomena—thus making us attentive to the way they appear to us, to their modes of appearance and givenness. What Husserl calls the "phenomenological reduction" allows us neither to escape the sensible in favor of the intelligible nor to leave the movement of becoming for the stability of the idea; instead, the reduction makes it possible for the temporal character of the given and the process of phenomenalization at the origin of what we call "reality" to appear. What Husserl calls "transcendental" phenomenology testifies to the *irruption* [*surgissement*] of what transcends or exceeds consciousness—namely, the *birth* of the object constituted by consciousness as what confronts it.

Husserl therefore does not remain within the static point of view of a phenomenology that aims only to take account of the ready-made object or a simple empirical "given"; starting very early on, he develops a genetic phenomenology that seeks to elucidate the process at the origin of the subject-object opposition. The whole phenomenology of temporality that Husserl develops in the 1905 lectures on internal time-consciousness can be viewed as a phenomenology of the *advent* [*avènement*], of the subject's coming-forth [*advenir*] into the world and to itself. In the 1905 lectures, Husserl wants to bring to light what he calls the "true and definitive absolute"—namely, the mysterious intimacy of consciousness and time at the origin of the constitution of world and object. This is a paradoxical task, since it implies making the condition of all appearing appear—thus highlighting what Merleau-Ponty called "the segregation of the 'within' and the 'without'"[6]—this process that gives birth to consciousness and world and that is never already realized or "ready-made,"[7] but on the contrary is always in the midst of being made and in constant becoming. What Husserl tries to reconstruct retrospectively [*après coup*] with the help of the concepts of protention, retention, and originary impression is the very movement of temporalization, which remains "invisible" in principle and "inapparent" in its very becoming—and which Kant, who always affirmed the invisibility of time and who saw consciousness's process of object-constitution in the transcendental schematism, had well understood, calling it an "art concealed in the depths of the human soul."[8]

The phenomenology of the *advent* of subject and world must therefore be a phenomenology of the *inapparent* in the strict sense, according to Heidegger's expression.[9] But time's inapparence or invisibility in its "eventual" dimension does not refer to a transcendent order of the perceived; it is instead a dimension of the perceived in genesis. The limit that phenomenology encounters as it pursues its task is therefore not exterior to the perceived, but is instead discovered only within and through it. Merleau-Ponty will later emphasize that it is not a question of an absolute invisibility, but rather of the invisible of *this* world—that is, of the dimension of invisibility implied in the visible itself and that therefore can be elucidated only from within.[10] And that is why, in the unfinished book *The Visible and the Invisible*, Merleau-Ponty sketches out the program of an "ontology from within," an "intraontology" that does not break with, but is instead the true completion of, the *Phenomenology of Perception*.

But is this phenomenology of the advent, mixed together with an ontology that remains interior to phenomenality itself and that seeks to make its procedural and dynamic character appear, also a phenomenology of the event? To think the coming of time—its *advenire*, its coming-forth, its coming toward us—is not yet to think its sudden irruption—its going outside of itself, connoted by the verb *evenire*, *ex-venire*, from which we get the substantive noun "event." What exactly is an event? Perhaps we can characterize it initially simply as the unexpected, which comes-on [*survient*] and happens by surprise, "befalls" us—thus as an accident in the proper sense.[11] The event is thus always a *sur-prise*, something that suddenly and unexpectedly takes hold of us, and in accordance with the excess of a yet-to-come [*à-venir*] that will come to us despite any expectation, tension, or intention. The *eventum*, which arises from the coming, represents something irremediably excessive with respect to the usual representation of time as flow and appears as what dislocates and reconfigures time, rousting it from slumber and changing its direction. The *eventum* thus threatens the intimacy of synchrony—that is, the mutual implication of the different moments of time (retention and protention in Husserl, and similarly, thrownness and pro-ject in Heidegger). The exteriority of the *eventum* introduces a scission between past and future, and so makes the different moments of time appear in their dis-location, literally pro-ducing their difference, exposing this difference in the suddenness of its irruption. It thus constitutes time's dehiscence, its continuous coming-out-of-itself into the always *other* than itself—which is what Heidegger calls *ekstasis*, and which, precisely as this "always" of a noncoincidence with self, Levinas designates by the term *diachrony*.[12] Every event is, in this respect and as such, overwhelming—an event is not integrated like a specific moment in the framework of time, but rather makes the framework entirely change "style"—to borrow one of Husserl's favorite terms, used to speak of the "style" of experience.[13] The event is not produced in a world but is instead what allows the world itself to be opened. As such, it constitutes a moment of caesura and undermines the temporality that paradoxically makes continuity possible, since this noncoincidence with self (expressed by the possibility that I have to be open to events, to be radically transformed or even destroyed by them) is also what makes me a temporal and ek-sistant being. Openness to the accidental is therefore constitutive of human existence, granting it a "destiny" and making its life an adventure rather than the expected unfolding of a program.

We thus see that if a phenomenology is to obey its own injunction to return to the things themselves, it cannot remain as an "eidetic" phenomenology (that is, a thought of the invariances of experience); it must also open itself to what the young Heidegger called a "hermeneutics of facticity," an *interpretation* of what existence conceals and what is not reducible to the ideal, of the essentially variable and eventual. Such a phenomenology should therefore no longer aim to be merely the thought of being or essence, but must also be the thought of the *may*-be and of contingency—or in other words, it can no longer be only the thought of the a priori and its conditions for the possibility of phenomena, but must also be the thought of the a posteriori and its after-effect [*après-coup*]. Moreover, such a phenomenology should be—has to be—both of these because the question is to show how a phenomenology of the event (if it is possible) constitutes the most proper completion of the phenomenological project rather than an announcement of its destitution or impossibility, as thinkers of absolute exteriority and alterity (such as Levinas and Derrida) sometimes suggest.

What then in the Husserlian and Heideggerian phenomenologies make a "phenomenology of the event" possible? This is the principal question to which we should respond in a synthetic and organized manner in order to sustain the thesis that I have articulated here. But I will have to be content with some reflections on a possible phenomenology of expectation and surprise that could be developed on the basis of Husserl's and Heidegger's thought.

To be against all expectation, even when it had been somewhat awaited or anticipated, is the "essence" of the event, about which we could say without paradox that it is a "possible impossible or impossible possible." The impossible happens in a terrifying or marvelous manner: this is the event in its intimate contradiction, which comes to us always by surprise and unexpectedly. This surfeit or excess of the event is what a phenomenology would have to think, and in this respect the phenomenology of eventuality finds itself in a very similar position to the phenomenology of mortality. Isn't death always what happens prematurely and against expectation, an impossible that nevertheless happens, coming *to* us without coming *from* us, in the impersonal mode of an event that happens to others, and that is even the most universally repeatable event? We may say that death is the event *par excellence*, that which is never present, never happens in the present, is not open to a world, but instead forever closes the world. It constitutes neither a lacuna of temporality nor a diachronic moment that may be at the origin of a new configuration of possibles, but rather the pure and simple destruction of all synchrony and diachrony. This is why Heidegger legitimately defines death as possibility *par excellence* instead of as an event: because death remains an absolute future for us, a possibility that can never be realized—not even in suicide, which serves only to escape "actively" the essentially passive possibility of dying, the possibility that most profoundly characterizes human existence. But if death is the possible *par excellence*, as Heidegger underlines, this implies a redetermination of the traditional definition of the concept of possibility. In classical philosophy, the possible is what is not real and as such is less than the real, whereas here the possible is defined in light of death as what is unrealizable, incommensurate with the real, and thus more eminent than it. In the phenomenological perspective, the possible is an excess with respect to the real and as such is a "category" higher than the real. Rather than being a structure of things, as categories are, the possible is a structure of existence, or as Heidegger says, an "existential," because what is appropriate to human existence is not to be in the mode of *res* and *realitas*, but on the contrary in the mode of the possible, of having-to-be. Because I am mortal and because I exist, I have a constant relation to my own end and to my own death, I remain essentially in the mode of the possible—that is, in the mode of a structure of anticipation with respect to my own being, which remains always "in expectation."

Heidegger's determination of the possible as an existential or as a structure of existence had in truth already been prepared by the Husserlian intentional analyses. Husserl himself strongly insisted on what constitutes the originality of intentional analysis in contrast to ordinary analysis. Its originality arises from the particular character of intentional life, which can never be presented as a whole made up of givens, but rather only as an ensemble of "significations." What does it mean for consciousness to be in the mode of signification, rather than the mode of givenness? According to Husserl, this implies an "overcoming of intention in intention itself"; in other words, the intentional aim always and in principle exceeds what is given in the aim. Husserl writes in section 20 of the *Cartesian Meditations* that "the phenomenological explication makes clear what is included and only non-intuitively co-intended in the sense of the *cogitatum* (for example, the 'other side' of the object) by making present the potential perceptions that would make the invisible visible."[14] Far from being a theory of the correlation of *noēsis* and *noēma*, of *cogito* and its *cogitatum*, intentional phenomenology instead posits in principle the necessary overcoming of the intentional object, of the *intentum* in the *intentio*, which implies that the *cogitatum* is never present as definitively given, but as capable of becoming always more explicit on the basis of its objective meaning and its horizonal structure. By this, we understand that the original operation of intentional analysis consists in unveiling the potentialities implicated in the actualities—that is, in the actual state of consciousness. Intentional analysis can therefore be viewed as the basis for a true phenomenology of expectation, of tension toward an objective that remains open to confirmation or invalidation of its own anticipations by the unfolding of always new horizons. In simpler terms, excess is the rule, and in intuition there is always an excess whose *intentio* will never come to term, but that alone makes possible a signification that would be equal to its object (in the sense where an *intentio* adequates its *intentum*), or in a word, a saturation of intentionality as non-meanings. On this basis, it becomes understandable that in Husserl, there is a parallelism between the perception of the object and the perception of the other: in the two cases, some aspects are not currently directly perceived, but are "appresented"—that is, their existence is implied in what is effectively perceived (for example, the hidden faces of the cube or the lived experiences of the other). That there is something unpresentable is thus a rule of intentional phenomenology, since the idea of an exhaustive presentation of the *intentum* would destroy the structure of intentionality at its basis. The intentionality of the other must not be conceived as a particular case of the intentionality of the object, but rather as a matrix of intentionality, which can be unfolded only where my expectation is never completely fulfilled, where my intention is never entirely "filled in," and where the threat of nonfulfillment is never totally averted.

But if we can find a possible ground for a phenomenology of expectation in Husserlian intentional analysis and in Heideggerian existential analysis, as I have tried to do, could we likewise discover the elementary characteristics of a phenomenology of surprise in these two philosophies? And is the idea of a phenomenology of surprise itself thinkable without absurdity? We know that it is possible and even necessary to await what exceeds all expectation and, as one of Heraclitus's fragments says, to hope for the unexpected.[15] And there is no doubt that this opening to the future's indeterminacy has been thematized by both Husserl and Heidegger. But what happens when the excess implied in the event shatters the horizon of possibles, such that the very encounter of the *eventum* proves impracticable? What is it about these moments of crisis, of death in life, and of trauma, in which the range of possibilities is powerless to integrate the discordant event and thus collapses in its totality? Two examples could be invoked here—of mourning the loss of a loved one and of religious conversion—wherein the transition no longer supposes the relative loss of a certain number of possibles, but rather the radical loss of all possibilities that we call the world. What we experience in moments of crisis is *our incapacity to experience the traumatizing event in the present*, the surprise of which (even if it is expected, for example, in the case of the death of a terminally ill person) always remains whole and appears as absolutely unanticipated (and absolutely unable to be anticipated) to us. If expectation can be disappointed in the case of the nonfulfillment of anticipation, here our own experience is indeed more profoundly overwhelming than that of disappointment, which has always been more or less inscribed in the program of our anticipations. What comes on by surprise is totally "outside the program" and thus unexpected in the strong sense, countering and ruining the very structure of expectation. Such experiences are in truth very rare, since, as both Husserl and later Merleau-Ponty underline,[16] ordinary experience supposes both an original faith in the world's stability and the always present presumption that experience will constantly unfold in the same "style." Psychosis provides a particularly gripping paradigm for those moments of "existential crisis": the schizophrenic, for example, experiences the loss of the world (or the rupture of the "ordinary" linkages of experience),[17] and this dooms him to the impossibility of an encounter and to a sojourn in the terrifying. The capacity to be open to the event and to experience the reconfiguration of possibles that it demands of us is consequently lost. For it is the event itself that demands, after the fact, to be integrated into a new configuration of possibles, rather than we who decide freely to change from one world to another or to convert ourselves. Concerning the event, we can speak neither in the active voice, because we do not decide the event, nor in the passive voice, because the event cannot transform us and even "happen" to us unless we are disposed to it (and it is this disposition that is catastrophically absent in the psychotic); we can speak of the event only in the middle voice and in the past tense, in the mode of "it happened to me." We are never contemporaneous with the great events in our life, above all with the very first, our birth, which we did not will and which attests to the fact that we are not at the origin of our own existence, since for us *to be* means to be determined by a past that was never present, which can be appropriated only after the fact by taking on those determinations of ourselves that we have not chosen. There is thus within us a surprise regarding our own birth that is in a way constitutive of our own being, a permanent surprise of having-been-born that testifies to the absolutely unmasterable character of this proto-event. It is possible to think that in each event (in the strong sense of the term) this proto-event of birth is, as it were, repeated, giving it its character of a "first time," a radical newness; just as what is also repeated in it is the experience or rather the ordeal of the *après-coup*, of the originary delay that, as having-been-born, I would always have with respect to myself; and that I therefore also have this experience with respect to the overwhelming event, whose present, because of the suddenness of its irruption, does not coincide with itself, making it exit time, so to speak, and giving it over to a nonactuality that ruptures it from both the past and the future.[18]

Existence is not the master of such surprise and occurrence [*survenue*], which is not reducible to the advent of a simply flowing temporality; it is, in a way, the event that orders and commands here. But the very experience of such a "commandment" confirms that the event requires my collaboration and that I am not in total passivity with respect to it, even if its meaning is still opaque to me; indeed, I am always *attempting* to give meaning to or make sense of everything that happens to me, and only with respect to this effort, which is merged with my being in the world, can an event appear as "traumatic." Both Husserl and Heidegger were aware that there is a "passivity" in our intentional activity and a "facticity" of existence that can be taken on but not chosen: Husserl sketched out the theory of what he calls "genesis" or "passive synthesis," while Heidegger narrowly linked the facticity of existence (insofar as it is always already thrown in the world) to its necessary resumption in an adventive project that configures the being-in-the-world of an existing being. We must therefore not oppose phenomenology to the thought of the event, but rather conjoin them, so that the opening to the phenomenon can be merged with the opening to the unforeseeable. This paradoxical capacity of expectation and surprise—of the "passivity of our activity," as Merleau-Ponty says, or this "transpassability," according to Maldiney—is what phenomenology always treats in some way; and since Husserl, phenomenology's objective has always been to overcome the traditional opposition of passive and active. In a note in *The Visible and the Invisible,*[19] Merleau-Ponty evokes this passivity of our activity, or, according to Valéry, the "body of the spirit" about which "philosophy has never spoken." It is a matter of a soul understood not as active principle but rather as an always already passively opened "field," or of "time that fuses in us," such that "I am not even the author of this hollow made in me by the passage of the present into retention" and that "it is not me who thinks, no more than it is me who makes my heart beat." For Merleau-Ponty, only in the opening of this field of being that I passively am can something be registered as present or absent, and only at the heart of it can all our initiatives be born (no matter how new they are). Henri Maldiney, author of *Penser l'homme et la folie,* coined the term "transpassability" to designate how the human being lives its transcendence insofar as transcendence implies receptivity. Receptivity must be understood as "passability"—that is, as a *capacity* to suffer and submit, in the sense that it implies an activity immanent to the ordeal, to the *pathein,* consisting in opening the field of receptivity. This opening and this capacity of indeterminate waiting are exactly what psychosis lacks, as Maldiney emphasizes: "What is defective in psychosis is receptivity, which is not of the order of what is projected, but rather of reception and openness, which admits no a priori, and which, waiting without waiting for anything, stands open beyond all possible anticipation. It is what I call *transpassability.*"[20]

Phenomenology gives a unilateral privilege neither to the interiority of expectation nor to the exteriority of surprise and assumes neither a structure of revelation in the subject nor the revelation brought about by the object as a precondition. Instead, it tries to think the strange diachronic simultaneity of the two—which, in his own language, Heidegger had named *Ereignis* and which he understood as the co-belonging of being and the human and as the simultaneity of the call and the response.[21] *Ereignis,* this master-word of Heideggerian thought, has several meanings. In ordinary language, it means "event," but if one also understands it starting from its root, *eigen,* which means "own" or "proper" in German, then one can also give it, as Heidegger does, the meaning of propriation. Heidegger himself underlines that the etymology of the word does not refer to *eigen,* but to *Auge,* the eye, and that the ancient form of the substantive is indeed *Er-aügnis,* which means mere appearance in the sense of "leading to visibility," thus making possible a view onto something.[22] Because it makes something appear and stand out, *Ereignis* has come to take on the meaning of event. And ultimately, this last meaning takes account of all the other meanings that this word can hold because it indicates that-without-which there would be no event—namely, the *appearing* that we are party to without however being its instigators, on the basis of which every event comes at us.[23] Contrary to what some suggest today—namely, that the thought of alterity and of diachrony require a mode of thought other than the phenomenological—we must instead emphasize that there is no possible thought of the event that is not also at the same time in principle the thought of phenomenality.

11

Phenomenology and History
Dilthey, Husserl, Heidegger

Is it possible to come to an understanding of the historical dimension in its totality without relating it to an anthropological agency [*instance*]? This question may seem altogether meaningless at first glance, since it seems perfectly obvious that Karl Marx was right to claim that it is humans who make history.[1] Do we other moderns agree with his fundamental thesis that humans are by definition historical beings? What meaning should be given to the historicity of human beings? Does it mean the decline of the absolute in all its forms and the domination of the most unbridled form of relativism, or on the contrary, does it mean the birth of a new alliance between truth and history, between being and time?

History began to enter into philosophy with Kant and Hegel, becoming not only an object of philosophical reflection but also the very milieu of its unfolding, precisely in order to bring to term the permanent scandal raging in a plurality of philosophies about the unicity of truth. Immersed as we always are in the anthropological interpretation too often given of Hegelianism (the most astonishing example of which is Alexandre Kojève's reading of the *Phenomenology of Spirit*),[2] we have forgotten that the history about which Hegel spoke is not so much the history made by or subject to humans as it is the history of *spirit*—that is, of an eternal agency. In the Hegelian sense, there is history *because* there is the absolute, not *despite* it or in the space created by its absence. Hegel's point of view is not that of a "truth in the making" in the sense that truth could be produced only by humans, but rather that of a truth that requires humans and time in order to be unfolded and manifested and thus not remain a pure virtuality. In a paradoxical sense, which also testifies to the oft-misconstrued depth of Hegel's thought, the eternal is precisely what in itself requires the historical dimension—because the absolute is not only substance but also subject, not only in-itself but also for-itself, and because consequently it "needs" human embodiment and mediation.

We therefore cannot speak of anthropocentrism in Hegel's case, given that in his philosophy, the human is not the being who makes history, but rather the being *through which* history is realized, with infinite reason employing finite human passions to guarantee its own triumph. Yet the rise of anthropocentrism during the nineteenth century tossed this conception of history in the shadows. For the origin of the prevalence of historicism and the relativism it implies is the rupture of the link between truth and history. The philosophies of historicity developed in the climate of relativism that marked the failure of Hegelianism announce a new confrontation with Hegel and a new perspective on the relation of truth and history, which must not be confused with mere anthropocentrism. It is this new perspective on history that we see unfolding in the horizon opened by Husserl's phenomenology and prepared by certain aspects of "life-philosophy."

Let us first take up Dilthey's case, probably the most difficult to defend, since he seems closest to slipping into psychologism and historicism. He was, however, the first to have ennobled the concept of "historicity." His friend and correspondent Yorck von Wartenburg "invented" the term *Geschichtlichkeit* to qualify the genetic difference of the human in comparison to the rest of nature.[3] It is remarkable that the concept of historicity originally takes its meaning from a Christian and Lutheran perspective that is not without analogy to Hegel's philosophical Christianism. For Yorck, Christ is the principle of history because he incarnates a supernatural life shared by all humanity, but that can be found neither in Greece (which was unaware of history and is "*ungeshichtlich*") nor in Jerusalem (where supernatural life is still considered as concentrated in God alone).[4] This philosophical Christianism proceeds from Yorck's opposition to the positivism and mechanism of the then-reigning *Weltanschauung*. Like Dilthey, Yorck aspires to take hold of reality in its vivacity, its *Lebendigkeit*, and to combat every form of metaphysics as yet another attempt to eternalize and stabilize the relatively intemporal elements that every representation contains. For Yorck, being as such is nothing more than a particular manifestation of life,[5] and the true question is to think life in itself. Dilthey, who is almost a pantheist, obviously does not share this philosophical Christianism, but like Yorck, he identifies the two concepts of *Geschichtlichkeit* and *Lebendigkeit*, history and life.[6] And also for him, it is not possible to look in the background of life for a stable entity to serve as support: every reference to an intemporal transcendence comes from the transposition of the concept of substance into the world of living experience. Yorck's philosophical monotheism and Dilthey's immanentist pantheism are two different versions of the same philosophy of life, which refuses to proceed on the basis of intemporal entities that could be separated off from the very process of becoming.

But what is the origin of the prestige granted to the concept of life? As the first commentator on Hegel's youthful works, Dilthey cannot be unaware of the importance of the concept of life in Hegel (from the Berne and Frankfurt, as well as the Jena, periods)[7]—that is, during a period when Hegel, although already engaged in the construction of his system, found more interest in describing the human condition than in devoting himself to the study of pure speculation. The idea of life, which is synonymous with infinity and totality, with the nonseparation of the one and the multiple, is common to every current of thought in German idealism inherited by Dilthey. The importance of the concept during this period is due to the fact that it refers to a being able to produce itself and its own mobility, an autonomous being rather than a universal and abstract being.[8] Dilthey himself speaks of "*Leben überhaupt*" and of the unity of life in general, disseminated in an infinity of living beings. The concept of life ultimately clarifies the concept of historicity, and it becomes clear that what life and spirit have in common is precisely infinity. Dilthey had admittedly defended the rights of finite consciousness against Hegel,[9] but without denying spirit the potential infinity implied in the idea of the universality of understanding. The philosophies of historicity—in particular Hegel's, Dilthey's, and Yorck's—certainly see that there is a link between life and death but are unable to see the very foundation of history itself in death and finitude. For these philosophies, what makes historicity possible is always an Absolute capable of overcoming its own limitations.

We encounter the same schema of thought in Husserl's philosophy. Fink was the first to show the similarities of the Hegelian and Husserlian manners of thinking the subject of history.[10] We can find a philosophy of history in the *Crisis*, and a simplified version of it constitutes the tenor of appendix XXVI,[11] where Husserl distinguishes three different levels of historicity, apparently analogous with Hegel's threefold schema.[12] There are admittedly some Husserl commentators who think that in reality he was absolutely unable to think history in itself.[13] There is no doubt that the 1911 article on "Philosophy as Rigorous Science" had been written in opposition to Diltheyan historicism in order to affirm the ahistoricity of logical laws and logical truth. Husserl nevertheless states in what follows that transcendental phenomenology must be complemented by a genetic phenomenology,[14] which contends that all reality is constituted by absolute subjectivity. The genetic relativity of scientific truth is thus demonstrated despite the fact that the *meaning* of this truth remains absolute irrelativity itself, since meaning and genesis are obviously not at all the same thing. What Husserl tried to show in his last works is the "absolute historicity" of the life of consciousness—or at least this was the program that he announced in 1930 in a letter to Georg Misch, the author of *Lebensphilosophie und Phänomenologie*, Dilthey's son-in-law, and the editor of his works.[15] Husserl finds the theme of "life" in the perspective of the *Lebenswelt*, which dominates all of his late philosophy, but we can wonder whether he, more than Dilthey, had really been able to think life in its concreteness and facticity, for he also thinks life as infinity. The subject views itself as finite as long as it has not achieved the transcendental reduction, but as soon as it understands itself as infinite subjectivity or as the origin of all reality, its own finitude disappears and gives way to the infinite life of the transcendental ego.[16] It is true that this infinity has a teleological nature and that it is the correlate of the "regulative" idea of truth, which is an "idea in the Kantian sense." There is a transformation of the Hegelian schema of the philosophy of history: spirit's return from its alienation opens onto the infinity of time, onto the infinite traditionality of science. In *Experience and Judgment*, Husserl explains that the eternity of truth should instead be understood as an "omnitemporality"—that is, it should be referred to the eminently historical subjectivity that constitutes it.[17] Knowledge of the eternal is therefore interpreted as a form of human existence. But is Husserl in a position to think human existence as a whole, even in its very root? It seems not, as the very few passages where Husserl speaks of death seem to demonstrate. He speaks of the immortality of humans in the sense that they have inherited something from all previous evolution and will continue to contribute something to all future evolution. There is thus the possibility for the dead to survive in the memories of the living.[18] But Husserl states that the transcendental ego, unlike the human who "inevitably dies," is "necessarily immortal" because it cannot be born from nothing (like all other things in the world) and cannot return to nothing.[19] For the ultimate subject, there is neither birth nor death, but rather an awakening to natural and worldly life as equally unjustified as the suspension of natural life (that is, death).[20] The ego's being is outside of time, and for this reason, it can neither be born nor die, since birth and death are intratemporal events that remain unintelligible and unmotivated. In the same manner, Dilthey saw the "enigma of life" in death, which is something that by definition life cannot understand.[21] Husserl's absolute ego "descends" into time, just as does Hegel's spirit, and this is why Husserl is not truly able to understand the absolute historicity of consciousness. Transcendental phenomenology and genetic phenomenology seem to be incompatible in the end: a first constitution of the world, which is not in itself historical, is required if the transcendental reduction is to maintain its rights, for otherwise the distinction between subjectivity and nature on which the *epokhē* is grounded would be entirely deprived of validity.[22]

There may well be an attempt in Husserl's phenomenology, as there is in Dilthey's thought, to make room for the finitude of human existence, but only in Heidegger are finitude and historicity thought as essentially linked to one another, with mortality constituting the hidden ground of the historicity of existence.[23] There is history—which is certainly not to be understood as the narrative of what happened (for which the Germans use the word *Historie*, derived from Greek), but rather as the very process whereby there are events (which is what *Geschichte* names in German)—only if the "subject" of history is finite. Is Heidegger therefore confronted by a new species of "historicism" and led to a relativistic point of view? This was probably Husserl's reaction when, during his attentive reading of *Being and Time* in the summer of 1929, he saw in it a return to the anthropocentrism that he had fought throughout his life.[24] In the subsequent years, Husserl shows himself just as capable of perceiving the historicity of truth, of demonstrating that history in its deep sense depends on the possibility of the infinite repetition of ideality, and of forming a new idea of what constitutes traditionality in the sense that the traditionality of truth encompasses not merely a limited group of humans, but all of humanity.[25] He came to see in history not the simple unfolding of events in time, but the process of the retention and transmission of meaning through a humanity understood as the factual anthropological index of subjectivity and intersubjectivity in general.[26] History can no longer be viewed as made by humans qua factual beings, but rather by transcendental subjectivity itself, which establishes its kingdom in the world on the basis of this "revolution in historicity" that constituted the birth of philosophy in Greece.[27] Nothing could be more foreign to Husserl than the idea of a historicity that would originate in facticity.

But everything depends on what we understand by "facticity." For Heidegger, what he calls the "facticity of existence" does not mean that the human being is one being among other beings of the same or different species as a given presence or as the *Vorhandenheit* of mere things. Instead, it means the "fact" that the human has to become responsible for its own being,[28] understood not as "substance" but as possibility, a being-able-to-be, a *Seinkönnen*. The human is a being who has to become what it is, who has to transmit to itself the possibilities that it inherits. This is why the structure of its being is historical. Historicity does not mean the extrinsic fact of the ego's immersion in the "nightmare" of history,[29] as if the human were at the mercy of circumstances and events and captive to a history similar to an Odyssey; instead, historicity means the very essence of human existence that temporalizes itself as *geworfener Entwurf*, thrown projection, and that consequently has to transmit or hand down to itself the possibilities that it inherits and that it chooses to "repeat."[30]

Heidegger calls this self-transmission of its own heritage "destiny" (*Schicksal*), and he sees the very nucleus of history in it. He then concedes that historicity is in this sense nothing more than a more concrete elaboration of temporality.[31] But this then casts new light on the originary phenomena of temporalization. To be originarily temporal and not merely intratemporal means for human being that its existence has a destinal structure—that is, that it is characterized by an internal self-traditionality. Are we once again led back to a solipsist point of view, in that the recognition of the destinal structure of ipseity could not take account of history, which in its full sense implies intersubjectivity? This could be the case if the ipseity about which Heidegger speaks in section 64 ("Care and Selfhood") were purely and simply identified with the ego in the traditional sense—that is, with an isolated subject. Ipseity is not, however, the substantial ground of personality, but is rather conquered by the impersonality of the "one" that constitutes the first level of existence. Existence is "initially and most often" an impersonal existence in the everyday world of preoccupation, and this implies that being-with-others, *Mitsein*, is a primitive determination of Dasein. As a result, the "subject" of history is not the isolated individual, but rather a collective identity, an ensemble of heirs from a determined period, which Dilthey described as a "generation" sharing a common destiny, a *Geschick*. Heidegger sees the "complete and authentic" form of historicity in this notion of a common destiny.[32] Heidegger does not elaborate this point concerning the collective dimension of history very far in *Being and Time*, but his whole conception of historicity would be unintelligible were it to remain in a solipsist point of view. There is a relation of belonging between the living and the dead, and this relation is the ground of true tradition. And this true tradition in turn becomes explicit only in "repetition."[33]

But what does this word "repetition" (*Wiederholung*) mean? Not the simple reproduction of a model of life that had been realized in the past, but the fact of seeking (*holen*) a possibility of existence in the past and of *replying* to it.[34] History is no longer understood as the domain of reality, but rather as the domain of possibility because it is the dimension within which a dialogue among humans is made possible. This is why true history must be understood as the "recurrence" of the possible,[35] which does not mean the return of identical events, but rather the essential *continuity* of history. This perhaps constitutes the postulate of the Heideggerian analysis. But it must be clearly explicated. First, continuity *is not given*, but *is only possible* at the level of authentic existence. The concern is thus not so much to observe the continuity of history but rather to create it. And next, this continuity presupposes—and does not neutralize—death. This is the most important point: history cannot become the refuge of all the disappointments of the ideal, of those who tried to find in it a new form of transcendence or a new possibility of survival for the individual. History is, in contrast, the mode of existence of a being *destined to die*. The dialogue that takes place between generations does not abolish the finitude of those who participate in it; on the contrary, finitude is what gives them the possibility of questioning and replying to one another. Mortality is not, for Heidegger, a limitation in the negative sense, but rather a "capacity" that opens—rather than closes—being-in-the-world, because the possibility of the impossibility of existence in general (that is, death)[36] is the very ground of all presence in the world. The finitude of human being is no longer opposed to the infinity of being or viewed as able to be overcome in the end, as was the case for Hegel and even for Dilthey and Husserl. To the finitude of humans corresponds the finiteness of being itself, which is only unveiled through the transcendence of human existence as the capacity to be in relation to nothingness.[37] Being is not, for Heidegger, an absolute that requires the human in order to be unfolded and to become "effective." Being is in itself neither God nor a human product, but rather the finite partner of humans, and it requires human beings not only to become self-conscious, as was the case with Hegel, but also simply "to be," because there is being only as long as humans exists,[38]—that is, in accordance with an eminently temporal mode.

It is not easy to understand how a finite and temporal being can differ from a being produced by humans, themselves finite and temporal beings, but this is the culminating point of Heidegger's thought in the period following the publication of *Being and Time* in 1927. What makes understanding this narrow relation between being and time even more difficult is the fact that the third section of the book, which was supposed to have the title "Time and Being," was never published because, as Heidegger explained later, it was not possible to articulate the passage or transition from the exposition of the temporality of existence (sections I and II) to the explication of the temporal "nature" of being itself using the language of metaphysics in which, however, this passage had to be accomplished.[39] The "turn" in question must not be understood as the dialectical reversal of the negativity of finitude into the positivity of a being that unconditionally wills its own effectivity, as was the case with Schelling's and Hegel's absolute idealism,[40] but rather as the transmutation of values opposed to eternity and temporality in light of an "assumed" finitude. For now the human being has to assume not only its own finitude, but also and above all the *finiteness* of being itself. This is where the true "turn" takes place: in the capacity to think in different terms the finitude and historicity of the human being as counterpart of the finiteness and historicity of being itself, always obeying the phenomenological method and gaze, "seeing" the event of being and of existence against the background of a more essential and more fundamental belonging of being to the night of nothingness. It is on this basis that Heidegger will speak of a "history of being" (*Seinsgeschichte*) and not just a history of man, of a dispensation of being (*Seinsgeschick*) and not just of the destinal structure of human existence. For it is being that destines the human to become the placeholder of being as *Da-sein*, rather than a human who by its own transcendence makes being surge forth.[41] History then becomes a dimension of being itself, and not merely a dimension of the human, but in a manner entirely unlike the Hegelian history of the absolute, thus refusing the authority of anthropological agency to history. This authority is given to being not in order to dispossess the human of its own power to "make" history, but rather in order to insist on the co-belonging of the human and being in this dimension that, after the turn, Heidegger will call *Ereignis*, appropriating event.[42]

In the course of this history, whose central agency, as in Hegel, is not man, being is dispensed in multiple ways, thus determining epochs. These epochs are not figures of spirit, as they are in Hegel, but are instead the different forms of the forgetting of being[43]—that is, the determinations of the *beingness* [*étantité*] of beings: Plato's *idea*, Aristotle's *energeia*, Descartes's *certitudo*, Hegel's absolute knowledge, Nietzsche's will to power are thus all names for beings [*l'étant*] as a whole. Epochal history is thereby identified with metaphysics itself, insofar as metaphysics is nothing other than the advent of the forgetting of being. For being can be dispensed only by withdrawing itself, and what it dispenses by its withdrawal is beings.

How do we think this retreat or suspension (*epokhē*) of being insofar as it is also dispensation and donation or givenness? Here is what Heidegger states on the subject in his course on Nietzsche's metaphysics in 1940: "Being itself occurs [*west*] essentially as such keeping to itself [*le se-retenir-soi-même*]. The essence of Being itself does not take place behind or beyond beings, but—provided the notion of such a relationship is permissible here—*before* the being as such."[44] This retention of being therefore does not refer to any afterworld. For the withdrawal of being is not a simple "mode" of a being preexisting in its plenitude and is not exterior to being, but is being itself. Heidegger similarly insists in his course the following year on the fact that "the history of being is neither the history of the human and a humanity nor the history of human relation to beings and to Being. The history of Being is being itself, and only Being." But he also adds that "the human is drawn into the history of being" because "Being claims the human being for its grounding in beings."[45] It is therefore not at all a matter of thinking history on the basis of the human as autonomous agency; instead, we must think it on the basis of the response that the human gives to the claim of being. Because "what is, is what takes place," and because the advent of Being can be given only in the form of withdrawal, "what happens is the history of Being, Being as the history of default [*des Ausbleibens*]."[46] The default of Being—that is, history *as* being—is what remains unthought and determines the metaphysical character of all historical reflection of the human being on his situation. But this withdrawal of being, whereby it is refused while being concealed, is at the same time that by which it is unfolded as promise. For withdrawal nonetheless remains a relation (der Entzug bleibt ein Bezug), which implies that being "needs" its own unconcealment, not as something foreign to it, but as something required by it as being. This is what allows Heidegger, in these pages of a properly speculative character, to claim that "Being advenes in default of unconcealment, it can only be 'needy,' its history a 'calamity' [*die Not*]."[47] Insofar as it promises itself in calamity and need, this being—which is no longer thinkable as the figures of subject or substance and about which Heidegger is quick to say that it is *das Un-ab-lässige*, the incessant, and consequently *nötigend*, necessitating—is thus pure advent, pure happening, *Geschehen*.

In an only recently published text from the same period, Heidegger writes significantly that "history is history of being, and for this reason history of the *truth* of being, and therefore history of the *foundation* of truth, and thus history as *Da-sein*; and because Da-sein instantiates being only by the vigilance of a humanity, human being is historical. Its historicity unfolds in its belonging to the truth of being."[48] History is the "ground of the truth of being" in the sense that the truth of being "needs" this foundation that comes forth as Da-sein by the human's response to the call and sending of being to which he belongs. The history of being may thus be understood only as this ground of being whereby being comes to its "essence"—that is, to its default, whose foundation occurs in Dasein—that is, in the human understood not as autonomous agency but rather on the basis of the claim of being. Heidegger had already strongly emphasized in an earlier text that "be-ing comes to truth only on the ground of Da-sein."[49] Only on the basis of such a belonging to being can we truly understand what the expression "the history of being" means. As Heidegger specifies once again, "the history of being means the history whose unfolding 'is' being itself. Not the 'history' that being traces out, nor the 'history' that can be drawn in it, nor even redrawn as a mass of opinions 'about' being. The history of being is the unfolding of being."[50] History is thus the name of being as no longer thought in the horizon of metaphysics, which always prefers beings to being and permanence to becoming.

What then becomes of the relation of truth and history? Hegel had highlighted the temporal dimension of truth, which, as essentially a process, can be found only at the end and is only the result. Husserl developed the idea of a truth that, like logical idealities, can generate a history, in that what had once been formulated can be indefinitely repeated; and he saw a model for temporality itself in the omnitemporality of truth.[51] Heidegger went further still in the same direction: truth is relative to the human being. From *Being and Time* onward, Heidegger says of truth what he had also said of being—namely, that there is truth only insofar and only as long as the human exists.[52] Does this mean that truth is "subjective," and if so, are we once again led back to relativism? Absolutely not, at least if we are capable of doing what Heidegger constantly tries to do—namely, thinking the human being on a basis other than the solipsist subject. Relativity does not here have the Protagorean meaning that makes the individual the standard of what is true and false, but instead means that the human can be understood only as starting from its *relation* to being itself—and this relation is what Heidegger calls "truth," in the sense of the discovery of what *is*.[53] The human has the capacity to discover what is, insofar as it is, and so does not remain prisoner in a world deprived of its own representations. The human being is initially just as much in truth as in nontruth.[54] This is why Heidegger, unlike Husserl, does not need to presuppose a transcendental subject different from the empirical subject as the only possible ground of science and truth. Such an ideal subject is a pure construction, a phantasmagoria with respect to the only existing subject—namely, the human being in its facticity. The idea of an eternal truth, which is part of the heritage of Christian theology but not of philosophy, must therefore be eliminated.[55]

The facticity of human existence, rather than the infinity of an ideal transcendental subject, is the true a priori of philosophy and of science. For Heidegger, to exist means to be originarily both in truth and in nontruth, and not (as is the case for the entire metaphysical tradition) *to be originarily only in illusion*, according to the archetypal image of the human condition that one finds in Plato's allegory of the cave. We thus need not escape our mortal condition in order to attain the eternity of truth, nor do we have to neutralize history in order to posit the foundations of science or to find the foundations of empirical history in a transcendental history in a Husserlian manner. The facticity of human existence (that is, the fact that we have not chosen to enter into existence) and the historicity of human existence (that is, the assumption, or in Heideggerian language, the repetition of facticity) are the only sources of truth, and in their authentic modes, they may also be the sources of non-truth. Mortality—which is the true principle of individuation since only death as unconditional possibility isolates the individual in-itself[56]—constitutes the foundations of truth and history. The recognition of human finitude, just as much as the recognition of the finiteness of being, does not mean the impossibility of a history of truth; instead, it announces the possibility of a new alliance of truth and history. For history is neither the real nightmare of the cave-dwellers nor the irresistible process of the rationalization of the world, but rather the free perpetuation of the co-belonging of the man and being in their reciprocal finitude.

12

History and Hermeneutics
Ricoeur and Gadamer

A ten-day conference dedicated to Paul Ricoeur's work was organized at Cerisy in August 1988 by Jean Greisch and Richard Kearney around the theme of "Les metamorphoses de la raison herméneutique." There, David Carr, author of a remarkable study on Husserl's *Crisis*,[1] focused his intervention on the question of the philosophical status of the story. I would like to begin by citing the first lines of his conference:

> A question that the reader of *Time and Narrative* might pose is the following: what finally is the philosophical status of narrative? Is it an epistemological principle or is rather, or at the same time, an ontological concept? This question is particularly important for the reader who is interested in the implications of Ricoeur's theory for the philosophy of history. For such a reader, the question could be formulated thusly: is narrative only a characteristic of historical knowledge, or is it rather, or also, constitutive of the historical reality aimed at by this knowledge? In other words, to recall a classical distinction, does it apply to the *res gestae* as well as to the *historia rerum gestarum*?[2]

The response Carr gave to this question demonstrates that narrative structure, which, as Ricoeur shows clearly, is both overcome and maintained in historical science, is subtended by a "narrativity of the first order," which is also of the very mode of existence of whoever (a person or a social entity) is constituted as a subject. This amounts to claiming, in a very Heideggerian manner,[3] that the epistemological function of narrative is *founded* on or *derived* from its originarily ontological character. Carr's concern was to show that the two epistemological and ontic functions of narrative distinguished by Ricoeur are intimately intertwined on the properly *ontological* level of the intrinsically narrative model of historical existence or—to use language that Heidegger himself borrows from Yorck von Wartenburg and Dilthey—of *historiality or historicity*, of *Geschichtlichkeit* itself. For if the epistemological function of narrative consists in the "narrative's configuration of time,"[4] with the act of narration constituting the possibility of a historical knowledge, then just as the use of narrative categories becomes "highly analogical" for scientific history[5] (in which the argumentative procedures interfere with the properly narrative schema),[6] so too is the "ontic" function of narrative a "refiguration of time by narrative," which (by the influence that it has as text and the reception that historical "actors" make of it) contributes to the constitution of historical reality itself, to the re-creation of that which is "our confused, unformed, and at the limit, mute temporal experience."[7] Yet this ontic function granted to narrative necessarily leads to questioning the mode of being of historical reality, as Carr underlines: "Of what nature must historical reality be, that is, the reality of political and social events and actions in time, in order that it may receive and assimilate in its existence these narrative interpretations of the past? In other words, what is the 'form' of reality that allows for a reception of narrative 'content' and sometimes a change in content influenced by the narratives of historians?"[8]

Ricoeur's reflection on history is principally focused on the status of historiographical knowledge and *texts*, and in this regard, as Carr emphasizes, "Ricoeur's theory overcomes conventional epistemology because the relation between historical knowledge and the real past is not a relation of *representation* or correspondence,"[9] but rather a "re-creative" or reconfigurative relation. For Ricoeur, the intersection of the epistemological field and the analysis of its relations with the ontic plane of historical reality is what constitutes this "long way," whose ultimate goal is no longer epistemological, but rather "ontological" and "hermeneutic," as the title of the last chapter of *Time and Narrative III* attests ("Towards a Hermeneutic of Historical Consciousness"). It is here that "refiguration" takes on a properly ontological meaning, since Ricoeur's concern is a "strategic decision" to "reverse the order of the problems" and thus to begin *not* with the question of the reality of the past (which is supposed by history-as-science, which is always defined as history of the past) but rather with this "project of history" that constitutes the level of the *res gestae*, of a history in the making, which has as a corollary the capacity to be affected by the past, which constitutes the properly ontological level of "reception" and of historical "transmission."[10] This "turning" or "shifting" movement—the term is Ricoeur's[11]—that makes us turn or shift from epistemology to ontology is nothing other than the opening of the hermeneutic dimension itself, insofar as this not only is defined on the basis of a method of interpreting texts, but also constitutes the interpreter's fundamental mode of being, in both his or her relation to the texts transmitted and in his or her relation to others and to self.

It was Gadamer who most forcefully expressed the linkage of epistemology and ontology in the intermediary dimension of hermeneutics: "At the beginning of all historical hermeneutics, the abstract antithesis between tradition and historical research [*Historie*], between history [*Geschichte*] and knowledge, must be discarded," because "the effect of the constantly living tradition and that of the historical investigation form a unity of effects [*eine Wirkungseinheit*] where the analysis would never be able to discern an intertwining of reciprocal effects [*ein Geflecht von Wechselwirkungen*]."[12] Gadamer specifies that this abolition is permitted by the fundamental presupposition (common to the understanding of the human sciences and to the survival of traditions) of being addressed (*angesprochen*) by the tradition, which implies that our relation to what is transmitted is always one of implication rather than "an objectifying process" that would have us view "the contribution of the tradition as something other or alien."[13] Historical consciousness, or rather historiographical consciousness, does not represent something absolutely new in history (*Geschichte*), but is only a new form of the relation to the past that constitutes the historiality of the human being. For Gadamer, this traditionality is what constitutes the very essence of the sciences of spirit, the human sciences as opposed to the natural sciences. We must not underestimate here that the meaning of the objects of historiographical investigation, as the meaning of the contents of the tradition, takes the form of a speech addressed to us and manifested in the form of the voice: "our historical consciousness [*geschichtliches Bewusstsein*] is always filled with a variety of voices in which the echo of the past is heard. It is present only in the multiplicity of such voices: this constitutes the essence of the tradition of which we want to share and have a part."[14] This implies that historiographical research is at the same time a historical (*geschichtliche*) experience of transmission and that it does not concern an identifiable object, as is the case with research in the natural sciences: "Precisely this is what distinguishes the human sciences from the natural sciences. Whereas the object of natural science can be described *idealiter* as what would be known in the perfect knowledge of nature, it is senseless to speak of a perfect knowledge of history, and for this reason, it is not possible to speak of an 'object in itself' to which its research would be directed."[15] The absence of an object for historical research implies that what this research investigates and seeks to understand is therefore not radically distinct from itself and that, as Dilthey strongly emphasized, there is an identity or homogeneity of the subject and object that makes historical knowledge possible: "The first condition of possibility for historical science [*Geschichtswissenschaft*] is that I myself am a historical [*geschichtliche*] being, and whoever is studying history is the same as whoever makes it."[16]

This relation of belonging thus defines the very space of traditionality as a field within which something like an address by the voice is made possible. But this voice is less the voice of the other than it is the voice of the thing itself, about which the interlocutors have an understanding (*Verständigung*)—for as Gadamer underlines, "the task of hermeneutics is to clarify the miracle of understanding, which is not the mysterious communion of souls, but a participation in a common meaning,"[17] because "whether in the understanding of a text or in a conversation with another person who presents us with the object, the way in which understanding comes about lies in the *coming-into-language of the thing itself*."[18] The tradition is not a pure order of events; it is "language," and "it speaks of itself in the second-person familiar," in the sense that it constitutes for us who belong to it a true interlocutor rather than an object. And although it is in itself free of any relation to intentional consciousnesses,[19] the content of meaning constituting the tradition nevertheless has "something to say to me."[20] Moreover, that its object is a person implies that historical experience understood in this way is a moral phenomenon arising from the Kantian imperative that demands the recognition of the other, and of the self, as an end-in-itself. This means that historical consciousness must not seek to become master of the past, objectifying and instrumentalizing it while disengaging itself from the dialectic of reciprocity that defines the mode of the relation to the other: "it is like the relation of the I and the Thou. Whoever by reflection is disengaged from the reciprocity of such a relation modifies it and destroys its moral authority. Thus whoever by reflection disengages himself from the living relation to the historical tradition destroys the true meaning of this tradition in exactly the same way."[21] Historical consciousness therefore must not view its own historicity as an obstacle to knowledge lest it be closed to an understanding of the tradition, but rather view it as what makes knowledge possible.

Belonging to the tradition as a condition for understanding it, however, cannot be defined by familiarity alone and must equally include the *strangeness* arising from the nonnegatable temporal distance, without which the thing's alterity and separation that lets it be meaningful for us could not appear to us. Only in the tension between familiarity and strangeness can transmission be achieved as an act of language, as a speech addressed to us, which implies the appearance of a discontinuity *in* the historical continuity and the appearance of the objective moment *within* the very community linking us to the tradition: "The intermediary place between strangeness and familiarity that a transmitted text has for us is that place between being an historically intended separate object and being part of a tradition. The true home of hermeneutics is in this intermediate place."[22] This intermediary position defines the hermeneutic task as the task of elucidating the conditions that permit understanding, which, as Ricoeur underlines, implies that "the properly critical question 'of distinguishing between true prejudices, by which we understand, and false ones, by which we misunderstand,' becomes a question internal to hermeneutics itself,"[23] and also implies, as Gadamer recognizes, that "a hermeneutically trained mind will consequently include historical [*historische*] consciousness."[24]

Temporal distance allows not only for the elimination of sources of error that frustrate attempts to understand the true meaning of what is transmitted; it also makes possible the awareness of prejudices that guide understanding and thus effects a sort of *epokhē*, a suspension of the validity of prejudice by making the prejudice appear as such in its alterity. We grasp here what constitutes the very root of understanding insofar as it in principle requires the temporal distance and alterity of what is understood. For understanding does not consist in a mere reproduction of a meaning already effected in the past (since the meaning of a text is not something that the author could have mastered), but is rather what escapes from the author, not occasionally but in essence,[25] and is what can be given only in the figure of alterity and in temporal distance. There is therefore never a possible coinciding with meaning or a possible mastery of it; it is always what is given-to-the self as a coming-from-the-other, and this is why Gadamer insists on the eminently productive (and not merely mimetic) character of understanding: "it is enough to say that we understand in a different way, if we understand at all."[26] The task of hermeneutics subsequently consists in showing the strangeness of the very familiarity with what is transmitted; we might say that it incites one to see "oneself as an other," since it is the condition both of understanding and at the same time of opening this dialogical space, which is the space of the transmission of meaning. A truly historical consciousness must therefore be open to its own historicity and to the historicity of another because, as Gadamer claims, "only then will it not chase the phantom of a historical object, which is the object of progressive research, but learn to see in the object the other of what is one's own [*das Andere des Eigenen*] and thereby to understand both. The true historical object is not an object at all, but the unity of this 'one' and the 'other,' a relationship in which exist both the reality of history and the reality of historical understanding."[27] Openness to the alterity of the selfsame has the structure of a question because *to question* is to put to the test possibilities of meaning that are not already realized and to be engaged in the infinite process of confirmation and invalidation of what is already understood, which we call experience.

The historicity constitutive of human finitude is most closely approached with the concept of experience to the extent that experience "is in absolute antithesis to knowledge and to that kind of instruction that follows from general theoretical or technical knowledge."[28] Gadamer wants to give back to experience its original content (which is ontological and not ontic) by recognizing its properly historical dimension, which is radically denied in the scientific horizon of basic experiences due to the principle of repetition, which guarantees the objectivity of knowledge:

> In fact, the main deficiency of experience hitherto—and this includes Dilthey himself—is that it is entirely oriented toward science and hence takes no account of the inner historicity of experience. The aim of science is to objectify experience so that it no longer contains any historical element. Scientific experiment does this by its methodical procedure. The historical-critical method, moreover, does something similar in the human sciences. Through the objectivity of their approaches, both methods want to guarantee that these basic experiences can be repeated by anyone. Just as in the natural sciences experiments must be verifiable, so too must the whole process be verifiable in the human sciences. Hence, there can be no place for the historicity of experience in science.[29]

Experience in the proper sense is not of the order of knowledge and is in no way confused with experimentation in the positive sciences precisely because it is not an ontic experience of this or that and because it cannot in essence be experience of the repeatable or of the same thing. Experience is rather always the experience of the unexpected for the person who, by virtue of that dialectical return to self that defines the essence of experience, has acquired a horizon within which the new can be announced. Despite what Hegel, who had so carefully analyzed it, says of the dialectic of experience, it does not reach completion in a definitive knowledge but rather "in the opening to experience sustained by experience itself." And Gadamer specifies that "this is a person who is called 'experienced' and has become such not only through experiences, but is also open to new experiences."[30]

Such a dialectical definition of experience, which for consciousness consists in knowing itself in what is foreign to it, leads to an emphasis on its necessarily painful character, which does not come solely from what is acquired in an experience on the negative path of disappointed expectation, but also and at the same time from the discovery by consciousness of its own limits and its constitutive incapacity to master time and to decide its future. This is why the "authentic" experience belonging to the historical essence of humans must essentially be understood as the experience of human finitude—that is, the experience of the historicity appropriate to us: "*Eigentliche Erfahrung ist somit Erfahrung der eigenen Geschichtlichkeit*: authentic experience is therefore the experience of one's own historicality."[31] Such is the result at the end of Gadamer's discussion of the concept of experience.

But we should not remain with a solely negative grasp of this finitude and historicity. For Gadamer historicity is essentially understood as a being-affected by history or a being-exposed to the efficiency of history,[32] and this fundamental passivity implies that it can never return in an absolute knowledge of itself. There is here incontestably a superior "power of history" (*Macht der Geschichte*) over the finite consciousness that we have of it, which, as Gadamer vigorously underlines, implies that " 'historical being' means that self-knowledge can never be complete [Geschichtlichsein heisst, nie in Sichwissen aufgehen]."[33] But the fundamental passivity of being affected by history, which can never return in total consciousness of *Wirkungsgeschichte*, may nonetheless be understood precisely because it defines our intrinsic historicity as the effect of an activity that is ours, but of which we do not have a direct intuition. Referring to the Gadamerian theme of the consciousness of being exposed to the effectivity of history (*Wirkungsgeschichtliches Bewusstsein*), Ricoeur very judiciously remarks in a note that we can find "a precedent of the notion of being-affected by history in the Kantian notion of auto-affection."[34] This "paradox" of an auto-affection of the subject by its own acts, in the absence of every direct intuition of these acts, which reveals that "we are temporally affected as much as we act temporally,"[35] more adequately discerns the "productivity of the subject" constituting the essence of historicity.[36]

In such a perspective, time can no longer be thought unilaterally in its dimension of *distensio*, which rightly names as its correlate the principle of continuity that is the narrative structure of the tale, alone susceptible to configuring what is thought from itself as power of dissemination and original alterity. Time must instead be conceived as power of growth, as the internal capacity of auto-configuration. It is noteworthy in this respect that Gadamer credits Droysen, the eminent representative of the historicist school and a penetrating methodologist who was not satisfied with an empiricist point of view on history, with the merit of having seen the essence of history in continuity, which, unlike nature, includes the moment of time.

Gadamer remarks that Droysen liked to cite Aristotle's definition of the soul, of the *psychē*, in *Peri psychēs* (417b5) as *epidosis eis autō*, growth in itself. In opposition to the purely repetitive form by which nature is given, history is characterized as growth, which supposes both a preservation and overcoming of the preserved. This internal productivity of history presupposes memory and consciousness and thus makes history not only an object of knowledge but also a being determined by self-knowledge. This is what pushed Droysen to claim that knowledge of history "is the knowledge of itself" (Das Wissen von ihr ist sie selbst).[37] After relating Droysen's views, which take consciousness of continuity alone as the foundation of history, Gadamer adds that "it would be quite wrong to see this only as an idealist prejudice. Rather, this a priori of historical thought (*geschichtliche Denken*) is itself a historical reality" (*geschichtliche Wirklichkeit*).[38] The continuity in which Droysen sees the foundation of history is not imposed afterward on the phenomena in order to provide disjointed lived experience with a unified meaning; rather, this continuity constitutes the fundamental structure of historical reality itself, to which empiricism in its blindness to the a priori (Husserl spoke on this point of a "blindness to ideas") has no access.[39]

Should we then do as Foucault does and associate "the privilege of continuity . . . with the ambition of a constituting consciousness and mastery of meaning"?[40] And must we necessarily view this coherence or cohesion of life, this *Zusammenhang des Lebens* of which Dilthey spoke, as the work of a consciousness?[41] "Nothing obliges us to tie the fate of the point of view emphasizing the continuity of memory to the pretensions of a constituting consciousness," Ricoeur notes, invoking as a valid alternative to the notion of sovereign consciousness, transparent to itself and master of meaning, the Gadamerian finitude of a consciousness exposed to the effectiveness of history.[42] For the Foucauldian notion of the Archive can appear more than any other to be diametrically opposed to the Gadamerian notion *par excellence* of traditionality, precisely because it raises the document in a radically anti-hermeneutic manner to an "object in itself" of history. In this respect, the formula defining the intentions of *Archaeology of Knowledge*, which Ricoeur cites in *Time and Narrative*, is significant: "the document is not the fortunate tool of a history that is primarily and fundamentally *memory*: history is one way in which a society recognizes and develops a mass of documentation with which it is inextricably linked."[43] What remains specifically unquestioned here is the nature of this relation of non-separation between the document and the social subject, even though the "instrumental" status of the document is refuted as having arisen from the "idealist" conception of history. The "new history" can privilege discontinuity and ruptures only by literally silencing the document and by no longer treating it "as the language of a voice now reduced to silence,"[44] thereby finding, as Ricoeur perspicaciously underlines, a physicalist paradigm as the model of human time, recalling "the Eleatic conception of time, which according to Zeno comes down to making time something composed of indivisible minima."[45] We would rather speak, with Ricoeur, of the "apparent antithesis" between discontinuity and continuity in history[46] and characterize, as he does, traditionality as a "dialectic of innovation and sedimentation" or as "a discontinuity corresponding to the moment of innovation and continuity to sedimentation."[47] For as we have already noted, traditionality is characterized by the "polarity between familiarity and strangeness" arising from the process of the objectification and scission of historical life and its results,[48] which Yorck von Wartenburg, that thinker *par excellence* of *Geschichtlichkeit* (even better than Dilthey and Husserl), knew how to elucidate.[49] The "continuity of life" (*Zusammenhang des Lebens*) is only, and can only be, that which includes discontinuities by "overcoming" them and this "dialectical" conception of traditionality can rightfully be maintained only on the condition (which both Gadamer and Ricour observe) of renouncing the totalization of experience in an absolute knowledge, which, according to Gadamer, would seal off the opening constitutive of experience and of renouncing this totalization of meaning,[50] which, according to Ricoeur, would amount to constituting the intrigue of intrigues that, upon rendering all other intrigue superfluous, would complete the *Aufhebung* of time itself in the form of an all-encompassing philosophical logic.

To conclude, we should return to the definition that Droysen borrows from Aristotle of *Geschichtlichkeit* as *epidōsis eis autō* (growth in and from out of itself) and to pose again David Carr's question of a possible parallel between hermeneutics and narrativity. If, as he suggests, narrative can be viewed as a species, and even the most important species, of hermeneutics, and narrativity is an eminent form of understanding, then what other meaning could we give to this *epidōsis eis autō* except that which consists in understanding this growth on the basis of *Sprachlichkeit*, the profoundly language-like [*langagière*] essence of historicity? For this is how we can begin to glimpse what Carr was positing—namely, that "self-constitution can be conceived as self-narration,"[51] since this growth of historical existence is the work of language, which always speaks at the same time both of itself and of something else and which is its own meta-language, rendering it no longer possible "to clearly separate life and the activity of recounting this life."[52]

PART IV

Finitude and Mortality

13

Phenomenology and the Question of Man
Patočka and Heidegger

> To think the truth of being at the same time means to think the *humanitas* of *homo humanus*. What counts is that *humanitas* is in the service of the truth of being, but without humanism in the metaphysical sense.
>
> **—M. Heidegger, "Letter on 'Humanism,'" in *Pathmarks***

In one of his last texts, dedicated to "Heidegger, thinker of humanity,"[1] Jan Patočka claims that Heidegger is the thinker who realized Dilthey's idea of "understanding the human on the basis of the human" by starting from what separates the human from all other beings, without recourse to anything foreign to humanity.[2] For Heidegger, the human is the only being capable of truth, which at first sight has the air of a truism, but in fact refers to an entirely new manner of posing the problem of truth. It is no longer a matter of the traditional view of judgment as the place of truth, or of logic as the science treating it, but rather, "after a hiatus of several millennia,"[3] of phenomenologically understanding that truth is the place of the dis-covering of things as they are, and that this dis-covery is effected in the human being, implying that it is not something we humans decide, but rather that it decides us. It is true that in his "Letter on Humanism," Heidegger sees humanism as a form of metaphysics, for this "humanist" prejudice, in the current sense of the word, consists in seeing truth as a purely human affair, something within our power and to which we would be inclined. Yet to understand the human in such a perspective, as modern humanism does, is precisely *not* to understand the human on the basis of itself—that is, on the basis of a finitude that prevents the human from becoming master of truth. Radically approaching the problem of truth therefore led to a conception of the human entirely unlike the conception to which we are accustomed and that comprises the foundation of the entire subjectivist tradition since Descartes and Kant. As Patočka underlines in response to a question from the audience, this implies "demolishing all traditional logic, all traditional psychology," "something that in general one dare not even envisage."[4] This is why Heidegger's thought is revealed only in the future: because something comes to the fore as possibility for us in what he thinks.

Some years earlier, during interviews and seminars at Medard Boss's residence in Zollikon before an audience of medical students and young psychiatrists,[5] Heidegger had been led to emphasize that the method that alone provides access to human phenomena is the phenomenological method, not the Cartesian method of the natural sciences, the absolutization of which in the form of the dominant sciences today—that is, cybernetics—leads to the "destruction of the human being."[6] For in order to understand human illness, what is required of the doctor and the therapist is to experience himself or herself as Dasein, which implies the putting out of play of the inadequate representations that we normally have of humans: "the most difficult task is demanded of the investigator, that is, to make the transition from the projection of the human being as rational animal to the projection of being-human as Dasein."[7] As a thinker of the crisis in which we live, rather than as an academic,[8] Heidegger engages in dialogue with practitioners with the hope that they will be more open than are philosophers and theoreticians to the "revolution in thinking" that the task requires, a revolution comparable to the Galilean discovery of the region of nature, but much more difficult than it, a revolution that will make the properly human continent appear in contrast to traditional anthropological representations of it.[9] Anthropology, along with psychology and psychopathology, have until now viewed the human as an object in the broad sense—that is, as something subsistent—and have left in the shadows the question of the human's mode of being and of what properly constitutes its *humanitas*, which Heidegger defines as "the free relation of the human to what he encounters." Heidegger understands phenomenology as a "hermeneutics of facticity"[10] because, in opposition to the impartiality of the Husserlian transcendental spectator, it consists for Dasein of *being engaged* in the manner of being that is already its own, and of properly *performing* it,[11] therefore bringing to light the humanity of the human, who is only the "administrator" of a freedom more original than it.[12]

Should we be surprised by such agreement between the Heidegger of the Zollikon Seminars, who openly identifies with the Husserlian method while inflecting its meaning as an analytic of Dasein,[13] and Patočka, who views Heidegger's transformation of transcendental phenomenology into ontology less as a reversal than as the completion of Husserl's fundamental intention?[14] What would truthfully be more astonishing, and even worrisome, would be to have to renounce discovering a common orientation of these two thinkers who are both identified with phenomenology. This is why Patočka wants to bring out the unifying elements subtending their opposition, not in order to end up in some eclecticism, but rather by adopting a critical attitude with respect to *both* doctrines,[15] to make the profound meaning of phenomenology appear as a "reflection on the crisis of thinking,"[16] which is also a crisis of humanity. Patočka is a member of what was not a "school," but a "movement"—the phenomenological movement—and like Eugen Fink and later Merleau-Ponty, he refused to oppose Husserl and Heidegger and wanted to maintain the unity of phenomenology, thus obeying what had once been Husserl's sentiment, which he had often expressed in the 1920s: "phenomenology: that is I and Heidegger, and no one else."[17] In this respect, Fink is an exemplary personality; as Husserl's private assistant and closest collaborator from 1928 until his death, he had from the beginning of the 1930s begun to develop an original thinking very strongly marked by the Heideggerian problem of being-in-the-world.[18] It is with Fink that Patočka, arriving in Freiburg in 1933, will discuss Husserl's texts. He recognizes in Fink's "art of the question" an "obvious similarity with Heidegger" and will quickly discover that it is worked out in secret by contrasting these two thinkers. And although Husserl once tried to force him to choose between attending Heidegger's courses and participating in discussions with himself and Fink, Patočka will continue to follow Heidegger's seminar without really having the time to devote himself to his thought because the phenomenological problematic preoccupied him so much.[19] Later, upon returning to Prague, the question of the relation of these two thinkers will become an almost daily subject of reflection and discussion.[20] And it is again the problematic character of the relation that constitutes the theme of one of Patočka's last texts, the 1976 manuscript written in German and published after his death under the title "What Is Phenomenology?," that I would like to now take as a focal point for the following reflections.

For Patočka, there is no doubt that the unity of the phenomenological method is the catchphrase requiring us to "go back to the things themselves . . . to the things such as they appear and show themselves . . . while abstaining from all speculation"[21]—that is, from an entire recasting of the constructions appropriate to the sciences of experience and the mathematical project as abstract ontology. This "triumphant advance of construction" that ends up at our own technical civilization is "without danger in itself" in that it is not at the origin of a conception of the being of beings, which has been the case since the seventeenth century, when, as Heidegger notes, with Descartes, the thing itself, the *Sache selbst*, became the subjectivity of consciousness.[22] When Husserl, who still belongs to this tradition, tried to go back to the original experience that serves as the ground for all construction, he thought that through the procedure of reduction he had once and for all brought to the fore the question of originary givenness, but he nevertheless continued to place this originary givenness in the immanence of consciousness and to understand deconstruction as a purely reflective undertaking. Even though he coined the catchphrase *Zur Sache selbst*, he is not able to go directly back to appearance precisely because he restores the transcendent noematic sphere to the immanence of the subject,[23] implying a profound difference between Husserlian questioning and the response given to it.[24] In effect, a *subjectivist* response is given to an *ontological* question, which is hardly new in light of what Descartes already discovered. But because Husserl's question is an ontological question, the idea of phenomenology "imperiously demands" to be enlarged into ontology as Heidegger understands it.[25] If "ontology is possible only as phenomenology,"[26] this can be true only in the sense of an "asubjective" phenomenology, which, in contrast to Husserlian transcendental phenomenology, is not grounded on "the self-apperception of reflective consciousness."[27] Although Husserl claims, against mentalism, that there are indeed things themselves that originarily appear to the ego, he nevertheless remains attached to the idea that objectifying reflection constitutes access to the psychical, and, among other things, he makes the result of this objectification (i.e., "lived experiences") into the very foundation of appearance.[28] Yet the ego has a manner of being, profoundly different from that of the thing, that makes its appearance in an act of perception impossible. Because the phenomenal field is in no way "given" to a pure theoretical gaze—or to the gaze of the *Kosmotheoros* of which Merleau-Ponty speaks—it is instead structured by the *practical* project of an ego that is never entirely given to itself. If appearing things "are in the first place nothing but the pragmatic possibilities of action,"[29] then this implies a nonexteriority of the "subject" in relation to the context within which it appears in a structurally incomplete manner. This is why it can never be grasped by an external objectifying reflection, but only by an essentially practical reflection, which can take hold only of the movement of the ego that carries it toward the world, or only of its essentially "ekstatic" character.[30]

This reflective self-apperception thus proves impractical at the same time: I can take hold of myself only in a reflection that Merleau-Ponty had qualified as "thick," since this reflection cannot tear me away from the practical context from which I am inseparable. As Heidegger constantly emphasizes in *Being and Time*, I can understand and take hold of myself only on the basis of the world, which is a fundamental structure of "my" being. Grasping something in the reflective gaze of a *res cogitans* is therefore only a dogmatic prejudice that comes from "abstract ontology," whose obfuscating character (with respect to "pure" phenomena) the Heideggerian "destruction" of the history of ontology has the task of disclosing because, as Patočka notes, the *epokhē* may indeed allow access to the thing itself and may "beat back the prejudice of the mode of absolute and transcendent being, which is in the mode of *res extensa*,"[31]—but by itself, it is not up to the task of separating out every preconceived idea and of purifying subjectivity of all historical sedimentations that dissimulate its originarily practical character. We must then follow Heidegger, adding "destruction" to the reduction and adding to the *epokhē* a historical approach that brings to light the nonoriginary character of the theoretical attitude and of the comportment of representation on which the Cartesian ontology is based. Patočka reproaches Husserl for not having viewed history as *free* action and resoluteness. In the course of his path as a thinker, Husserl is led to give more and more place to genetic (in contrast to static) analysis, conceiving it as a transcendental genesis that "knows only the apprehensible structures in the reflection of an impartial and disinterested onlooker, of a subjectivity essentially without history in our sense of the term."[32] For Husserl, the disinterested onlooker remains the condition of possibility for the phenomenological attitude. The situation is completely different for Heidegger, who takes as the starting point for all ontological questioning the interest [*intéressement*] in being that is constitutive of the human. What distinguishes the latter is the fact that it is not conceived as "a case and instance of a genus of beings understood as objectively present (*Vorhandene*)" and is therefore not indifferent to its being; on the contrary, "there is" its own being for the human.[33] Patočka strongly underlined the "practical" and thus originarily "ethical" character of the mode of being of Dasein, whose "essence" resides in its existence—that is, in its "having-to-be" [*Zu-sein*]:[34] "His own being is given so that he respond to it, not so that he contemplate it. He must carry it, complete it, and the human *is* only insofar as he accepts this task or relegates it, flees it, dissimulates it. Or, in other words, Dasein (= the essence of human life) *is* in view of itself."[35] Patočka clearly sees that the ontology of *Vorhandenheit* (that is, Greek and modern ontology), conforming to what Kant called the "scholastic" concept of philosophy, is alone opposed to ethics, whereas Heideggerian fundamental ontology, since it is not the ontology of a subject understood as theoretical agent of representation but rather as an "essentially responsive and acting being,"[36] is the same as what Heidegger calls "originary ethics" in the "Letter on Humanism."[37] For it is not solely Dasein's originary temporality that Heidegger highlights by showing that all behavior presupposes a "for-the-sake-of-which" (*Umwillen*)[38]—which Kant had moreover already expressed by his concept of *Endzweck*, final goal[39]—according to which a primacy is granted to the ekstasis of the yet-to-come, the future [*à-venir*]; the phenomenon of responsibility is also thereby understood as the constitutive structure of a being able to understand itself only by responding to itself, since its facticity, far from being assimilable to a *factum brutum* of natural being, must instead be understood as what constrains the human to take over or take upon itself its own being (*Faktizität der Überantwortung*).[40] Being-human subsequently appears as the unity of a task in which the free and ethical "subjective" essence is the same as a comprehensive essence, which, as Patočka rightly emphasizes, situates Heidegger in line not only with the post-Kantians (especially Fichte) but also with Kant himself, who tried "to overcome the dualism of the representing ego and the freely acting ego."[41] Patočka grants a capital importance to the interpretation of responsibility on the basis of the phenomenon of facticity, a point from Heidegger's early philosophy that, Patočka notes, is never developed: "Heideggerian philosophy ontologizes responsibility, thereby abolishing the modern distinction between ethics and ontology, a stale distinction that is in large part responsible for the false moralism of modern times and that motivates the attacks directed by Nietzsche against moralism."[42]

Because Husserl's phenomenology continues to be situated in the framework of the abstract ontology of the moderns by presupposing consciousness as something ultimate,[43] it grants primacy to the representative and theoretical agent, to intellect, whereas Heidegger's phenomenology starts from a primacy of freedom, allowing him to conceive history not as a spectacle unfolding before our eyes, but rather as the responsible realization of the relation (to self and to the other of self) that the human is: "history is not a theoretical gaze, but responsibility."[44] Heidegger does not conceive this freedom as a power of the subject or an aspect of human essence, but rather as what opens us to what essentially characterizes us—that is, the understanding of being, which "is not our work, but ourselves, we who are existence-in-appearance."[45] It is therefore the case that freedom possesses the human rather than, inversely, the human who possesses freedom. And freedom is not the power of beginning and creation that Kant granted to practical reason in opposition to theoretical reason, but rather the freedom to let a being be as it is, and thus a "freedom for truth," the truth of being and not only of beings, which supposes a radical "no" opposed to the naïve evidence of what one takes, "proximally and for the most part," as being.[46]

Heidegger demonstrates that freedom is essentially negative in nature—that it is precisely the experience of "an absence of every link imposed by beings," by analyzing the fundamental attunement of anxiety, thus allowing him to find in existence a justification for the possibility of the *epokhē*, which remains ungrounded in Husserl, as if it "fell from the sky."[47] Whereas doubt is negation of the world, the *epokhē* is the simple neutralization of the world, but for Patočka is an annihilating behavior to the extent that it is grounded on the power to be distanced from all activity, and in particular, the theoretical activity of judgment. As such, it is grounded on the "fundamental disposition that forbids and closes off all address in general,"[48] which, though manifesting the impossibility of all theoretical or practical behavior, nevertheless, as disposition, remains a dis-covering of the totality of the world,[49] not as the ensemble of beings, but as the opening of appearance as such. What Dasein experiences in anxiety is its own transcendence, rendering it foreign to the universe of thingliness while also allowing the latter to appear. This opening of appearing—the world in the existential sense, which is in no way an entity—is "the withdrawal of being imposed in the figure of nothingness."[50] What Heidegger seems to propose is a "negative phenomenology" based on transcendence, which would do justice to the appearance of appearing beings, but which Husserlian constituting phenomenology is unable to do because it remains based on this "integrally positive being" incapable of overcoming, which is consciousness.

Heidegger's thinking as a "philosophy of finite freedom" cannot see phenomenality as the accomplishment of a subjective constitution.[51] But by emphasizing the "practical" character of the presence in the world of what is no longer a "subject," but rather an existence, Patočka tries to demonstrate that phenomenality cannot be the work of our freedom, thus showing that he is in closer agreement with Heidegger than he thinks; Heidegger had never made transcendence into a mere "capacity" of Dasein, and "we are led to error" only if we misconstrue the originarily passive character of what Heidegger calls a "project."[52] In contrast to what Husserl had wanted, this implies that the relation of the human to the world is not an *act* (thesis or belief) that we can suspend in an intellectual manner, but rather a *behavior* that engages the entirety of an existing being as "thrown project." For Patočka, Heidegger's philosophy is "the only consequential doctrine up to the task of justifying the autonomy of the being opposed to every kind of subjectivity, even that which flows from the current materialist conception of the relation between object and subject as resting on the operant action of causality in the exterior world,"[53] and this is precisely because a "phenomenology of finitude" can be erected only by breaking with the idea of an absolute mastery of phenomenality.[54] In relation to the phenomenology of infinitude—which Husserlian phenomenology still is, founded on a reduction understood as a conversion of the noetic, subjective domain into a reality—"Heidegger reverses the situation: the event of being, the eclosion of the phenomenal domain, the 'temporalization' of time and the clearing of the world (world = light) are what makes humanity and the birth of the human possible."[55]

14

The Phenomenology of Finitude
Heidegger and Patočka

In the course of these last few years, it has been a pleasure to discover that among all the readings undertaken in Europe and elsewhere of Heidegger's work, one of them, which is also the work of a great philosopher and not merely an epigone, was able to touch on and take the true measure of the coherence of Heideggerian thought. Should we be astonished that such a reading comes to us from Eastern Europe, from that "engaged" thinker Jan Patočka? In order to move with such assurance directly to the keystone of Heidegger's thought, to the assumption of finitude with which it engages, it was perhaps necessary indeed that the simple act of thinking become a high-risk undertaking and no longer, as it so often is in our "democratic" countries, a purely "cultural" activity. I would like to try to evoke Patočka's reading of Heidegger simply by emphasizing a number of texts that have formed the underpinnings of my own discovery of Patočka's work.[1]

The first of Patočka's texts that attracted my attention is in the second volume of *The Crisis of Meaning*, a text that establishes a parallel between Masaryk and Heidegger (and not just Masaryk and Nietzsche), a comparison that Patočka says "speaks to what is best and most profound about Masaryk,"[2] referring to the book of Emanuel Rádl, published in 1910, in which Masaryk is classed next to Nietzsche, that other philosopher of life, as the renovator of the *vita activa*.[3] Not that Masaryk had been an "existentialist before the letter" (which is Machovec's thesis in his book on

Masaryk published in 1968),[4] because we do not find the thought of existence in Masaryk, who was marked by positivism. But what we do find instead is an existence that acts.[5] For "*Masaryk is an excellent example of an existence that acts. Being and Time* gives a schema, and Masaryk's action is the completion of it."[6] Patočka sees in the act, in his act of the foundation of the state,[7] the very achievement of Heideggerian "resoluteness." It was indeed as a *thinker* that Masaryk founded a state, and although politics is not thought, they are narrowly linked in that they are both "the manifestation of the responsible life, raised above mere life for the sake of life."[8] This implies that thought may not be content to be a simple view on a given situation and that it requires the "active" engagement of the one who sees—"Masaryk," Patočka notes, "was the only man among all the Czech people to have a clear conception of the global situation, the only man who knew and sensed that he saw what engaged him"[9]—and who by his action shows everyone that there is a possibility of authentic existence, a possibility to get over the crisis, which in its depth is nothing but each individual's indecision or incapacity to act in a situation that has objective components independent of the individual, but that the individual nevertheless has to assume and for which he is responsible.[10]

As Heidegger showed in his analysis of authentic concern,[11] it is only by assuming our own responsibility that we can give others back theirs: "Masaryk's act must be interpreted as a responsible gesture of courage, which does not alleviate others of their responsibility, accomplishes nothing in their place, but that *invites* each to assume his *own* responsibility in himself, thus demonstrating an action that, in a situation that we tend to regard as blocked, withered, and demoralizing, discovers, in virtue of its resoluteness, possibilities that pusillanimous minds do not see."[12] For Patočka, this is what forces the expression *sub specie aeterni* out of Masaryk's mouth, a phrase that qualifies the modality of his act. It is not a matter of a Platonism of the eternal essence of the state,[13] which would still refer to pure contemplation, but rather of a gaze bearing on "the totality of the possibility of life, and on the basis of this, on the extreme possibility of death."[14] Such a gaze gets rid of an invalid possibility of responsible life, which can thus not be imitated in a servile fashion, but which remains an example to follow, an address to all those who come after him, an incitation to live and to act, *sub specie aeterni*—that is, *sub specie mortis*.[15]

Now it is in *Being and Time* that Patočka finds the expression of such "engaged thought," because, for Heidegger, the finite temporality of existing is the source of philosophical thought, and because ontology can therefore never be detached from its concrete *existentiell* root, which implies the decisive abandonment of the Platonism of "eternal truths" and the recognition of a practical and ethical dimension inherent to all so-called "theoretical" thought.[16] Patočka expresses this quite clearly when he states: "first philosophy for Heidegger is a philosophy of responsible acts that draws its provenance from conscience [*Gewissen*]. Conscience is the choice of self *sub specie mortis—sub specie aeterni*. The acts are part of *action*, and action proceeds from conscience. The exterior act does not have its origin in an exterior *stimulation*, but in *interiority*, in the *interior action* that is *conscience*."[17]

For Patočka, the philosophy of *Being and Time* is thus an eminently practical philosophy that implies the risk of *existentiell* engagement in a situation that is never "a situation in general" but instead always such-and-such a given situation.[18] Patočka therefore sees in Heidegger's first work, just as Marcuse did in 1928,[19] the expression of a "concrete" philosophy that breaks with the ahistoricism and "theoreticalism" inherent in the philosophical tradition, which promotes the model of what Merleau-Ponty characterized so well as the ideal of the *Kosmotheoros*, the surveying-thought that still rules in Husserlian phenomenology, founded as it is on the primacy of pure intuition. Because as Merleau-Ponty will underline later, the gaze is not born from nowhere, and the seer is essentially implicated in what he sees. Well before Sartrean existentialism, Heidegger underlined that resoluteness, which must be understood as the taking charge of the openness that Dasein is,[20] is in no way a flight from action but rather the authentic openness to factual possibilities, which then lose their contingency in order to become the properly existential *situation*, the *Da-* of Dasein,[21] which is never a Dasein "in general" but always one that is each time my own, according to the fundamental structure of *Jemeinigkeit*.[22]

This explains why the disclosure of the situation can be effected only in the resoluteness that is the assumption of being-guilty, *Schuldigsein*, in the existential sense, which eminently characterizes a being "in debt" or "at fault" (*schuldig*) in a constitutive manner, since it "has yet to be" and must "become what it is"—in Kantian terms, it exists in the "practical" mode of *sollen*. Patočka very clearly understood that it is only on the basis of this engagement in the practical dimension of existing that the possibilities that Dasein inherits by taking them on are discovered and that Dasein can glimpse only by choosing them in the instant—that is, in the authentic mode of the present, inseparable from the future and from having-been, which constitute the standing in resoluteness of the ekstatic relation to the possibilities that Dasein encounters in the situation.[23] He writes:

> The *instant* as time of action. Disclosure of the *situation*. Possibilities that glimpse that upon which it acts. The instant is that about which

"we are not free to let ourselves be frustrated"; Kierkegaard: heaven is open. The instant *does not perish* as a "now"—because from then on, it *remains* in the past as unshakeable as it is *renewable*.[24]

Authentic temporality is an "agitated" temporality, and because of this, it is "irrevocable," not in the sense that it would have access to an eternity exterior to factual existence, but in the sense that it is born from the confrontation with eternity over which we can never become master, which Patočka names the "glacial regard of eternity—the possibility not to be, from which we cannot extract ourselves."[25] This "irrevocability" of what one does as a being authentically in view of death can alone be "repeated" as a possibility of having been and that a Dasein, essentially turned toward the future (because it is in the mode of *sollen*, because it has yet to be), is able freely to accept again.[26] Patočka thus understood what many other commentators on *Being and Time* did not clearly perceive—namely, the essential finitude of temporality as constituting the ground of the historiality of Dasein—that is, of its manner of being intrinsically historical that makes it exist while transmitting to it the possibilities it inherits at birth and that it has yet to accept.

The second text that prompted a lively interest in me is a short manuscript entitled, "Martin Heidegger, Thinker of Humanity."[27] It contains Patočka's immediate reaction upon hearing of Heidegger's death in May 1976, and what particularly strikes me is the fact that Patočka, in this immediate posthumous elegy, does not characterize Heidegger as a thinker of being but rather as a thinker of humanity. We should bring this text together with a passage from the televised interview of Heidegger (conducted by Richard Wisser in 1969) wherein he invokes the critics who "claim that Martin Heidegger concentrates so much on 'Being' that he sacrifices the human condition, the being of the human in society and as a person," to which Heidegger responds that "this critique is a gross misunderstanding" because the question of being presupposes a determination of the essence of the human; more, the idea at the basis of his thought is that being needs the human, and inversely, the human can be itself only in the opening of being, which implies that "we cannot pose the question of being without also posing the question of the essence of the human."[28]

But to say that Heidegger is "the thinker of humanity" is to underline what Heidegger himself brought to light in the "Letter on Humanism"—that is, that the Western tradition has not managed to think *humanitas*, but only *homo animalis*: "Metaphysics thinks human being on the basis of *animalitas* and does not think in the direction of its *humanitas*."[29] What clearly emerges here in Patočka's manner of presenting things in this short text is that the traditional definition of the human as *animal rationale* proves insufficient to think the specificity of human life. What renders life human is its capacity for truth, and in this, Heidegger is in agreement with the whole ontological tradition that sees reason as what is proper to humans. But the ontological tradition considers that judgment, the work of human reason, is the "place" of truth, which is itself conceived as the adequation of thought and reality, of the statement and the thing. Against this, Heidegger, relying on Husserl's discovery in the sixth *Logical Investigation* (as Patočka emphasizes), claims that "truth is the place of judgment,"[30] which implies that truth "takes place" outside of judgment or before judgment, that it is originally the discovering of things as they are, and that this "discovering" comes from the pre-predicative level of human comportment in general—that is, from the level of an existence defined as the understanding of being.

What is therefore effected in the human's ekstatic existing is the disclosure of things as they are, which implies that the human must be understood on the basis of the understanding of being instead of viewing the understanding as a property or particular capacity of the human, which the philosophical tradition had always tried to do by seeing in reason a characteristic "distinction" of the human animal. Patočka suggests that from *Being and Time* onward, Heidegger is on the path to a new conception of truth—a truth that would possess the human rather than the inverse, which Heidegger will say explicitly staring in the 1930s—in "On the Essence of Truth," a lecture given in 1930, but published only thirteen years later, and above all in the "Letter on Humanism" from 1946. Heidegger criticizes metaphysical humanism in the later text precisely because this humanism viewed truth as "a purely human affair," "something that the human takes on with his own power," as Patočka says, which amounts to making truth into a property of the human—that is, of adding it as a specific difference to a being that essentially belongs to animality. To think the human as *animal rationale* is not to take account of human singularity or, as Patočka underlines, "to understand the human on the basis of itself." To do so, we would have to renounce conceiving it as "master of truth," a thesis that is at the foundation of all modern humanisms. The relation to truth must instead be conceived as what constitutes what is most appropriate to humanity and as what on the basis of which the human becomes understandable. In this way we arrive at a concept of truth unlike the one that understands truth as adequation, the latter being a traditional concept that, as Heidegger shows in "On the Essence of Truth," consists in its modern form in making objects conform to thought rather than making thought conform to objects, which was the Greek and medieval position.[31] This other conception of truth is one of "truth not as something about which the human may decide, but rather as that which decides the human," according to Patočka's own terms.

Thinking the human on the basis of itself—that is, on the basis of its relation to being, or of this truth that it is—leads to a conception of the human entirely unlike the conception constituting the subjectivist tradition since Descartes and Kant. Patočka specifies that this new conception "means demolishing all traditional logic, all traditional psychology," and not only the history of ontology—"something we cannot even envisage" because the concern is not only to make a *tabula rasa* of historical doctrines of the "past"—which Heidegger underlines when he speaks of *Destruktion*[32]—but also of the present—that is, of psychology and logic as we conceive and practice them today. And it is not by chance in this text that Patočka first cites Dilthey as the thinker whose fundamental idea is realized by Heidegger—namely, the idea of explaining the human on the basis of itself without recourse to anything foreign to humanity. Because Dilthey's is precisely the one who, in his attempt at a "critique of historical reason," wanted to think the "historiality" of humans—that is, their non-subsisting being, while marking a strict distinction between the historical and the ontic (made on the advice of his friend Yorck von Wartenburg, as Heidegger recalls in section 77 of *Being and Time*, which is entirely dedicated to the investigations and ideas of these two thinkers), and by proposing to ground an entirely new psychology, a "comprehensive" psychologic, whose premises he finds in the second volume of Husserl's *Logical Investigations*,[33] and which we may believe is fully realized in the analysis of *Gemüt* in the existential analytic of *Being and Time*.[34] Patočka had understood the unity of the phenomenological method as a path to an "a-subjective phenomenology," because the modern notion of the subject inevitably transposes with it the notion of substrate, thus accomplishing what Patočka characterized as "the admixture of thingliness into the properly human." Phenomenology can follow its catchphrase and go right to the things themselves only if, in accordance with the Diltheyan project, it completes the "destruction" of Cartesian ontology that, as an abstract ontology, does not take account of the implication of the "subject" in what is always presented to it as a pragmatic possibility and never as a pure object of theoretical perception. By emphasizing the practical character of the presence to the world of what is no longer a subject but rather an existence, Patočka shows that Heidegger completes phenomenology by breaking with the idea of an absolute master of phenomenality: this is the only way to obey the imperative of going back to the things themselves, which are no longer absorbed into the all-powerful thought that thinks them, but instead acquire their true autonomy in relation to what is no longer a "constituting" agency or the identity of knowledge, but rather the experience of a finitude that stands the test of the excess of a being whose withdrawal manifests its absolutely nonappropriable character. And it is this very "phenomenology of finitude" that is forcefully expressed in the texts that Patočka devoted to technology.

The last text I would like to evoke here is Patočka's Varna lecture from September 1973. In a text written shortly after,[35] Patočka underlines that Heidegger's thought testifies to the fact that we are entering into a new epoch of history, an epoch determined by another relation to being: "what comes to birth today is not a theological metaphysics of history, but the first truly radical attempts to situate philosophy in finitude."[36] Finitude therefore seems to Patočka to constitute the master idea of Heidegger's thought in both its early and later phases; and it also constitutes the difference between Husserl and Heidegger because Husserlian phenomenology still tries to understand the infinity of the mind, certainly not in a dialectical fashion, but rather on the basis of a "transcendental empiricism of an altogether singular species," allowing transcendental subjectivity to ground itself by means of the reflexive conversion of the gaze. Yet this supposes the suspension or putting out of play of the relation of the human to the world, which Husserl conceives as an act, a thesis, or a primordial belief (*Urdoxa*) on which all other possible intentionalities of consciousness are grounded. The *epokhē* must be freed by a "pure" consciousness, "purified" of its "natural" commerce in the world, allowing consciousness to appear as the absolute with respect to which the being of the world is only relative.[37] In contrast, Heidegger shows the impossibility of any transcendental phenomenology that, in unconscious agreement with Hegel, thinks the absolute as subject—which rightly leads Patočka to speak of the "highly speculative idea of the reduction" in Husserl.[38] For Heidegger the relation of the human to the world is not an act, not even an authentic act like Husserlian *Urdoxa*, but rather a manner of being, which is not "put out of play," because outside of it we are nothing, and because the reduction would then be a pure and simple destruction of existence itself, which can in no way be conceived as arising from any "absoluity" whatsoever. Existence is finite—that is, dependent with respect to the facticity that it discovers and to a phenomenality in relation to which no position of withdrawal is possible. This is what leads Patočka to claim, by contrasting the Heideggerian position with the Husserlian, that "either phenomenology is phenomenology of finitude or there is no phenomenology."[39] Heidegger's thought gives access to the *double* finitude of being and Dasein—that is, to the overcoming of the metaphysics of absolute subjectivity by means of a return to the Kantian position, which is at the same time also the deepening of it.

Yet in the Varna lecture, Patočka shows that Heidegger and Husserl agree in seeing a danger in the essence of technology because technology puts the relation of the human to the truth, and consequently humanity as such, into play: "the discovery that rules in the essence of technology necessarily loses sight of unveiling as such, dissimulating as never before the originary essence of truth and thus prohibiting the human from the access to what he himself is—a being who can be in an originary relation with truth. Forced to assure, calculate, and exploit the grounds, we repress outside the field of vision what makes it possible: man now knows only some singular truths of a practical sort, while the truth itself is unknown to him."[40] But the danger presented by technology is not as menacing in Husserl's eyes as it is in Heidegger's. For Husserl, the supremacy of technology—that is, the fact that modern science becomes a *techne*, an art of the exact calculation of nature—simply means a repression of intuitive experience insofar as it is the originary source of truth. And the remedy for this "spiritual" crisis, which is the loss of "vital" meaning for science,[41] consists in leading formalized theoretical truths back to their originary foundation, the intuitive ground of the lifeworld. In contrast, for Heidegger, the crisis is serious in other ways and so profound that, as Patočka underlines, it "could not simply be overcome by a radicalization of reflection."[42] There is no simply "spiritual" remedy for this crisis, which is the crisis of being itself—that is, of that which in the human understands being and makes truth possible. For Heidegger, the epoch of modern technology is menacing precisely because in this epoch, the human appears as the master of beings, as unconditional mastery, and is therefore deprived of what essentially constitutes him as an existing finitude. Because modern technology in its essence commands a universal disclosure of beings, a discovering without remainder that includes the discovering agent itself, the human who, as master of technology, thereby becomes the slave of it.[43] What is therefore threatened is the very humanity of the human—that is, his essential finitude.

It is on this basis that Patočka's own thought unfolds: the call to sacrifice as the most radical accomplishment of humanity, as the assumption of finitude, and as the revelation of effective freedom. By sacrifice, which allows the human to have a view on its own finitude, the human conquers its authentic humanity.[44] For sacrifice implies what the technical world profoundly denies or negates—namely, the distinction of rank within beings, the idea of a highest.[45] And Patočka underlines that "the mere fact of speaking of sacrifice thus refers to an understanding of being entirely different from the understanding worked out exclusively by the technological era."[46] Sacrifice therefore constitutes the preponderant experience of our epoch insofar as it "checks" the integral calculability reigning today and thus brings the limits of technology to light. It announces the transformation of the relation of humans to truth and attests to the opening of another dimension. For one does not sacrifice oneself for any thing because all things are now caught in the web of integral calculation; rather, one sacrifices oneself in fact for "nothing"—that is, nothing thingly [*rien de chosique*]: "sacrifice takes on the meaning of an explication of the authentic relation of the human's essence to what grounds his understanding, to what makes the human be human, and its being radically finite is neither cause nor force, is not the ground of reason for a being. Whence the necessity for the human to respond to being and to sacrifice himself to it, in order thereby to conquer his humanity in an authentic manner."[47]

Sacrifice testifies to the human nonmastery over beings, to true freedom that is the freedom to make the truth come forth [*advenir*]. This is why it is pure protestation; it makes nothing come forth, promises no positive "value," but makes the properly human dimension appear in its very disappearance. There is a paradox of sacrifice, identical to that of Greek tragedy: "the paradoxical idea is that we win by consenting to a voluntary loss."[48] Those who have to bear the costs of the technological domination of the world are not reducible to a mere fund of available forces; they are also the victims who are voluntarily immolated so that what they esteem as higher than themselves can come forth. But this "naïve" sacrifice aiming at objective gain and presenting itself as a sort of exchange of one being for another today demands being repeated and radicalized in the form of a sacrifice whose stakes are nothing positive. As Patočka underlines concerning those who have tried to repeat the experience of sacrifice and thus to shield it from the forgetting in which the technical understanding of the world (which reduces everything that is to something useable) wants to hold it, "without wanting to neglect or minimize the historical or social objectives that they can propose, we may say that the center of gravity is elsewhere."[49] There is sacrifice in the radical sense, not merely for the happiness of generations to come or the most disadvantaged, although such a sacrifice always takes place for all and by all, but rather in order to make a dimension appear that would otherwise remain submerged—namely, the dimension that lets the human be human and that is neither infinite power nor a transcendent foundation for it. This dimension is instead radically finite because it requires the sacrifice of the human in order to appear, the sacrifice of the openness thanks to which there is something in general rather than nothing at all.[50]

The radical and paradoxical figure of the human within the inhumanity of the technological world means, according to Patočka, that sacrifice could become the starting point of a renewal of our understanding of the world, of what, following Hölderlin, Heidegger called the *Kehre* from menace to salvation; it can be what saves—*das Rettende*—that is, what makes finitude appear in what is proper to it, no longer as lack and weakness but rather as resource.[51]

15

Worldliness and Mortality
Fink and Heidegger

"Worldliness and mortality," *Weltlichkeit und Sterblichkeit*—the title sounds better in German and somewhat recalls the course that Fink gave in the Summer Semester 1949 and then again some seventeen years later, under the title *Welt und Endlichkeit*, "World and Finitude," edited by Franz-Anton Schwarz and published in 1990 by Königshausen and Neumann. We know that it takes up in an original manner the theme of Heidegger's course (attended by Fink) in the Winter Semester 1929–30 course entitled *Fundamental Concepts of Metaphysics: World, Finitude, Solitude*,[1] which Heidegger dedicated in memoriam to Fink, who had died on July 26, 1975 (the text was not published until 1983). In the announcement for the 1949 course, which is reproduced in Schwarz's postface to *World and Finitude*, Fink specified that he proposed "the systematic task of the exposition of the problem of the world" and added, "yet where the world becomes a problem and is experienced in what is proper to it, the question of the finitude of every being is posed."[2] The problematic of finitude thus appeared inseparable from the problem of the worldliness of the world—that is, from the recognition of the non-thingly status of the world and of what Fink called "cosmological difference,"[3] which is both different from and similar to Heideggerian ontological difference. But if thinking worldliness is also *ipso facto* thinking finitude, or more exactly, the *finiteness* of things (since the concern here is not directly for the assumption of finite being that occurs only in humans, but rather for the effectively finite character of all that is, insofar as all that is takes part in the world, finding both its origin and its end in it), then we can likewise wonder whether the thought of worldliness by itself implies the thought of the mortality of the thinking being and if the world and death are for Fink as intimately linked as the world and finitude are.

In 1964, Fink dedicated an entire course to a meditation on the unthinkable character of death in Aristotelian, Leibnizian, and Hegelian metaphysics;[4] he also developed at length (in the essay on philosophical anthropology from the cosmological point of view, which constituted the focus of his 1955 course on the *Fundamental Phenomena of Human Dasein*) the idea that death, along with work, the battle for domination, love, and play, properly characterize the humanity of humans,[5] arguing that these "fundamental phenomena" constitute "ontological models" on the basis of which humans understand nonhuman things because "the relation of human existence to the world narrowly attaches the finite understanding that we have of ourselves to the understanding of beings distinct from us, and thus narrowly links together anthropology and ontology."[6] But the question arises of knowing whether death—and as is clearly said at the end of *Metaphysik und Tod*, it is in death, which is "maybe what is most human about the human," that finitude finds its "most acute expression and most bitter taste"[7]—constitutes a more fundamental characteristic of the "relation to the world," of the *Weltverhältnis* that we are, than the other "fundamental phenomena" that Fink invokes.

Among these, it is play that seems to furnish an "operational model"[8]—more appropriate than work, struggle, or love, which are existentially just as originary as it—to make the worldliness of the world appear, precisely because in play the human is not dealing with another equally real being, but rather with something unreal, which makes play be always something more than any random intraworldly behavior. "In human play, an *ekstasis* of Dasein towards the world comes forth,"[9] Fink claims in his 1960 book *Spiel als Weltsymbol*, which means that in intraworldly play, human Dasein is always already dealing with something more than the merely ontic level of finite things and is always already open to non-beings in such a way that the merely human sphere cannot close in on itself, as is still the case in work, which opposes humans to matter, and in struggle or in love, which confronts humans with an alter ego. It is therefore the *irreality* of play that gives us access to the ontological in-finity of the world because, in the appearance of play, the whole is in some way given within itself, and the world is reflected, so to speak, in a particular intraworldly arrangement.[10] The imaginary scenery of play, which is both more and less than the sensible real (specifically, more from the ontological point of view, and less from the ontic) thus has the remarkable virtue of piercing this "opening" in the intraworldly tissue, the "window on the absolute" that Fink already invoked in citing Hegel in his 1929 *Dissertation*,[11] an opening and window by which an ontic vicarity of the ontological, a finite image of the infinite, a symbolism of the world all become possible.[12]

But here already the difficulty of thinking the cosmological difference on the model of the ontological difference comes to light. Because, as Fink clearly says in his 1956 Krefeld lecture on "World and History," the relation to being and the relation to the world are not the same thing,[13] and so for him, cosmology must encompass ontology rather than the inverse, insofar as it is the world that constitutes what is most originary and includes being and nothingness within it.[14]

It is a question of thinking the *in*-finity and the *non*-entitiness [non-*étance*] of the world, and thus of arriving at an idea of nothingness that is not drawn from the consideration of the being of beings, even though "speculation on being and nothingness remains most often captive to the perspective of the finite being of fragmentary intraworldly things, even where, as in Hegel, nothingness is conceived as nihilation, as 'negativity.'"[15] Such a thought of nothingness as "that which is altogether other than beings," as Heidegger says in the "Postscript to 'What Is Metaphysics?,'"[16] is also what Fink is looking for, in particular in his course from Summer Semester 1958 on *Alles und Nichts*, where he already called the Hegelian thought of the "determinate nothing" into question:

> The nihilation [*Nichtung*], (either as an-nihilation [*Ver-nichtung*] or as limitation) is a fundamental event in all finite things, and as such it has an ontological importance, which until now has found its highest conceptual expression in the Hegelian concept of "negativity." The question remains open, however, and is still without response. And perhaps it is a question that still has not yet been posed, a question of knowing whether a philosophical understanding of nothingness can be obtained on the basis of the ontic phenomena of "nihilation"—or if inversely the worldly nothing [*das welthafte Nichts*] precedes all the intraworldly phenomena of nihilation.[17]

This nothing, which is the world (and we must recall here that Heidegger, adding a rubric to Kant's table of nothing, called it a *nihil originarium* in his last course at Marburg),[18] and which is announced in the irreality of intraworldly arrangements, and which constitutes the groundless ground of the ensemble of the phenomenal, is, for Fink, a dimension just as originary as being. And according to Fink, it is because Heidegger had not sufficiently insisted on this co-originarity of nothingness and being, of absence and presence, that cosmology finally had to subordinate itself to ontology. "It is rather in the way that shadows belong to light, not as absence of light, as the night without ground, that the movement of concealment [*Verbergung*] belongs to being," Fink explains in "World and History," while recalling that for Heidegger, who thinks being on the basis of *logos*, the clearing, and not concealment in itself, is truly how being reigns.[19] One ought not be too quick to claim that in Heidegger, *lēthē* is not understood in its abyssal "essence," because even in the "first" Heidegger, we already find, at the very moment in 1929 when his reflection is concentrated on the nothing, a thought of the abyss and a foregrounding of the abyssal character of Dasein.[20] Of the "second" Heidegger—who devotes the entirety of his 1942–43 course on *Parmenides*[21] to a meditation on *alētheia* on the basis of what he later calls its "heart,"[22] namely, *lēthē*, and who is the thinker of *Enteignis*, depropriation, as what is most appropriate to *Ereignis*, appropriation[23]—we can hardly say that he sees in veiling only the "weighty shadow" of the clearing without at the same time completely missing the "turn" that led him to a thought of the meaning of the being of beings, to the truth of a being so essentially defined by the withdrawal that it can "give," as Fink will also underline,[24] only the space-time of phenomenality.[25] We could show (and Fink would be no doubt in agreement with this, as we will see shortly) that from *On Being and Time* onward, by the emphasis placed on Dasein as being-toward-death, the luminosity of the clearing is placed opposite the abyssal depth of an equally co-originary closing.

In truth, as the passage from "World and History" already cited makes clear, Fink's reservations with respect to the Heideggerian thought of being are essentially based on the fact that "Heidegger's concept of BEING is thought essentially on the basis of language, of logos."[26] Fink therefore wants to take his distance from what we could very generally call the "logocentrism" of Heideggerian thought because, with this logocentrism, "being is in danger of becoming a 'thing for thought,' of 'volatizing itself into a concept,'" and we would risk "letting escape the spatio-temporal character of being understood mundanely."[27] Through understanding the world as existential and as horizon, the young Heidegger is not only threatened by a "bad" subjectivation of the world,[28] but moreover, according to Fink, the domination of logic over the understanding of being can proceed by paths other than the route of theory—for example, those practical and affective paths of work, struggle, love, or play: "these are existential phenomena that constitute the horizons of meaning for the interpretation of the world. It is not only as a native speaker of language that the human interprets the world, but also as warrior or worker, lover or player."[29] It is because the understanding of being is nourished by sources both clear and obscure that the logical path does not possess exclusivity, and this authorizes Fink to see the plurality of paths taken by the understanding of being as "operant models" on the basis of which we think without always being able to think the models in themselves.

The opposition *logos-mythos*—which Heidegger refutes, correctly seeing the idea that *mythos* was destroyed by *logos* as "a prejudice of history and of philology inherited from modern rationalism on the basis of Platonism"[30]—seems in some way to constitute the background of the distinction of the thematic and the operant for Fink:

> Many ontological relations presented through the lens of arduous abstractions in universal language become transparent in analogies and metaphors, and receive a fullness of meaning in the language of the warrior, the worker, the player, or the lover. This is not a remnant of mythology, but it is rather the myth itself that is a spontaneous beginning form [*eine unbefangene Vorform*] of the understanding of being from an existential inspiration. Being, becoming, being born, and dying let themselves be formulated in comparisons that are extended, much like elastic or suspension bridges, over the abyss of the unsayable, but these comparisons have limited resistance and break under excessive weight.[31]

Whereas Heidegger, in his enterprise of a "deconstruction" of logic,[32] appeals to a more originary (pre-Platonic) sense of *logos* that is no longer opposed to *mythos*, Fink, who is no less Heraclitean than Heidegger,[33] seems to want to find in the "symbolism" of myth and poetry the resource for a "cosmological" thought, which philosophy could not access, insofar as philosophy is confused with a metaphysics remaining captive to intraworldliness.[34] Fink wants to develop an authentically "existential" anthropology that, in contrast with traditional philosophical anthropology,[35] is not developed by taking the phenomena of language, reason, freedom, or history as a guiding thread, but rather the coexistential structures of death, work, domination, love, and play, which more profoundly take account of the principles of the sociality and finitude of human Dasein.[36] The criticisms he addresses to Heidegger therefore aim less at opposing him and opening a wholly different path than at trying to go further than he on the same path. Heidegger "achieved a breakthrough in the direction of a concept of world that no longer depends on the human, but on which perhaps man depends, a concept of world that can truly be called 'cosmological.'"[37] Fink's concern now is to penetrate this still unexplored country of cosmological thought and to determine the philosophical task as the critical task of an examination of the complete arsenal of ontological conceptuality on the basis of an authentic understanding of the world.[38]

Fink's course on *World and Finitude* ends with a question: "is a nonmetaphysical thought of the world possible?"[39] This question requires in an essential way that mortality be taken into account. Metaphysics had not been able to think death, no more than it could think the world—and it is in the forgetting of the world that metaphysics necessarily developed because, for Fink, it is the world that, like Heideggerian being, possesses in itself the fundamental character of self-withdrawal.[40] The 1964 course, which had consisted in questioning the great metaphysics of becoming and perishing, ends in silence and in the absence of a response.[41] Could we therefore legitimately think that there is at least an analogy between the withdrawal that so intimately characterizes the being of the world (and about which Heraclitus's fragment 123 already spoke: *physis kryptesthai philei*; nature likes to hide itself)[42] and this absolute absence that is death? It is true that the withdrawal of the world, like the withdrawal of being, does not mean an escape to the supersensible, but rather a foregrounding of intraworldly beings,[43] whereas death is a pure and simple end of the world itself, at least for the thinking being who dies.

There is, in truth, something that demands a careful clarification. One the one hand, we find in Fink the idea that the world is imperishable, in great fidelity with Heraclitus, that thinker of the uncreated world and the always living fire.[44] The last sentences of *World and Finitude* read, "What the poets and thinkers say is transient human speech. Human wisdom and poetry can be dissipated, but the world, the play of being, 'remains.' Space and time, the openness of the sky and earth, the 'seeming' of being, the space of play wherein all beings arise and fall, are imperishable. Words fade away, but the silent and unsayable play that opposes earth and sky cannot be born and cannot perish."[45] But on the other hand, Fink also frequently emphasizes the fact that the world is not only the place where all things emerge, but also the domain of the decline of everything that has emerged, and is therefore decisively marked by finiteness.[46] In this respect, we must cite the last lines of *Alles oder Nichts*: "the world is not only the worldly presence of appearing, it is also UTOPIA, the no man's land of the Nothing, to which the mysteries of love and death refer." The concern is therefore not to remain with the usual idea that we have of the world as domain of presence and dimension of appearing. We must also see in it "the nameless domain of absence, on the basis of which things come to appear and disappear again" and to understand that "Hades and Dionysus are the same."[47] It is because the world is *Ur-Ereignis*, "original event," that all things are granted appearance and individuation and is also what takes them back. Greek mythology knew how to think this unity of *Welttag* and of *Weltnacht*—of world as day and world as night, of what gives and what takes—in the figure of Persephone, who plays the great game of intertwining life and death.[48]

For if, as Heidegger has shown, the imminence of death is experienced as a condemnation to extreme individuation where nothing can "accompany" us any longer, Fink wonders whether, at the height of distress, the death mask can be suddenly transformed and whether what terrifies the living may become a deliverance for the dying, for whom death takes on the face of what frees them from the bonds of individuation and the chains of finitude,[49] because, for the dying, death means not only the abandonment of corporeal individuation, but also the abandonment of self-relation, as well as leaving behind the rule of difference and withdrawing into the inessential and the enigma of nothingness.[50] Because this enigma concerns not only the "objective" being that we are, but also the very understanding that this being has of being, human thought is tempted to nourish itself with the reassuring vision of a beyond and tends to interpret death as a "passage" that guarantees the perdurance of the "person."[51] There is thus a "double experience" of death, referring not only to the individual experience of death but also to its "authentic" social experience in the cult of the dead. This double experience is the experience of the simultaneously exposing and sheltering essence of death, which both exposes the individual to extreme solitude and leads the individual back into the original protective ground of the One-All.[52] This intertwining of exposure and sheltering explains why death is always intimately united with love. Fink follows Heidegger in claiming that only humans are mortals—that is, the only beings in the universe who relate themselves to death insofar as they are doomed to it, but he adds that we are also the only beings in the universe capable of loving—that is, of escaping from the solitude to which our individuation condemns us. The "fundamental phenomena" of work, struggle, play, love, and death are, as we have already seen, strictly "human" because they imply an understanding of being and are grounded on a relation to the world, a relation of which only humans are capable. But this by itself does not mean for the Heideggerian thought of being that being is a product of humans, or that the world is an anthropological given or a structure of existence; in contrast, it means that the human is the only being who sees in the world the origin of all things and who can *be related to* this origin,[53] implying that he assumes the finiteness that he shares with all beings: the human is thus the finite being who expressly takes hold of itself in its finitude[54] and who consequently has the possibility of wanting becoming and of saying yes to all that is perishable.[55]

What intimately unites love and death for Fink is their common reference to the "original and unformed ground of all life and being."[56] We find in Fink's Nietzschean thought an adherence to a "philosophy of life" that has no allegiance to any biologism, but that nevertheless views human life as something eternal and indestructible;[57] this infinity of human life is what Fink says is celebrated in the "mysteries" of ancient Greece.[58] Love, which for him constitutes the very foundation of sociality, is not only an altruistic attitude that orders Christianity, but also an ekstatic attitude whereby we rejoin the *supra*-individual life constituting the chain of generations and the infinite series of always new forms of human life. This is why loving does not mean only being united with an other, but also feeling one with the original infinite life from which all finite forms of life emerge and to which they return in the end. It is this occasional and fleeting glance at the immortality of the species that constitutes the properly "panicky" experience of love;[59] the animal is deprived of this experience because, though it also participates in the eternity of the species, it does not "exist" as such and does not feel the intimate sentiment of its belonging to the species.[60] For in such moments, it is not a question of "abolishing" (*aufheben*) mortality, but rather of conceiving it as constituting the very presupposition of eternity: "only a mortal being can therefore have the knowledge, through death, of the eternal return and regeneration of existence, of repetition in the child."[61] There is therefore no experience of love that is not at the same time an experience of death, and it is in the intertwining of these two experiences that we find the one true eternity and immortality, not what is beyond time and beyond death, but rather what comes about [*advient*] in time and through mortality itself.[62]

By accentuating mortality and the finitude of the human, it has no doubt now become clear how Fink can maintain the claims about the infinity and immortality of human life as well as the claim about the imperishability of the world without renewing the transcendentalism of the philosophical tradition or succumbing to the naturalism of nonphilosophy. As he underlines at the end of *Metaphysik und Tod*,[63] his concern is not to take sides in the conflict opposing these two overly rigid philosophical motifs of transcendentality and the ontic, precisely because what is supposed in both cases is the possibility of a knowledge of being-human as it is "in itself" in either its "objective" or "subjective" form, whereas what characterizes the human is precisely that it cannot attain total knowledge of itself and that, as Heidegger already said, "so abyssally does the process of finitude entrench itself in Dasein that our most proper and deepest finitude refuses to yield to our freedom."[64] Because such "absolute knowledge" of our finitude fails us,[65] there is the unthematizable for us. For our knowledge of ourselves is in movement; it "is produced" *at the very moment* when it tries to take itself as a theme, it eludes its own consideration through its own operation, and the "transcendental" illusion of philosophy no doubt always remains the illusion that believes it possible to be able to subsume the very movement of ontology in an ontology of movement.[66] But these "operant models," by means of which we think and that constitute those "shadows" of philosophical thought that it can never jump over,[67] do not arise from a pure and simple enclosure in anthropomorphism, even though the philosophical task still consists for Fink in their incessant critique in a still very Kantian sense. For we could legitimately speak about them in terms of an *ontomorphism* or of a *cosmomorphism*, since it is impossible to say whether the human interprets things in his image, or inversely, whether the image he makes of himself is the reflection of the things.[68] Because the human is always already coimplicated in what he thematizes, and because he has always already entered into what the philosophical tradition itself has designated as a "hermeneutic circle," access to the whole is only ever possible *through* a thinking being. This is why work, struggle, love, and play, which are strictly human phenomena, are *at the same time* also paths for the understanding of the world. But is it possible to say similarly that death also constitutes such a path for understanding the world?

For what is announced with death is the impracticable path of the nothing about which Parmenides's poem speaks, and Fink meditated on this no less than he did on Heraclitean "worldliness."[69] Parmenides is no doubt the thinker of this forgetting of the world who most closely characterizes Western thinking, and it is with Parmenides that Heidegger says that the phenomenon of the world has been leapt over (*übersprungen*);[70] but for this same reason, Parmenides is the thinker of the exclusion of the nothing outside of being,[71] of the strict antinomy of being and nothing on which the ontological era is grounded.[72] In Parmenides's poem, the non-path of the absolute nothing is announced—this "path of shadows" that, precisely because it is impracticable, nevertheless remains a path; for although Fink barely suggests it, it is perhaps on the basis of the nonviable alone that the multiplicity of the paths of the understanding can be unfolded. Death remains rigorously unthinkable, and this is no doubt what paradoxically makes it the operant model *par excellence*, by means of which we can understand "everything," precisely because death itself absolutely escapes from understanding. But a "model" that is merely "operant" is like a universal key that is useless when there are no doors or windows; for as Fink says so well, we are held prisoner in the world, and it is not possible to be delivered from this cosmic enclosure.[73]

Death is therefore perhaps what is most human in the human, only because nothing can be thematized in death, for as Heidegger already forcefully said, it refers to *Jemeinigkeit*, to this "each time my own" of existence, in which Fink sees a problem,[74] because according to him, it implies the determination of being-human as monadic subjectivity and egoic ipseity.[75] In opposition to the unilaterality of the Heideggerian interpretation that, still heir to the metaphysics of subjectivity, gives primacy to death, Fink wants to give value to the double aspect, individual and social, of death[76] and to conjoin the perspective of the dying with the perspective of the survivor.[77] We can, however, wonder whether with this conjoining he does justice to what he himself calls "the systematic and architectonic motif of the 'equilibrium of the world,' " which led the metaphysical tradition since Aristotle to couple genesis and corruption in the absolute process of becoming uniting being and nothingness within itself, thus managing to "subsume, generalize, and disarm human death."[78]

If the human is this "strange creature in the midst of beings who has a knowledge of death and who is certain of his mortality," and if "human death is the great indicator—of the absolute nothing, which is nowhere and not in time, which does not rival the worldly totality of spatiotemporal appearing, but which, as the silent night of Hades, only draws into an ultimate problematicity all that appears, all that shows itself and shines on the surface,"[79] then we may perhaps see that what Fink calls the human's "consecration to death" is what opens the human *par excellence* to the unthinkable other that is the world,[80] which also "strangely escapes the grasp of thought, refusing it and rendering all concepts decrepit."[81] And we may perhaps understand with Fink, but also with what is greatest in the metaphysical tradition, that death, the "absolute master," is nothing extrahuman,[82] is only *what* in the human, as Rilke said, risks the human, "more still than the plant or the animal . . . more than life itself, for one breath more," and saves him by giving him "being without shelter" and thereby making him capable of "saying yes to it."[83]

16

The "Last God" of Phenomenology

Husserl and Heidegger

Although it is formed of two Greek roots, the term "phenomenology" itself appears only very late in the philosophical tradition. It had probably been coined by Lambert, who, in his *Nouvel Organon* of 1764, baptized "phenomenology" as a discipline whose task is to allow the recognition of appearances and to furnish the means to escape them and arrive at the truth.[1] In the 1770 letter accompanying the copy of the *Dissertation* he sent to Lambert, Kant, situating himself in the framework of the traditional opposition between the sensible and intelligible worlds, also recognized the necessity of elaborating a "*phaenomenologia generalis*" as a "propadeutic discipline that would preserve metaphysics from all intrusion by the sensible."[2] We again find the hint of an opposition between phenomenology and metaphysics in his 1772 letter to Marcus Herz, but by this time, Kant had already begun to turn his back on the traditional solution of dogmatic metaphysics, which consists in making humans participate in divine understanding; and by denying philosophy any recourse to what he calls the "absurd" hypothesis of the *Deus ex machina*,[3] he tries to lead philosophy back to its original perilous situation of no support on earth or in heaven and of having to give itself its own laws, as he says in the *Grounding for the Metaphysics of Morals*.[4]

Philosophy must therefore become atheistic in the proper sense of the word—that is, it must endure the absence of the divine and take the finitude of the human as its unique starting point. But this implies that the science of the sensible can no longer be viewed as a merely negative propaedeutic to metaphysics and that knowledge of the phenomenal can no longer be knowledge of simple appearance, but must instead be knowledge of a truth that remains relative to human finitude. And in 1781, in what is no longer called a "general phenomenology" but rather the "transcendental aesthetic," Kant strictly distinguishes appearance from phenomenon, defining the latter as the thing as it is for an *intuitus derivativus*—that is, for a noncreative and thus receptive intuition, in opposition to the thing-in-itself, which is the correlate of a divine and creative *intuitus originarius*. Kant thus clearly no longer subscribes to the thesis of the opposition of the sensible and intelligible worlds since, as a passage from the *Opus Postumum* cited by Heidegger in *Kant and the Problem of Metaphysics* shows,[5] phenomenon and thing-in-itself correspond to two different gazes cast on the same thing. We can thus rightfully consider, as both Husserl and Heidegger do,[6] that although Kant did not preserve the term phenomenology, the whole of the *Critique of Pure Reason* is nevertheless a phenomenology—that is, a discourse on the thing *qua* phenomenon.

In the post-Kantian horizon that once again fundamentally calls into question the difference Kant maintained between the two modes of human and divine intuition, the term "phenomenology" reappears with Hegel, who sees in appearance a characteristic of being itself. The *Phenomenology of Spirit* nevertheless constitutes only a first part of science, that of appearing knowledge, at the level of which the opposition of being and appearing persists, whereas metaphysics proper, the *Science of Logic*, is possible only from the point of view of absolute knowing and thus of the identity of being and appearing. For phenomenology to become the very name of philosophy and not merely a propaedeutic for it, the Husserlian claim that there is no being other than being-for-us is necessary. Husserl also refuses the Kantian distinction of the two modes of intuition, not in order to put himself in the point of view of the absolute in a Hegelian manner, but rather in order to generalize the *intuitus derivativus* and attribute it to God himself, which is the only way not to posit a being behind the phenomenon.

Husserl is not content merely to recognize as the "principle of principles" the originary presence of the thing to consciousness; he also excludes the concept of a God who would escape the laws of intentionality. When in *Ideas I* he distinguishes the perception of a transcendent thing that must be given in "sketches" from the perception of a lived experience given immediately, he vigorously underlines that this remains true for all consciousnesses, human or not. For him it would be "an error of principle" to imagine that perception could not attain the thing itself or that the thing itself could not be given to us in its being, thus implying that the idea of a God possessing the perception of the thing in itself, a perception denied us finite beings, is nothing less than "nonsensical."[7] Perception of the thing implies in principle a certain inadequation, and "no God can alter this in any way, any more than he can change the equation 1+2=3 or the stability of any other essential truth."[8] The perception of space has its laws, and these possess an absolute validity: "Thus we see," Husserl explains, "that not only for us human beings, but also for God—as the ideal representative of absolute knowledge—whatever has the character of a spatial thing is intuitable only through appearances, wherein it is given, and indeed must be given, as changing 'perspectivally' in varied yet determinate ways, and thereby presented in changing 'orientations.'"[9] The same goes for inner experience, a sure knowledge of which, Husserl maintains against skepticism, can be obtained through reflection. Moreover, God is also "subject to this absolute and transparent necessity," such that "even God could win a knowledge of his consciousness and its content only through reflection."[10]

Husserl's non-Cartesianism appears very clearly here: far from decreeing them, God himself is bound by eidetic truths. But as Husserl takes care to specify, the concern is not to transport the debate to the theological plane, but rather, by remaining on the epistemological plane, to make use of the idea of God as an "indispensable pointer in the construction of certain limiting-concepts which even the philosophical atheist cannot dispense with."[11] In this perspective, God cannot be what determines consciousness from the outside, but rather, like the world, is what can have meaning only for me, as Husserl contends in the *Formal and Transcendental Logic*: "the subjective a priori precedes the being of God and world, the being of everything individually and collectively, for me, the thinking subject. Even God is for me what he is in consequence of my own productivity of consciousness."[12]

God is not only a limiting-concept for philosophy, but is also what is revealed to religious consciousness as an absolute transcendence. Yet phenomenology cannot take the immediately given as a starting point: the pure phenomenon, the "thing itself" to which we must return, instead requires the putting out of play of all the contents of experience in order to appear. The transcendental reduction thus bears not only on the whole of the natural world, but also on all the products of culture, and in particular on custom, law, and religion.[13] The bracketing of the God of religion represents a specific problem in that God is "an 'Absolute' in a totally different sense from the Absolute of Consciousness," and at the same time is "a transcendent in a totally different sense from the transcendent in the sense of the world."[14] The Absolute Being of consciousness is immediately grasped in the immanence of lived experience, whereas, though the idea of a worldly God is impossible, the immanence of God in absolute consciousness is not the same as lived experience, but is indirectly announced in it.[15] It is announced not only in the "admirable teleology" that manifests both the factual order of the world as it is constituted and the development of life and humanity, but also in religious consciousness. In all these cases, however, the transcendence of God still belongs to the domain of fact, which explains why it may and must be reduced.[16]

Although Husserl abstains from any theological thesis in this first phase of transcendental phenomenology, it seems that a certain concept of God became impossible from the phenomenological point of view. A God who is indirectly announced in the sphere of absolute immanence can no longer be absolutely transcendent or determined from the exterior of consciousness. A God who must obey the eidetic laws can no longer be conceived as a creative God. When, starting in the 1920s, the figure of God reappears in Husserl's unpublished texts,[17] it is no longer a matter of a God having lost all of his classic attributes. In the 1935 "Vienna Lecture," Husserl claims that "in the concept of God, the singular is essential,"[18] and this is not a matter of a mere affirmation of a monotheism, but rather of the recognition that on the side of the human, the validity of the concept has to be experienced as an "absolute interior bond."[19] The same is true for Husserl and for Kant: after the destitution of a metaphysical God who assumes the functions of supreme ontological guarantor in classical philosophy, a new figure of God reappears, which, as a postulate of practical reason, finds its meaning only on the basis of the presence of the moral law in the consciousness of a finite being for whom it necessarily has the meaning of a categorical imperative. Likewise, for the later Husserl, transcendental consciousness discovers God in itself as its own internal depth.

We understand why Husserl can claim that at this level, a mixture is produced between divine absoluity and philosophical ideal, which explains why God becomes the "bearer of the absolute *logos*."[20] It is thus philosophy itself that leads to God or, more precisely, to the recognition of this divine depth of consciousness, which, as Husserl underscores in a manuscript from the 1930s, implies that "philosophy (always becoming more concrete) and theology (always becoming more philosophical) coincide at infinity."[21] Philosophy thus constitutes the nonconfessional path leading less to the being of God and more to the recognition of his meaning as deity. There can be no doubt about the meaning of Husserl's words recorded by Edith Stein: "The life of the human is nothing other than a path to God. I tried to arrive at this point without help from theology, its proofs and methods; in other words I wanted to attain God without God. I had to eliminate God from my scientific thinking in order to open the way to those who, like you, did not know the surest route of faith passing through the Church."[22] God as absolute *logos* does not "exist" and is nothing other than absolute reason coming to itself in an infinite process, and history itself can be viewed as "the process of self-realization of the deity," as Husserl says in another manuscript from the 1930s.[23] At the end of the account, the idea of God is for Husserl identical to that of a perfect and totally rational humanity: as the absolute logos toward which all finite being is necessarily oriented, God is only the "infinitely distanced human."[24]

Even while it opens itself to these metaphysical questions that had remained in the background during the first phase of the constitution of transcendental phenomenology, at the end of its road, Husserlian phenomenology unfolds a discourse that is more "theiological" than properly theological—but this does not in any way mark a "religious" turn for phenomenology. Religion certainly represents for Husserl the culmination of a culture, but a culture that remains pre-philosophical, as he explains in one of the articles published in a Japanese review in the early 1920s.[25] And if he goes as far as recognizing that true religion properly so called is a breakthrough of freedom,[26] it is nevertheless to philosophy that he returns to develop this tendency toward a freely produced culture. Even if we can reveal the resumption of a Christian theme in the idea of a community of love as the true realization of intersubjectivity in Husserl's work, this apparent "Christianization of phenomenology" does not intervene in any way in the dimension of revelation,[27] and at no moment can Christian theology be invoked as a foundation for Husserlian teleology.

Now concerning Heidegger, we can say that because he studied theology before dedicating himself to philosophy, he more directly approaches the relations between phenomenology and religion than Husserl does. While he certainly claims as clearly as Husserl that "nothing else stands behind the phenomena of phenomenology,"[28] he nonetheless devotes one of his first courses to an "Introduction to the Phenomenology of Religion," in which he wants to show that what constitutes the specificity of Christianity is a new conception of eschatology and a new experience of life in its facticity, on the basis of which alone the notion of God can acquire a meaning.[29] This does not, however, hinder him from claiming during the same period that "philosophy is in principle atheistic," meaning here "free with respect to all religiosity," or from suggesting that the very idea of a philosophy of religion is pure non-sense, especially if it does not take account of the facticity of the human.[30]

The concern to distinguish the religious dimension of faith radically from the dimension of thought and philosophy is what leads Heidegger in his Marburg years to a dialogue with Protestant theology. As the lecture he gave in 1928 ("Phenomenology and Theology") shows, his concern is not only to distinguish theology as positive science from philosophical questioning, but also to highlight the fundamental opposition between these two existentiell possibilities constituted by faithfulness, on the one hand, and the free taking-charge-of-oneself (which is philosophy), on the other, such that from this point of view faith remains the "mortal enemy" of philosophy. No mediation is possible in either direction, according to Heidegger, which leads him to declare categorically that the very idea of a Christian philosophy is a square circle and that there is no more a phenomenological theology than there could be a phenomenological mathematics.[31]

But starting in the 1930s, what becomes a question for Heidegger is the onto-theological essence of philosophy, which does not arise from the transformation of Greek metaphysics by Christian theology, but rather from the manner by which a being is manifested from the origin. Because metaphysics has an onto-theological structure, and because theology issues from philosophy itself, Christian theology was thus unable to take possession of Greek philosophy, and ran the risk of misconstruing the specificity of the existentiell possibility on which it rests, which is nothing but faith. As he explains in his 1936 course on Schelling, it is because Christian theology is the Christianization of an extra-Christian theology that it could not be secularized in its turn, since theology is possible only the ground of philosophy.[32]

On this basis, we contend that Heidegger (and this is true for Husserl as well) cannot remain in the same methodological atheism that he did at the time of *Being and Time* and that he is led to question what makes all discourse about God as such possible. In his 1947 letter to Jean Beaufret, Heidegger most clearly explains this point by claiming that "it is only on the basis of the truth of being that the essence of the being of the sacred can be thought" and that "only in light of the essence of divinity can it be thought or said what the word 'God' is to signify."[33] The dimension on the basis of which God and deity itself can be thought is thus the dimension of the sacred, of the *indemne*, since the word "*heilig*" in German specifically has the meaning of what is whole and exempt from all unilaterality and retreat into itself. Yet this horizon of indemnity is nothing but the clearing of the world, within which alone all things, and even God himself, can be announced and gain access to appearing.

This is what allows us to understand that for Heidegger, God and being are not identical, as he constantly reaffirms after finishing the "Letter on Humanism," but that does not mean, however, that the experience of God and of the divine can occur outside of the dimension of being. For the concern is rightly to denounce the contamination of the idea of God by the logic that sees God as the first foundation, or *causa sui*, in order to rise up to the idea of a "divine God" by leaving behind the God of the philosophers.[34] In his text from the mid-1930s entitled *Contributions to Philosophy* and dedicated to the thought of *Ereignis*, Heidegger named this God the "last God." And it is from this God, who cannot be without us, that we must await not so much "redemption," which is at bottom only the "subjection of the human," as the recognition of the human's belonging to being.[35]

The entire thematic of the "last God" presupposes a preliminary experience of the "death of God" in the Nietzschean sense, and even more, the experience of the "flight of the Gods," a recurrent theme in Hölderlin's poetry. Hölderlin is the one who tried to put the plurality of the manifestations of the divine, to which the Greek religion bears witness, into relation with the singular God represented by Christ, and so he is therefore the one who no longer unilaterally relates the dimension of the divine to Christianity alone. Yet Heidegger's concern is to find a new space for the manifestation of the divine in opposition to the "prolonged Christianization of God,"[36] which constitutes the very framework of our tradition. The "last God" of which Heidegger rather enigmatically speaks is, in contrast, presented by him as "the totally other over against Gods who have been, especially over against the Christian God."[37] For the divine can in no way find its space of appearance in cults or in the church, or in the inner experience of mass movements, but only in the "abyssal space of being itself"—that is, in the absence of ground of a being no longer opposed to becoming but thought instead on the basis of its essential historiality. The idea of a "last God" whose passage we must await, according to Heidegger, does not refer to any desired resurgence of archaic divinities, and is in no way in league with neo-paganism, as certain seem to think today. What is instead in question is the unfolding of an unheard-of dimension of the divine, which, as the Hölderlinian experience already showed, can be revealed only privatively and through withdrawal.

This God is the last, not as the last member of a series but rather because it simultaneously constitutes both the most extreme and the highest figure of time, and because in it is gathered the heterogeneous multiplicity of the experiences of the divine, as Hölderlin had sensed.[38] It is in this sense that there is "an absolutely unique unicity" of the deity, which is not at all the same as monotheism, which, like all species of "theisms," exists only on the basis of the Judeo-Christian horizon.[39] We must therefore not oppose the plurality of the Gods in flight of which Hölderlin spoke to the unicity of the God yet to come, for whom Heidegger wants to prepare the way; rather, and more profoundly, we must understand that the plurality of the Gods has nothing to do with number, but refers instead to the properly temporal dimension of a God who appears only in the instant of his disappearance, and who must therefore be originarily divided in order to "pass" into time. This thematic of a God who only "passes" implies that the Christian idea of divine infinitude is abandoned because, for Heidegger, what is unveiled in the sign that the last God addresses to us while passing is "the most intimate finitude of being."[40]

This theme of the finitude of being already announced at the end of the 1920s,[41] which tore being away from its independence with respect to history, is the ground for the new figure of the "last God" of which Hölderlin spoke. But this does not mean a lowering of divine transcendence to the level of human history, but rather a more authentic understanding of what the divine is, which is not adequately thought through the notion of "transcendence" or "overcoming." In the idea of a constant presence of the "eternal" Gods, as Hölderlin clearly saw, there resides the danger of idolatry whereby the Gods become mere human playthings. The last God is certainly not confused with *Ereignis*, the term Heidegger uses to designate the co-propriation of the human and being, but "he needs it"[42] because he can signal to us in passing only in this space of encounter, which is being, thought in its dimension of the event. This is why such a God commands nothing, in contrast to the moral God, and manifests itself only by withdrawing itself, in contrast to the God of revelation. It is this God who, while passing, simply signals to mortals, to those who are "capable of death"—that is, those who can see in their own finitude a resource rather than a limit. And such a God, who signals on the basis of death and who exists only through this sign addressed to mortals, is what calls for the "phenomenology of the inapparent,"[43] with which the later Heidegger is associated.

Acknowledgments

All of the chapters appearing in this book have appeared elsewhere, which we note here while expressing our thanks to the editors of reviews and editions who first published them and who have graciously allowed us to gather them here in the present form.

Chapter 1, "The Logic of Validity" (Husserl, Lotze et la logique de la validité) first appeared first appeared in *Kairos: Revue de Philosophie* 5 (1994): 31–48.

Chapter 2, "The Project of a Pure Logical Grammar" (Husserl et l'idée d'une grammaire pure a priori), appeared in *Grammaire, sujet et signification: Cahiers de philosophie ancienne et du langage* 1 (November 1994): 87–103.

Chapter 3, "The Problem of Pre-Predicative Experience" (Husserl et le problème de l'expérience antéprédicative), was a lecture given at the University of Liege on 21 March 1996.

Chapter 4, "The Phenomenological Gaze and Speech" (Le regard phénoménologique et la parole), first appeared in *Cahiers de L'École des sciences philosophiques et religieuses* 5 (1989): 39–58.

Chapter 5, "Reduction and Intersubjectivity" (Réduction et Intersubjectivité) was first published in *Husserl*, ed. E. Escoubas and M. Richir (Grenoble: J. Millon, 1989), 43–64.

Chapter 6, "Time and the Other" (Le temps et l'autre chez Husserl et Heidegger) appeared in *Alter: Revue de Phénoménologie* 1 (1993): 385–401.

Chapter 7, "Phenomenology and Therapy: The Question of the Other in the Zollikon Seminars" (Phénoménologie et la thérapie: La question de l'autre dans les *Zollikoner Seminare*), was first published in *Figures de la subjectivité: Approches phénoménologiques et psychiatriques*, ed. J.-F. Courtine (Paris: Editions du CNRS, 1992), 165–77.

Chapter 8, "Conscience: The Most Intimate Alterity" (Paul Ricoeur: Le soi et l'autre; L'alterité la plus intime), appeared in *Paul Ricoeur, L'herméneutique à l'école de la phénoménologie* (Paris: Beauchesne, 1995), 59–71.

Chapter 9, "Temporality and Existence" (La temporalité chez Merleau-Ponty), appeared in *Dimensions d'exister: Études d'anthropologie philosophique*, ed. G. Florival (Louvain: Peeters, 1994), 5:19–32.

Chapter 10, "Phenomenology of the Event" (Pour une phénoménologie de l'événement: L'attente et la surprise), first appeared in *Études phénoménologiques* 25 (1997): 59–75.

Chapter 11, "Phenomenology and History" (Phénoménologie et histoire), appeared in *Cahiers philosophiques, numéro spéciale: La phénoménologie* 81 (1999): 77–92.

Chapter 12, "History and Hermeneutics" (Histoire et herméneutique), was first published in *Paul Ricoeur: L'herméneutique à l'école de la phénoménologie* (Paris: Beauchesne, 1995), 219–33.

Chapter 13, "Phenomenology and the Question of Man" (Patočka et Heidegger: La phénoménologie et la question de l'homme), appeared in *Les Cahiers de philosophie: Jan Patočka, Le soin de l'ame* 11–12 (1990): 83–92.

Chapter 14, "The Phenomenology of Finitude" (Heidegger et Patočka: La phénoménologie de la finitude), first appeared in *Cahiers de L'École des sciences philosophiques et religieuses* 18 (1995): 99–114.

Chapter 15, "Worldliness and Mortality" (Eugen Fink: Mondanéité et mortalité), was first published in *Eugen Fink: Actes du Colloque de Cerisy-la-Salle*, ed. N. Depraz and M. Richir (Amsterdam: Rodopi, 1997), 323–49.

Chapter 16, "The 'Last God' of Phenomenology" (Le "dieu extreme" de la phénoménologie), was first published in *Archives de Philosophie* 63 (2000): 195–204.

Notes

Preface

1. Maurice Merleau-Ponty, "Preface," *Phenomenology of Perception*, tr. C. Smith (New York: Routledge, 1962), viii.

2. Recall that the full title of this last book, originally published in Prague in 1939, is *Experience and Judgment: Investigations in the Genealogy of Logic*; see Edmund Husserl, *Experience and Judgment*, tr. J. Churchill, J. Spencer, and K. Ameriks (Evanston: Northwestern University Press, 1973).

3. LI I: 249.

4. BT, 77–83.

5. ITC, 4–5.

6. Allow me to refer to my short book: Françoise Dastur, *Death: An Essay on Finitude*, tr. J. Llewelyn (London: Athlone Press, 1996).

7. This is Heidegger's formulation in section 7 of *Being and Time*. As for Husserl, he claimed in *The Idea of Phenomenology* in 1907 that the apprehension of the phenomenon—that is, of what is given in person (*Selbstgegebenes*)—is all that there is of the ultimate.

8. Merleau-Ponty had already understood this when, in one of his last courses, he stated this concerning the later Heidegger: "The 'non-theological mystique' is further from theology than from the philosophy of nothingness. . . . Heidegger is further than the nihilists from theological positivism"; Merleau-Ponty, *Notes de cours 1959–1961* (Paris: Gallimard, 1996), 119.

1. The Logic of "Validity" (Husserl, Heidegger, Lotze)

1. LI I: 214.

2. Ibid., 218.

3. Ibid., note.

4. Ibid., 224.

5. Husserl, "Review of Melchior Palagyi's *Der Streit der Psychologisten und Formalisten in der Modernen Logik*," tr. D. Willard, in *Early Writings in the Philosophy of Logic and Mathematics* (Dordrecht: Kluwer, 1994), 201.

6. Ibid., 201.

7. Ibid., 201–2.

8. Husserl, "A Draft of a Preface to *Logical Investigations*," in *Introduction to the Logical Investigations*, ed. E. Fink, tr. P. J. Bossert and C. H. Peters (The Hague: Nijhoff, 1975). Section 8 appears on 44–47. The draft originally appeared in *Tijdschrift voor philosophie* 1 (1939): 106–33 and 319–39.

9. Fink, "Editorial Remarks," in *Introduction to the Logical Investigations*, 13.

10. Husserl, "Draft," section 9: 48.

11. Ibid.: "Bolzano's propositions, ideas, truths 'in themselves' are anything but the meanings of 'ideal' unities. He would have firmly rejected the idea of a pure logic in my sense—and even more, in the sense of the pure logic to be 'elucidated' by a theory of knowledge."

12. Ibid., section 8: 45.

13. Ibid.

14. LI I: 43.

15. FTL, section 27: 88. Husserl shows here that the idea of a formal ontology is already present in the *Prolegomena* under the name of pure logic, and he restores his initial understanding of the formal in his *Philosophy of Arithmetic* of 1891, which, as imperfect as a first book can be, nevertheless consisted in a constitutive phenomenological investigation—that is, in an attempt to take account for the first time of those "categorial objectivities" (number and quantity) on the basis of the intentional constituting activity, which implies that their formal element has something in common with objectity in general (*Gegenständlichkeit überhaupt*) and the something in general (*Etwas überhaupt*).

16. A posthumous work by Brentano has the title *Die Lehre vom richtigen Urteil* (The Doctrine of Correct Judgment). It gathers together materials from courses given during 1884–85, when Husserl was attending them in Vienna.

17. Husserl, "Draft," section 6: 36.

18. Ibid., section 8: 46.

19. Ibid., 47.

20. Ibid.

21. Ibid.

22. On this subject, see the testimony of Georg Picht, "Die Macht des Denkens," in *Erinnerung an Martin Heidegger* (Pfullingen: Neske, 1977), 201.

23. Martin Heidegger, *Logik, die Frage nach der Wahrheit* (Frankfurt: Klostermann, 1976), section 9: 62–88; English translation by T. Sheehan as *Logic: The Question of Truth* (Bloomington: Indiana University Press, 2010).

24. Heidegger, *Towards the Definition of Philosophy*, tr. T. Sadler (London: Continuum, 2003), 106–9.

25. Ibid., 108.

26. Ibid.

27. Heidegger, *Frühe Schriften*, ed. F. von Herrmann (Klostermann: Frankfurt, 1972), 111: "So muss es demnach noch ein Daseinsform geben neben den möglichen Existenzarten des Physischen, Psychischen und Metaphysischen. Lotze hat für sie in unserem deutschen Sprachschatz die entscheidende Bezeichnung gefunden: neben einem 'das ist' gibt es ein 'das gilt.'" (There must therefore be another form of existence alongside the possible kinds of physical, psychical, and metaphysical existence. In the vocabulary of our German language, Lotze found the decisive designation for this: alongside a "that is" there is a "that is worth.")

28. BT, 146.

29. R. Herrmann Lotze, *Logic: In Three Books*, tr. B. Bosanquet (Oxford: Clarendon, 1888): *Logic* II, Book III, chapter 1: 177; translations of this work have been modified throughout.

30. Ibid., 183.

31. Ibid., 185.

32. Ibid., 187.

33. Ibid., 198.

34. G. W. F. Hegel, *Phenomenology of Spirit*, tr. A. V. Miller (Oxford: Oxford University Press, 1977), 48.

35. Lotze, *Logic* II, Book III, chapter 1: 199.

36. Ibid., chapter 2: 201.

37. Lotze, *Logic* I, Book I, chapter 1: 14.

38. Ibid., 15.

39. Lotze, *Logic* II, Book III, chapter 2: 203.

40. Ibid., 204.

41. Ibid., 207.

42. Ibid., 208.

43. Ibid., 209.

44. Ibid., 210.

45. Ibid., 212–13.

46. Ibid., 220.

47. Ibid., 221.

48. See Heidegger, *Logik, die Frage nach der Wahrheit*, 82.

2. The Project of a Pure Logical Grammar (Husserl)

1. The chapter reproduces without change the content of a lecture given March 14, 1992, in a seminar on "Philosophy and Language," directed by Antonia Soulez and Jan Sebestik. The seminar was dedicated to the genealogy of philosophical grammar starting in antiquity.

2. Martin Heidegger, *Frühe Schriften*, ed. F. von Herrmann (Frankfurt: Klosterman, 1972), 209.

3. LI II: 493.

4. Noam Chomsky, *Cartesian Linguistics: A Chapter in the History of Rational Thought* (New York: University Press of America, 1966), 39.

5. LI II: 529.

6. FTL, 49. Husserl refers in a note to Heidegger's thesis and mentions an article by M. Grabmann (1926) that establishes Thomas of Erfurt as the author of the *Grammatica Speculativa*, originally attributed to Duns Scotus.

7. LI II: 520, note 1, where apophantic logic is defined as the logic of enunciative meanings (*Aussagebedeutungen*).

8. It is in the *Formal and Transcendental Logic* that Husserl presents a more elaborated stratification of formal logic, which Suzanne Bachelard illuminates well in *A Study of Husserl's Formal and Transcendental Logic*, tr. L. Embree (Evanston: Northwestern University Press, 1990), 11ff. Three different levels of formal apophantic logic must be distinguished: the level of the logic of meaning or the pure morphology of judgments (that is, the level of the conditions of the meaning of the judgment); the level of the logic of noncontradiction (that is, the level of the conditions of the formal noncontradiction of the judgment); and the level of the logic of truth (that is, the level of the conditions of formal truth of the judgment). In the *Logical Investigations*, Husserl opposes only the level of pure grammar to the level of the logic of noncontradiction, without distinguishing material noncontradiction or falsity from formal noncontradiction or absurdity. As Bachelard underlines (7), all the examples that Husserl gives in the fourth *Investigation* are examples of material counter-sense (like the "square circle" or "all squares have five angles"), and it is only in the *Formal and Transcendental Logic* that he makes use of examples for formal counter-sense by abstracting from all matter of knowledge ("all As are Bs among which some are not B"). The demonstration of the autonomy of the second level constitutes the novelty of the point of view of the *Formal and Transcendental Logic*, which views the consideration of judgment, as a relation to a *possible* object, as also arising from *formal* logic, which in turn leads to distinguishing the attitude in which one is interested in judgments in themselves (the level of formal or analytic noncontradiction) from the attitude in which judgment is considered as the means to a possible objective knowledge (the level of material or synthetic noncontradiction). As for formal ontology, a specifically Husserlian notion that designates the "eidetic science of the object in general," it forms a correlate of this formal science of predicative judgment—namely, formal apophantic logic. The opposition, within formal logic, between apophansis and ontology, thus marks a duality of correlative orientations, one toward judgment, the other toward the object.

9. Bachelard, *Study*, 8–9.

10. LI I: 257: "that it is indispensable to envisage at the same time the grammatical aspect of logical lived experience."

11. Ibid., 250.

12. Ibid., 257–58.

13. Ibid., 292.

14. Ibid., 293.

15. LI II: 526. Note that the German says *reinlogische Grammatik: purely* logical grammar.

16. René Schérer, *La phénoménologie des "Recherches logiques" de Husserl* (Paris: PUF, 1967), 227.

17. See LI II: 529, where, citing Steinthal's works, Husserl remarks, "I refer especially to his beautifully precise statement of Humboldt's notion . . . from which it would seem that the views stated here are in some points close to those of the great thinker, whom Steinthal also respects."

18. See the book by Charles Serrus, *Le parallelisme logico-grammatical* (Paris: Alcan, 1938), in which we also find a critique of Husserl's point of view, accused of confusing the rules of grammar with the rules of logic. On this point, see Schérer, *La phenomenology*, 247.

19. LI II: 528 (trans. modified).

20. Ibid.

21. Ibid., 525.

22. Ibid., 526.

23. Ibid., 525.

24. FTL, 71.

25. LI II: 518.

26. The importance of the third *Investigation* and the theory of whole and parts that it lays out—an importance that is relevant not only to the fourth *Investigation*, but to the general problematic of the entire book, and even to every subsequent "noematic" analysis—has been remarkably illuminated by Robert Sokolowski in his article "The Logic of Parts and Wholes in Husserl's *Investigations*," in *Readings on Edmund Husserl's Logical Investigations*, ed. J. N. Mohanty (The Hague: Nijhoff, 1977), 94–111.

27. The notion of "truth in itself" that Husserl criticizes in the 1913 edition (see LI I: xvii) does not, however, necessarily refer to the idea of a *separation* of the real and the ideal, but rather to the idea of their correlation. What Husserl considers in 1913 as constituting the "imperfection" of the conception of truth as laid out in the *Prolegomena* is precisely the fact that it unilaterally overemphasizes the atemporality of truth and its independence from all knowledge of it (LI I: 300). As Alphonse de Waehlens has rightly noted (*Phenomenologie et vérité: Essai sur l'évolution de l'idée de vérité chez Husserl et Heidegger* [Paris: PUF, 1957], 15), Husserl, "carried away by a logicist sentiment" whose origins must be sought in his training as a mathematician, and that pushes him to hypostatize relations, tends to detach the true (in itself) content of the judgment of truth from its necessary correlate, the judicative act.

28. Schérer, *La phenomenology*, 228; see also 180. In the *Prolegomena*, Husserl insists on the fact that logic could not be defined as normative or

practical discipline, but rather as a theoretical discipline (LI I: 289ff). It is essential to see clearly that the ideality of meaning is in no way normative and refers to no "ideal" language, which Husserl vigorously underscores in sections 31 and 32 of the first *Investigation*. The concern there is not for an ideal to which one could conform (which supposes that one could somehow appresent it to oneself, or give oneself a "concrete archetype" of it [the "logical" dream of the combinarium in Leibniz's sense, the dream of a language of univocal meanings]), but rather for the ideality of the species, and it is absurd to imagine that it could ever be "practically" realized, since it would be a "metaphysical hypostasis" that would ruin the distinction between ideal and real. The example of color as *Spezies* is here, as always, the most clarifying: it is the sameness of red *in specie* that allows me to perceive this or that individual case of red, but red itself exists nowhere, neither in the world nor in our thought; it exists (ideally) only as "the unity of a multiplicity" of all real perceptions of red objects. When Husserl, in section 22 of *Ideas I*, responds to the reproach of "platonic realism" made against him by demonstrating that "blindness to the ideas" is a sort of incapacity to accept the most current perceptual evidence, he restores the properly philosophical attitude as incarnated by Socrates who, facing a Hippias "blind" to *the* idea (*eidos*) of beauty, distinguishes the beautiful in itself (*auto to kalon*) *from* beautiful things; Plato, *Hippias Major*, 298d.

29. I am depending here on the excellent article by James M. Edie, "Husserl's Conception of 'The Grammatical' and Contemporary Linguistics," in Mohanty, *Readings on Edmund Husserl's Logical Investigations*, 136–61. Like Edie, I also take into account, in addition to the fourth *Investigation*, the passages from FTL that treat of the pure morphology of meanings or purely logical grammar, and in particular the totality of Appendix I.

30. LI II: 467. In this paragraph, Husserl distinguishes the fragment (*Stück*) or independent part of the whole from the moment (*Moment*) or abstract and dependent part of the whole. What characterizes the moment is its inseparability from the whole and from other moments, exactly as is already the case in Hegel's *Science of Logic*, where the moment is defined as a nonautonomous term and can be posited only in its difference from other moments.

31. Ibid., 466.

32. Ibid., 517

33. Ibid.

34. Ibid.

35. FTL, 297.

36. Ibid., 309.

37. Ibid., 311.

38. Ibid., 310.

39. On the importance of the logical point of view of this operation, see Bachelard, *Study*, 33–34. The operation of nominalization of the predicate (the quality "P becomes S") makes appear the category of object as a constitutive

element of the proposition and thus evidences the interference of the formal apophantic and the formal ontological logics.

40. Schérer, *La phenomenology*, 149.

41. The article "Husserl's Conception," by James M Edie, makes this very clear, and I take account of these indications in the developments that follow.

42. Chomsky, *Cartesian Linguistics*, 40–41.

43. Ibid., 43. "Through the remarks made in the framework defined above, what Port-Royal's grammar brings out is that a deep structure subtending a phrase such as 'Peter lives' or 'God loves men' contains a copula expressing the affirmation, and a predicate ('living,' 'loving men') attributed to the subject of the proposition. Verbs constitute a sub-category of predicates; they are subject to a transformation that leads them to be melded with the copula in one word."

44. LI I: 514.

45. See Jacques Derrida's proposed translation for *bedeuten* in *La voix et le phénomène* (Paris: PUF, 1967) as *vouloir dire* (meaning-to-say).

46. Johannes Lohmann, "M. Heideggers 'ontologische Differenz' und die Sprache," *Lexis* 1 (1948): 49–106. This article, mentioned by Edie in "Husserl's Conception," has been translated into English as "M. Heidegger's 'Ontological Difference' and Speech," in *On Heidegger and Language*, ed. and tr. J. Kockelmans (Evanston: Northwestern University Press, 1972), 303–63.

47. Lohmann sees in it something as unique and as abstract in the Indo-European languages as is the root in the Semitic languages, which is not susceptible to any intuitive presentation and receives concrete form only in writing.

48. On this subject, see Derrida, "The Supplement of the Copula," in *Margins: Of Philosophy*, tr. A. Bass (Chicago: University of Chicago Press, 1982), 174–205, in passing. In this text, which admirably brings into focus the question of the relation of philosophical thought to a determinate form of language, Derrida is led to bring Benveniste and Heidegger into dialogue, opposing them to one another. The task of pursuing this dialogue while introducing a third voice into it—namely, Lohmann's—has yet to be carried out.

49. See Mohanty, *Edmund Husserl's Theory of Meaning*, 113.

50. Merleau-Ponty, "On the Phenomenology of Language," in *Signs* (Evanston: Northwestern University Press, 1972), 85: "Taking language as a *fait accompli*, as the residue of past acts of significations and the record of already acquired meanings, the scientist inevitably misses the clarity peculiar to speech, the fecundity of expression."

3. The Problem of Pre-Predicative Experience (Husserl)

1. See Husserl's letter to Albrecht from 1 July 1908, in Husserl, *Briefwechsel* 9 (Dordrecht: Kluwer, 1994), 41.

2. CM, 81.

3. EJ, 18.

4. Ibid., 47.
5. Ibid.
6. Ibid.
7. Ibid., 48.
8. Ibid., 49.
9. FTL, 211.
10. EJ, 7.
11. Ibid., 24.
12. Ibid., 63.
13. Ibid.
14. Ibid., 254–55.
15. Ibid., 261.
16. Ibid., 60.
17. Ibid.
18. Ibid., 108.
19. Ibid., 204.
20. Ibid., 11.
21. Ibid., 13.
22. Ibid., 16–17.
23. Ibid., 17.
24. Ibid., 19.
25. Ibid., 21.
26. Ibid.
27. Ibid., 19.
28. Ibid., 20.
29. Ibid.
30. Ibid.
31. Immanuel Kant, *Critique of Pure Reason,* tr. N. K Smith (New York: St. Martin's, 1929), 47: "The light dove cleaving the air in her free flight and feeling its resistance, might imagine that its flight would be still easier in empty space . . . meeting no resistance that might, as it were, serve as a support on which [she] could take a stand."
32. LI II: 817.
33. EJ, 27: We underline the "Aristotelian" character of the reference to the individual. There is no doubt that Husserl inherited this Aristotelian horizon of his problematic from his teacher Brentano.
34. Ibid., 26.
35. Ibid., 29.
36. Ibid.
37. Ibid., 30.
38. BT, 31.
39. EJ, 31.
40. Ibid., 30.
41. Ibid., 34.

42. Ibid., 53

43. Ibid.

44. Ibid., 54. [Trans. modified from "every sensuous experience" to "every simple experience."]

45. Ibid.

46. Ibid., 55.

47. Ibid.

48. Ibid., 56.

49. LI II: 503. Here Husserl recognizes that wanting to deduce occasional significations from language and wanting to describe any subjective experience whatsoever in an objective fashion are "manifestly vain" efforts.

50. CM, 92.

51. EJ, 57.

52. LI I: 266. Here Husserl claims that the phenomenological analysis that he is about to conduct has "its sense and epistemological worth . . . [independently of] the fact that there really are languages and that humans really make use of them in their mutual dealings."

53. CM, 38. On this subject of the relation between sensuous experience and linguistic meaning in *Experience and Judgment*, see the article by Maria Villela-Pétit, "Receptivité antéprédicative et familiarité typique," *Archives de Philosophie* 58 (1995): 603–15.

54. EJ, 58.

55. Ibid., 79.

56. Ibid., 112.

57. Ibid., 139.

58. Ibid., 71–72.

59. Ibid., 76.

60. Husserl, *Analyses Concerning Passive and Active Synthesis: Lectures on Transcendental Logic*, tr. A. J. Steinbock (Dordrecht: Nijhoff, 2001), 441 [trans. modified to correspond with Dastur's French quotation].

61. Ibid., 442.

62. On this subject, see Françoise Dastur, "Heidegger et le ton de retenue de la pensée," *Epokhē* 2 (1991): 309–24.

63. FCM, 343.

64. Ibid., 67.

4. The Phenomenological Gaze and Speech (Husserl and Heidegger)

1. Réné Char, *Oeuvres Complètes* (Paris: Gallimard, 1983), 716.

2. WPh, 49.

3. One possible translation of Fragment 50 reads, "He who hears not me but the *logos* will say: All is one."

4. Plato, *Symposium*, 203b, tr. S. Benardete (Chicago: University of Chicago Press, 1993), 33.

5. "All men naturally desire to know" is the first line of Aristotle's *Metaphysics*. Recall that the verb *eidenai*, constructed from the root *eidō*, which means "to see," attests that in Greek, and in all the European languages in general (cf. the Sanskrit Veda), knowledge [*savoir*] is essentially thought as a seeing [*voir*]; see Aristotle, *Metaphysics*, in *Basic Works of Aristotle*, tr. R. McKeon (New York: Random House, 1941), 689.

6. Aristotle, *Metaphysics*, Alpha 1.980a25 and Alpha 2.982b9, in *The Basic Works*, 689, 692.

7. *Metaphysics*, Alpha 2.982b29 and Theta 6.2048b18, in *Basic Works*, 692, 826.

8. *Metaphysics*, Alpha 2.982b12, in *Basic Works*, 692; Plato, *Theaetetus* 155d, tr. F. M. Cornford, in *Plato: Collected Dialogues*, ed. E. Hamilton and H. Cairns (Princeton: Princeton University Press, 1961), 860.

9. BQP, 154. In this course from Winter Semester 1937–38, Heidegger analyzed the essence of wonder (section 38) and, citing Hölderlin, noted that every thinking apprehension is a "sufferance" [*leiden*], a passion [*Leidenschaft*] that is situated beyond all activity and passivity in the usual sense and that it must be understood as a taking in charge by humans of what exceeds them.

10. WPh, 85: "In astonishment we restrain ourselves (*être en arrêt*). We step back, as it were, from beings, from the fact that they are as they are and not otherwise. And astonishment is not used up in this retreating from the Being of beings, but, as this retreating and self-restraining, it is at the same time forcibly drawn to and, as it were, held fast by that from which it retreats" [translation slightly modified; Heidegger's interpolation of the French phrase; "held fast" is given in the French translation used by Dastur as "*enchaîné*"].

11. WPh, 85 [translation slightly modified].

12. Martin Heidegger, *Parmenides*, tr. A. Schuwer and R. Rojcewicz (Bloomington: Indiana University Press, 1992), 145.

13. Heidegger, *The Principle of Reason*, tr. R. Lilly (Bloomington: Indiana University Press, 1991), 48.

14. VI, 170: "this perceptual world is at bottom Being in Heidegger's sense, which is more than all painting, than all speech, than every 'attitude,' and which, apprehended by philosophy in its universality, appears as containing everything that will ever be said, and yet leaving us to create it (Proust): it is the *logos endiathetos* which calls for the *logos prophorikos*."

15. Heidegger, *Principle of Reason*, 48.

16. BT, 138.

17. Ibid., 140.

18. Ibid., 142: "Alle Auslegung, die Verständnis beistellen soll, muss schon das Auszulegende verstanden haben."

19. This analysis of the *idea* is found in BQP, 60.

20. Heidegger, *Parmenides*, 148.

21. Ibid., 42.

22. BQP, 76. "Das Wesen wird nicht angefertigt, aber auch nicht wie ein vorhandenes einzelnes Ding beliebig angetroffen, sondern er-sehen, hervorgebracht. Woher—wohin? Aus dem Ungesichteten ins Sichtbare, aus dem Ungedachten in das fortan zu Denkende." It is the absolutely original character of essence, by which it makes possible every ontic vision, that leads Heidegger to define pro-duction of the idea a little further on as hypothesis, positing of the foundation of all beingness [*étantité*].

23. Ibid., 84.

24. Heidegger, "The Self-Assertion of the German University," tr. W. S. Lewis, in *The Heidegger Controversy: A Critical Reader*, ed. R. Wolin (Cambridge, Mass.: MIT Press, 1991), 33–34: "The Greeks did not assimilate praxis to theory, but rather understood theory itself as the highest realization of authentic praxis."

25. See Heidegger, "Mein Weg in die Phänomenologie," in *Zur Sache des Denkens*, ed. F. W. von Herrmann (Frankfurt: Klostermann, 2007), 86: "Als ich in der Nähe Husserls das Phänomenologische Sehen einübte."

26. Heidegger, "My Way into Phenomenology," tr. J. Stambaugh, in *On Time and Being* (New York: Harper, 1972), 78.

27. Heidegger, "Letter to Richardson," in *Through Phenomenology to Thought*, by William J. Richardson, 4th ed. (New York: Fordham University Press, 2003), x.

28. Heidegger, "Seminar at Zähringen," in *Four Seminars*, tr. A. Mitchell and F. Raffoul (Bloomington: Indiana University Press, 2003), 80.

29. Maurice Merleau-Ponty, *Signs*, tr. R. McCleary (Evanston: Northwestern University Press, 1964), 180.

30. Heidegger, "My Way into Phenomenology," 79.

31. See Husserl, "Présentation des Recherches logiques (1901)," in *Articles sur la logique*, tr. Jacques English (Paris: PUF, 1975), section 2: 205. [This short text appears not to be translated into English.]

32. Heidegger, "Seminar at Zähringen," first session, in *Four Seminars*, 67.

33. LI II: 783 and 774. On the meaning of this "in excess," see Jacques Taminiaux, *Dialectic and Difference*, ed. and tr. J. Decker and R. Crease (Atlantic Highlands, N.J.: Humanities Press International, 1985), 91.

34. LI II: 788.

35. Ibid., 789.

36. Ibid., 818.

37. See, for example, Friedrich Wilhelm Josef Schelling, "Of the I," in *The Unconditional in Human Knowledge: Four Early Essays*, ed. and tr. F. Marti (Lewisburg, Pa.: Bucknell University Press, 1980).

38. Ideas I, section 43: 123.

39. Ibid., section 24: 83.

40. VI, 273.

41. On this point, see Françoise Dastur, "World, Flesh, Vision," *in Chiasms: Merleau-Ponty's Notion of the Flesh*, ed. L. Lawler and F. Evans (Albany: SUNY

Press, 2000), 23–50; and in Dastur, "Monde, chair, vision," in *Chair et langage: Essais sur Merleau-Ponty* (La Versanne: Encre Marin, 2001), 69–107.

42. BT, 81.

43. Ibid., 33.

44. Heidegger, "A Dialogue on Language," in *On the Way to Language*, tr. P. D. Hertz (New York: Harper and Row, 1971), 9.

45. Heidegger, *Zur Bestimmung der Philosophie*, GA 56–57: 117. "Die bemächtigende, sich selbst mitnehmende Erleben des Erlebens ist die verstehende, die *hermeneutische Intuition*, originäre phänomenologische Ruck- und Vorgriffs-bildung, aus der jede theoretisch-objectivierende, ja transzendente Setzung herausfällt"; Heidegger, *Towards the Definition of Philosophy*, tr. T. Sadler (London: Continuum, 2002), 98. The 1923 course to which Heidegger alludes was published in 1988 as GA 63, *Ontologie (Hermeneutik der Faktizitat)*; English translation by J. van Buren as *Ontology: The Hermeneutics of Facticity* (Bloomington: Indiana University Press, 1999).

46. Heidegger, "Dialogue on Language," 9.

47. Ibid., 10.

48. Ibid., 29. In the 1953–54 dialogue, Heidegger cites the same passage from Plato's *Ion* that he had already cited in 1923 (GA 63: 9), which portrays poets as the messengers (*hermeneis*) of the gods. And already at this time, he understands hermeneutics in its original meaning as the announcement (*Kundgabe*) of Being because it was already a matter in 1923 (when he first begins to prepare *Being and Time*) as it was still in 1953 a matter of bringing to light (*zum Vorschein zu bringen*) the Being of beings "of such kind that Being even comes to appear (*zum Scheinen kommt.*)"

49. Heidegger, "The Essence of Language," in *On the Way to Language*, 72–73. See also the long note in Jacques Derrida, *Of Spirit: Heidegger and the Question*, tr. G. Bennington and R. Bowlby (Chicago: University of Chicago Press, 1991), 129–36 (note 5 to page 44).

50. VI, 120: "No question goes towards Being: if only by virtue of its being as a question, it has already frequented Being, and returns from it."

5. Reduction and Intersubjectivity (Husserl)

1. Edmund Husserl, "Author's Preface to the English Translation," in Ideas I: 5–6. [This text was written by Husserl in 1930 for Gibson's translation, then subsequently published as an appendix in *Husserliana* V (The Hague: Nijhoff, 1952), which corresponds to Ideas III. The only English translation of Ideas I (or III) that contains this text is Gibson's translation—Tr.].

2. We must recall with insistence that the famous claim in Appendix XXVIII to section 73 of the *Crisis*, which reads "philosophy as science, as serious, rigorous, and indeed apodictically rigorous science—*the dream is over*" (Crisis, 389), is not an assertion advanced by Husserl himself but rather, as the context of the rest of the appendix makes clear, a judgment held by the times: "a powerful and constantly growing current of philosophy which renounces

scientific discipline, like the current of religious belief, is inundating European humanity" (390). In order to remedy the crisis of the times, Husserl wants instead to reconnect with the "unitary meaning" of philosophy—that is, with its teleological meaning, which exists in the state of a project in all the great systems of the past. What has changed in relation to the 1911 manifesto "Philosophy as Rigorous Science" is simply the necessity for philosophical mediation now to pass through history: "there is no doubt . . . that we must engross ourselves in historical considerations if we are to be able to understand ourselves as philosophers and to understand what philosophy is to become through us" (391).

3. IP, 21.

4. Husserl, "Author's Preface," in Ideas I, tr. Gibson, 20.

5. IP, 21: "the most rigorous mathematics and mathematical natural science here have not the slightest advantage over any actual or alleged knowledge belonging to common experience."

6. Ibid., 21.

7. Ibid., 23.

8. See the excellent article by Alexandre Lowit, "*L'epokhē* de Husserl et le doute de Descartes," *Revue de metaphysique et morale* (1957).

9. IP, 19.

10. CM, 35.

11. IP, 33.

12. Ibid.

13. ITC, 245n1.

14. LI I: 261 (that is, section 6 of the "Introduction" to volume II of the original German edition).

15. IP, 64.

16. Husserl, Ideas I, section 86: 232–33: "From its pure eidetic standpoint which 'suspends' the transcendent in every shape and form, phenomenology comes inevitably on its own ground of pure consciousness to *this whole system of problems* which are *transcendental in the specific sense*, and for this reason, it *merits the title of transcendental phenomenology*."

17. LI I: 265: "Its aim is not to *explain* knowledge in the psychological or psychophysical sense as a *factual* occurrence in objective nature, but to *shed light* on the *Idea* of knowledge in its constitutive elements and laws. It does not try to follow up the real connections of coexistence and succession with which actual acts of knowledge are interwoven, but to understand the *ideal* sense of the *specific* connections in which the objectivity of knowledge may be documented. It endeavors to raise to clearness the pure forms and laws of knowledge by tracing knowledge back to an adequate fulfillment in intuition. This 'clearing up' takes place in the framework of a phenomenology of knowledge, a phenomenology oriented, as we saw, to the essential structures of pure experience and to the structures of sense that belong to these."

18. LI II: 541; "we limit the purely mental ego to its phenomenological content."

19. Ibid., 544–45. Here Husserl does not yet speak of the phenomenological reduction properly speaking, but of the reduction to the phenomenological (Reduktion auf das Phänomenologische).

20. Descartes identifies in the second *Meditation* his thinking self with his soul (*mens sive animus*); he thus thinks the cogito as the action of a consciousness as being part of the world or as able to be a part of it, because a representative consciousness, which is what Cartesian consciousness is, is necessarily posited as exterior to things and as therefore constituting with them the empire of exteriority, the *world*.

21. IP, 41.

22. Ideas I, section 49: "consciousness considered in its purity must be taken as a self-contained system of Being [ein für sich geschlossner Seinszusammenhang] as a system of Absolute Being in which nothing can penetrate and from which nothing can escape"; see Leibniz, *Monadology*, section 7: "Monads do not have windows through which something may enter or exit."

23. IP, 66.

24. Ideas I, section 50: 150; see also Eugen Fink, "Phenomenological Philosophy of Edmund Husserl and Contemporary Criticism," in *Husserl (Critical Assessments of Leading Philosophers)*, ed. R. Bernet, D. Wellton, and G. Zavota (New York: Routledge, 2005), 217: "In contrast to the psychological *epokhē* the phenomenological *epokhē* is not a method for delimiting (*Einschränkung*) an area within the world, but is rather a method for going beyond the world by removing limits (*Einschränkung über die Welt hinaus*): the totality of beings signified by the title 'world' is made a problem by viewing the world as a unity of acceptances lying within the life of the reductively disclosed transcendental subjectivity." The *epokhē* has the virtue not of positing limits but rather of opening to what does not know limits: to infinite intentional life.

25. Husserl, "Author's Preface," Ideas I, 7: "The change of attitude (*Einstellungsänderung*) which in this work is called the phenomenological reduction (transcendental-phenomenological we now say, to be more precise) is effected by me as the actually philosophizing subject, from the natural attitude as a basis, and I experience myself here in the first instance as 'I.' "

26. G. W. F. Hegel, "Introduction," *Phenomenology of Spirit*, tr. A. V. Miller (Oxford: Clarendon, 1977), 55: "Our account implied that knowledge of the first object, or the being-for-consciousness of the first in-itself, itself becomes the second object," and later, "the new object shows itself to have come about by means of a reversal of consciousness itself [durch eine Umkehrung des Bewusstseins selbst]."

27. IP, 54.

28. Fink, "Phenomenological Philosophy," 230: "If we can no longer interpret this transcendental life as being receptive, its true character still remains indeterminate. Its constitutive interpretation identifies it first as creation." We must nevertheless specify that Fink tempers the weight of the word 'enormous' (see Ricoeur's preface to the French version of *Ideas*, xxx) by

immediately adding "the apparent dryness of the doctrinal character of a determination of essence of constitution as productive creation matters little because it has at least the merit of underlining its opposition to the receptive character (requiring a being in itself) of the life of ontic-worldly (psychic) experience. (We cannot here clearly show that 'constituting' designates a relation, which is neither receptive nor productive, that would not attain ontic concepts, which the accomplishments of constitutive investigations alone can indicate.)"

29. Ideas I, section 43: 123.

30. See the very suggestive article by Rudolf Boehm, "Deux points de vue: Husserl et Nietzsche," *Archivio di Filosophia* 3 (1962): 167–81. Boehm brings the two thinkers together specifically on the basis of their conceptions of interpretation.

31. LI II: 860: "It is of the essence of perception that something should appear in it: apperception, however, *constitutes what we call appearance*. . . . The *house* appears to me in no other manner than that I apperceive actually experienced sense-contents in a certain fashion. I hear a *barrel organ*—the tones sensed are interpreted *as those of a barrel organ*. In the same way I apperceivingly perceive my own psychic phenomena, *the blessedness quivering through 'me,' the grief in my heart*, etc." In the second edition, Husserl replaced the term *Interpretation* with the Leibnizian term *Apperzeption*. Leibniz defined apperception as "the consciousness, or the reflective knowledge, of the internal state" (*Principles of Nature and Grace*, in "*Philosophical Papers and Letters*," ed. Leroy E. Loemker [Dordrecht: Kluwer Academic, 1989], 636–42) and sees what constitutes simple perception in it. In section 6 of the Appendix (LI II: 864–67), Husserl wants to establish the identity of the point of view of knowledge with what Brentano distinguished as internal and external perception. In the first edition, he establishes this identity by showing that all perception, internal and external, is *interpretation* in the same sense that he had already shown (in section 23 of the first *Investigation*) that all apprehension (*Auffassung*) is an act of interpretation (*Deuten*) since sensations (*Empfindungen*) need an objectifying interpretation (*objektivierende Deutung*) in order to become an intuitive representation (*anschauliche Vorstellung*). The term "apperception" designates the essence of all perception in the second edition because it has the advantage of characterizing lived experience in its purity—that is, disregarding every transcendental position.

32. In his translation into French, Ricoeur proposes as a title to this section "Fundamental Phenomenological Considerations," thus pluralizing, and weakening, what the German expresses with the radicality of the singular.

33. Ideas I, section 31.

34. Ibid., 97–98.

35. CM, 2: "Accordingly, the Cartesian *Meditations* are not intended to be a merely private concern of the philosopher Descartes, to say nothing of their being merely an impressive literary form in which to present the foundations of

his philosophy. Rather, they draw the prototype for any beginning philosopher's necessary meditations, the meditations out of which alone a philosophy can grow originally."

36. Ideas I, section 50: 140.

37. See Crisis, 154: "Characterization of a new way to the reduction, as contrasted with the Cartesian path."

38. Fink, "Phenomenological Philosophy," 223: "It can be formulated in certain theses. The phenomenological reduction is not primarily a method of simply 'disconnecting,' but one of *lending back*. It leads, through the most extreme radicalism of self-reflection, the philosophizing subject *back through itself* to the transcendental life of belief (a life which is concealed by the subject's human self-apperception) whose acceptance correlate, the world, '*is*.'" See also the excellent article by Rudolf Boehm on the reduction in *Vom Gesichtspunkt der Phänomenologie* I (Hague: Nijhoff, 1968), from which we have drawn much inspiration here.

39. Crisis, 155.

40. See "Author's Preface," in Ideas I, 10: "In the course of many years of brooding over these matters, the author has followed up different lines of inquiry, all equally possible, in the attempt to exhibit in an absolutely transparent and compelling manner the nature of such motivation as propels beyond the natural positive realism of life and science and necessitates the transcendental conversion or phenomenological reduction." See also the first version of a passage of *Erste Philosophie* II, Hua VII: 174, note 1: "For myself, I recognize that the first intuition that I had of the phenomenological reduction was of limited importance such as I described above [that is, as reduction to the proper transcendental ego]. During these years, I saw no possibility of transforming it into an intersubjective reduction. But finally, I saw how to open a path that had to be of decisive importance for the possibility of realizing a fully transcendental phenomenology and—at a higher level—a transcendental philosophy." On the multiplicity of the ways to the reduction, see Boehm's "Editor's Introduction," in Hua VIII, *Erste Philosophie Zweiter Teil*, xi–xlii, as well as the excellent article by Iso Kern, "Die drei Wege zur transzendental-phänomenologischen Reduktion in der Philosophie Edmund Husserls," *Tijdschrift vor Filosofie* 4, no. 2 (1962): 303–49.

41. CM, section 54: 117.

42. Husserl, *Erste Philosophie* 2, "Theory of Phenomenological Reduction," Hua VIII: 175.

43. Hua VIII: 129.

44. Ibid., 174.

45. Ibid.

46. Ibid.: "falls er nicht schon jene beflügelten Vorahnungen hat, die ihn alle wahre Aüsserlichkeit in der Innerlichkeit suchen lassen."

47. Cf. Crisis, "Author's Preface," 31: "If the author has been obliged, on practical grounds, to lower the ideal of the philosopher to that of a downright

beginner [*rechten Anfangers*], he has at least in his old age reached for himself the complete certainty that he should thus call himself an actual beginner [*wirklichen Anfanger*]. He could dare hope, were Methuselah's age granted to him, to be still able to become a philosopher . . . . The author sees the infinite open country of the true philosophy, the 'promised land' on which he himself will never set foot. . . . Gladly he would hope that those who come after will take up these first ventures, carry them steadily forward, yes, and improve also their great deficiencies, defects of incompleteness which cannot indeed be avoided in the beginnings of scientific work."

48. Landgrebe did indeed view as entirely legitimate the claim that Husserl had "taken a break" from Cartesianism starting in his 1923–24 courses on *Erste Philosophie* (see the last chapter, dedicated to these courses and entitled, "Husserls Abschied vom Cartesianismus," in Ludwing Landgrebe and Edmund Husserl, *Der Weg der Phänomenologie: Das Problem einer ursprünglichen Erfahrung* [Gütersloh: Mohn, 1963]). But if the *Cartesian Meditations* of 1929 cannot be viewed simply as a relapse into Cartesianism, they nevertheless take up again the Cartesian path that Husserl had certainly considered as problematic from at least the beginning of the 1920s and that he will abandon in favor of the "ontological" path of the Crisis only beginning in the 1930s.

49. Husserl, *Zur Phänomenologie der Intersubjektivität*, Erster Teil, *1905–1920* (Hague: Nijhoff, 1973), 1.

50. Ibid, xxxv: "Ausdehnung der phänomenologischen Reduktion auf die Intersubjektivität." [The text in question from this volume of the *Husserliana* is published as a single volume in English as *The Basic Problems of Phenomenology: From the Lectures, Winter Semester, 1910–1911*, tr. I. Farin and J. G. Hart (Dordrecht: Nijhoff, 2006).]

51. GPP, section 29, 61: "Going beyond the realm of absolute givenness as a necessary condition for the possibility of a phenomenological science."

52. Ibid., 62.

53. Ibid., 61.

54. Ibid., 62.

55. Ibid., 74.

56. Ibid., 101. We must recall here the importance of the phenomenological concept of motivation (see Ideas I, 134n1) that Husserl was already using in the first *Logical Investigation* (sections 2 and 3) in order to characterize the relation of indication (*Anzeige*) that links in a non-obvious manner an actual knowledge to an inactual knowledge.

57. GPP, 102.

58. Ibid.

59. Hua VIII: 164, Chapter 11: "The Second Path to Opening of the Sphere of Transcendental Experience."

60. Ibid., 189.

61. Ibid., 190.

6. Time and the Other (Husserl, Heidegger, Levinas)

1. See Emmanuel Levinas, *On Escape*, tr. B. G. Bergo (Stanford: Stanford University Press, 2003); the French title is *De l'évasion*.

2. See Levinas, "Preface," in *Time and the Other*, tr. R. Cohen (Pittsburgh: Duquesne University Press, 1987), 32.

3. See the title of the book Levinas published in 1974: *Otherwise than Being or Beyond Essence*, tr. A. Lingis (Dordrecht and Boston, Mass.: Kluwer, 1978).

4. See Levinas, *Totality and Infinity: An Essay on Exteriority*, tr. A. Lingis (Pittsburgh: Duquesne University Press, 1969), 304: "Morality is not a branch of philosophy, but first philosophy."

5. See TO, 75: "right away this means that existence is pluralist. The plural is not here a multiplicity of existents, it appears in existing itself."

6. MFL, 139: "Zerstreuung des Daseins als solchen, d.h. das Mitsein überhaupt." On the sense of this dispersion, see Jacques Derrida, "Geschlecht I: Sexual Difference, Ontological Difference," in *Psyche: Invention of the Other*, ed. and tr. P. Kamuf and E. Rottenberg (Stanford: Standford University Press, 2008), 2:19–23.

7. Ideas I, section 49: 139.

8. Ms. B IV 6, "Zur Lehre des transzendentalen Idealismus," Husserl Archive, International Centre for Phenomenology and Continental Philosophy, Katholieke Universiteit, Leuven.

9. Ideas I, section 80: 195.

10. CM, section 10: 24

11. Ideas I, section 81: 216.

12. Edmund Husserl, *Zur Phänomenologie der Intersubjektivität: Texte Aus Dem Nachlass*, Dritter Teil, *1929–1935*, Hua XV, ed. I. Kern (The Hague: Nijhoff, 1973): xlvii (manuscript dating from March 1931).

13. Hua XV: xlv.

14. ITC, section 39: 84. [Note that the English translation proposes "horizontal intentionality" instead of "longitudinal"—Tr.]

15. Heidegger, "On the Essence of Ground," tr. J. Sallis, in *Pathmarks*, ed. W. McNeill (Cambridge: Cambridge University Press, 1998), 125n66 (text of note is on 371).

16. Husserl articulates this very clearly in manuscript E, III, 2 from 1920–21 and again in manuscript C 10 from 1931, Husserl Archive.

17. Immanuel Kant, *The Critique of Pure Reason* (B 225), tr. N. K. Smith (New York: St. Martin's, 1929), 213.

18. ITC, section 31: 66.

19. Hua VIII: 471: "The ego as objective has no place in subjective time, but it is according to the form of time that belongs to it omnitemporal."

20. Ms. C 1, Husserl Archive; cited by Klaus Held, in *Die lebendige Gegenwart* (Cologne: 1963), 107.

21. Ms C 2 III, Husserl Archive.

22. Ms. C 7 1 (1932), Husserl Archive.

23. Held, *Die lebendige Gegenwart*, 172.
24. Hua VIII: 175.
25. Ibid., 86–88.
26. GPP, 61–63.
27. Ibid., 100.
28. Hua VIII: 153.
29. Ms C 16 VII, Husserl Archive; cited by Held, *Die lebendige Gegenwart*, 186.
30. TO, 79.
31. Cf. Hua XV: xlix (Manuscript C 3), Husserl Archive.
32. CM, section 49: 107.
33. Hua XV: xlix.
34. Husserl, *Ideas Pertaining to a Pure Phenomenology and to a Phenomenological Philosophy*, Second Book, *Studies in the Phenomenology of Constitution*, tr. R. Rojcewicz and A. Schuwer (Dordrecht: Kluwer, 1989), 109.
35. Husserl, *Analyses Concerning Passive and Active Synthesis: Lectures on Transcendental Logic*, tr. A. Steinbock (Dordrecht: Kluwer, 2001), 467.
36. Ibid., 467.
37. Ideas I, section 89: 240.
38. Heidegger, *The Concept of Time*, tr. W. McNeill (London: Blackwell, 1992), 21–22E.
39. Ibid., 21E: "Time itself is meaningless: time is temporal."
40. PCT, 20.
41. Heidegger, *Concept of Time*, 6E. *Jeweiligkeit* does not have here the sense of "perpetuity," a term proposed by the French translators, but rather refers to the essentially temporal and transitory character of the "I am." The English translator chooses "specificity" as a translation and appends an informative note (24En8).
42. BT, 40. The French translation of *Jemeinigkeit* that F. Vezin proposes, "être-à-chaque-fois-à-moi," being-each-time-my-own, seems felicitous in this context. [Stambaugh proposes "always-being-my-own-being" (ibid.)—Tr.]
43. Ibid. Marginalia B: "Jemeinigkeit meint Ubereignetheit." The marginal notes that Heidegger added to his own personal copy were reproduced in the *Gesamtausgabe* edition in 1977. [Stambaugh gives this phrase as "in each case my own means being appropriated."—Tr.]
44. PCT, 236.
45. Ibid., 154.
46. We certainly find in Husserl the affirmation that the monadic ego is not a general impersonal subject, such as is the subject of critical philosophy, but that it is instead the "de facto transcendental ego" (CM, 69). Phenomenology cannot, however, be installed at the level of this (absurd) transcendental empiricism because any transcendental analysis must also be an eidetic analysis. Yet the necessary transition of the de facto transcendental ego to the eidetic ego is difficult to undertake, precisely because "the extension of the eidetic ego is

[uniquely] determined by the variation of my ego" and because neither reality nor even the possibility of an other ego is presupposed: "I modify myself in the imagination, myself, I phantasy myself as if I were otherwise, I do not phantasy others" (CM, 72). The eidetic ego obtained on the solipsist plane is, however, the essence of every other ego: even if Husserl does not need to presuppose a de facto community for this, it is already necessary from the beginning for him to admit a transcendental plurality of subjects.

47. MFL, 139.

48. PCT, 238.

49. ["Isolation" here translates the French *esseulement*, which itself is used to render Heidegger's *Vereinzelung*, translated by J. Stambaugh in *Being and Time* (Albany: SUNY Press, 1996) as "individuation."—Tr.]

50. BT, 127.

51. Heidegger, *Concept of Time*, 21E.

52. Ibid., 21: "*die einzige Diesmaligkeit seines einzigen Schicksals in der Möglichkeit seines einzigen Vorbei.*" [The sentence in the text is a translation of Dastur's French. The phrase is translated in *The Concept of Time* as follows: "this one singular uniqueness of its singular fate in the possibility of its singular past" (21E).—Tr.]

53. MFL, 209. [Translation modified to reflect Dastur's French.—Tr.]

54. BT, 113.

55. Ibid.

56. PCT, 237.

57. Eugen Fink, "Les concepts opératoires dans la phénoménologie de Husserl," in *Husserl: Cahiers de Royaumont* (Paris: Minuit, 1959), 214–30. This text also appears in Fink, *Nähe und Distanz: Studien zur Phänomenologie* (Freiburg: Alber Karl, 2008), 184–85.

58. BT, 79.

59. MFL, 188.

60. Ibid.

61. BT, 117.

62. Ibid., 58.

63. IP, 28–29.

64. BT, 117.

65. See the letter from Heidegger to Husserl dated 22 October 1927 in Husserl, *Phenomenological and Transcendental Psychology and the Confrontation with Heidegger*, tr. and ed. T. Sheehan and R. Palmer (Dordrecht: Kluwer, 1997), 139.

66. BT, 246.

67. Ibid., 285–86.

68. Ibid., 288.

69. TO, 93: "Just as in all the philosophies of communion, sociality in Heidegger is found in the subject alone; and it is in terms of solitude that the

analysis of Da-sein, in its authentic form, is pursued." It seems that Levinas does not see that this "collectivity of the side-by-side" is not a collectivity of isolated subjects, but a union on the basis of what alone is common: the lonely commonality in death—a difference in identity or, as Hölderin had said, *a hen diapheron eautō.*

70. MFL, 139.

71. Ibid., 207–8.

72. Ibid., 138: "Mannigfaltigkeit gehört zum Sein selbst."

73. TO, 31; my emphasis.

74. TO, 90. Even if for Levinas, "the problem does not consist in rescuing eternity from the jaws of death, but in allowing it to be welcomed" (78), the question remains: "how do I assume my own death?" For Heidegger the concern is always not to assume one's death but to exist, which means letting death become master of existence. Hegel, in *The Phenomenology of Spirit*, had already called death "the absolute master."

75. TO, 92.

76. This has been analyzed particularly well by Werner Marx, in "Les mortels," *Le Cahier du Collège International de Philosophie* (Paris: Osiris) 8 (1989): 79–104.

7. Phenomenology and Therapy: The Question of the Other in the Zollikon Seminars (Heidegger and Boss)

1. Medard Boss, "Zollikoner Seminare," in *Erinnerung an Martin Heidegger* (Pfullingen: Neske, 1977), 31–45.

2. Martin Heidegger, *Zollikoner Seminare*, ed. Medard Boss (Frankfurt: Klostermann, 1987); *The Zollikon Seminars: Protocols, Conversations, Letters*, ed. M. Boss, trans. F. Mayr and R. Askay (Evanston: Northwestern University Press, 2001). The volume contains Heidegger's corrected protocols of the seminars at Zollikon between 1959 and 1969, stenographs of personal interviews between Heidegger and Boss (1961–72), and letters between them from 1947 to 1971. The question of the other is not a theme treated explicitly by Heidegger in the seminars or in the interviews with Boss; it appears only sporadically, for example in the interview in Taormina in April–May 1963 (ZS, 160). It nevertheless seems to me that this question is one of the keys to reading these texts, which are all presented as dialogues. We can wonder what a "famous" philosopher went seeking in Zollikon and what this Sisyphean work (Boss's description, ZS, xvii) would bring him, a work that would consist in ridding the audience members' minds of those psychological and psychopathological theories impeding them from being open to the properly human dimension of their medical practice. We could also obviously include in the account the growing dogmatism of an old man whose political debacles had led him from great intellectual solitude to proffering his views to young minds unaccustomed to philosophical matters. But we could also take the project

seriously, a project that involves leaving the philosophical ivory tower and engaging in dialogue with practitioners in the hope that they will be more open than theoreticians to the "revolution in the mode of thinking required by the task, comparable to but infinitely more difficult than the Galillean discovery of the region of nature, of making the properly human continent appear" (ZS, 210–11). This is the side I take here, while attempting what Heidegger called a "positive critique," which consists not in denigrating but rather in showing what is worthy of being questioned (*das Fragwürdige*) (ZS, 76–77). Yet what seems to me to be worthy of questioning is precisely the situation of what issues from the seminars, this common "becoming aware" (*gemeinsame Besinnung*) that constitutes the performative aspect of the dialogue. Because this situation is that of a being-together (of a *synousia,* without which there is no thinking), we would have to speak of the question of *others* and recognize at the outset that a simplification of reflexive thought translates a plurality into a duality; we would have to say that "the problem of *the* other is a particular case of the problem of others" (VI, 81) and that this is all the more true for a thought that, instead of considering the originary relation with the other as a face-to-face without intermediary, describes the relation with others by the preposition *mit* and initially sees others as most often not distinct in themselves, and among whom one is also a self (BT, section 26).

3. The beginning of Boss's "Preface" to the *Zollikon Seminars* reproduces parts of the text from 1977.

4. Boss, *Erinnerung an Martin Heidegger*, 31–32.

5. We must here underline that despite the weak case that Heidegger seems to make of the philosophical virtues of the Latin language, it is in a fable of Hygeia that he discovers, by the intermediary of Goethe and Herder, a preontological testament in favor of the ontologico-existential interpretation of Dasein as care (SZ, section 42). Yet what this fable makes clearly appear is that the double sense of the term *cura*, which means both care and concern, corresponds to "a basic constitution in its essentially twofold structure of thrown project" (SZ, 185).

6. Medard Boss, *Grundriss der Medizin: Ansätze zu einer phänomenologischen Physiologie, Psychologie, Pathologie, Therapie und zu einer daseinsgemässen Präventiv-Medizin in der modernen Industrie-Gesellschaft* (Bern: Hans Huber, 1971) 523. This major work by Boss is not translated into French; the English translation is *Existential Foundations of Medicine and Psychology*, tr. Stephen Conway and Anne Cleaves, with an introduction by Paul J. Stern (New York: Jason Aronson, 1979), 273. Another major work by Boss, *Einführung in die psychosomatische Medizin* (Bern: Hans Huber, 1954), has not been translated into English, but is translated into French as *Introduction à la médicine psychosomatique* (Paris: PUF, 1959).

7. ZS, 223. In the Preface to the *Zollikon Seminars*, Boss states that during the eight years he dedicated to elaborating his *Grundriss*, Heidegger gave the same kind of careful attention (*Sorgfalt*) to the revision and editing

that he had given to the seminar protocols: "He corrected them very carefully, made some minor additions here and there, and occasionally added major additions in German handwriting." Several pages of protocols and book manuscript abundantly corrected by Heidegger are reproduced in the book at 3, 188–94, 212, and 222–25. Similar hand-corrected manuscript pages appear in the German edition of the *Grundriss*, but not in the English translation.

8. The performative dimension of Heidegger's thought is already perceptible in his first writings. It is inseparable from the project of a "hermeneutic of facticity" (which is the title of a 1923 course published in GA 63 [1988] and translated as Heidegger, *Ontology: The Hermeneutics of Facticity*, tr. J. van Buren [Bloomington: Indiana University Press, 1999])—that is, of an understanding of existence that remains inherent to the accomplishment (*Vollzug*) of existence, and it is this nonobjectivizable relation of accomplishment and time (*kairos* rather than *chronos*) that Heidegger, taking a term from Dilthey and Yorck von Wartenburg, will call *Geschichtlichkeit*, historiality. This is the reason that in *Being and Time* the thematization of the question of being does not have the sense of a reflexive objectification, but only of an expression, an *Ausdrücklichmachen*. Phenomenology, in becoming hermeneutics, breaks with the reflexivity of the Husserlian *Auslegung* and with the status of the "disinterested onlooker" that Husserlian phenomenology reserves for the philosopher.

9. To say that this method is Greek is to say that it is philosophical and that it is ordered by what Husserl called in the *Logical Investigations* "the principle of presuppositionlessness." The Cartesian method, on the other hand, is mathematical: instead of letting what shows itself be purely present, it is instead measured by mathematical evidence (ZS, 110). When Husserl, for example in *The Idea of Phenomenology*, insists on "the totally new dimension of philosophy" in relation to all natural knowledge, including "the most rigorous mathematics" (IP, 21), he is in some way only restoring the very famous Platonic opposition between mathematics, which can rise above hypotheses, and philosophy (the dialectic) as the science of the *anhypotheton*. We must note, however, that in the *Zollikon Seminars*, what is not directly apparent is that for Heidegger, the essential opposition is not so much between Plato and Descartes as it is between the Greeks and the Romans. Boss is therefore led to view Freud (a theoretician more than a practitioner) as "a late descendent of the Roman spirit" (!) because for him "phenomena were only interesting as signs of a play of forces" (Boss, *Einführung in die psychosomatische Medizin*, 6). The concept of force, without which the Freudian notion of the psyche is not thinkable, comes from the Roman incapacity "to represent a thing other than by an object born of a painful operation, an effort" and issues directly from their "anthropomorphism of nature" (ibid). This indeed represents the hypothesis of the Freudian "dynamic."

10. Heidegger, *Heraclitus*, GA 55: 398; English translation by Marnie Hanlon (London: Continuum, 2011).

11. See "The Turning," in Heidegger, *The Question Concerning Technology and Other Essays*, tr. W. Lovitt (New York: Harper and Row, 1977), 42; see also "The Question Concerning Technology," in ibid., 38: "To save is to lead back in essence in order to make it appear for the first time in the manner appropriate to it"; and "Building, Dwelling, Thinking," in *Basic Writings of Heidegger*, ed. D. F. Krell (New York: Harper, 1977), 310: "to save is not only to tear away from danger, it is properly to liberate a thing, let it return to its proper being" (etwas in sein eigenes Wesen frei lassen). It is only this ancient sense of the word *retten* that must be read in the famous phrase of the *Spiegel* interview in 1966, "Only a God Can Save Us"—that is, liberate our essence and make it appear. That this has very little in common with any theology could be shown by an attentive reading of an essay by Hölderlin called "On Religion" (written in Winter 1796–97). Hölderlin does not say anything there that the Heraclitus fragment analyzed by Heidegger in the "Letter on Humanism" does not already say: *ethos anthropos daimon*, which Heidegger translates as "the human being dwells [inhabits], insofar as he is a human being, in the nearness of the god [the inhabitual]" (See Heidegger, *Pathmarks*, ed. W. McNeill [Cambridge: Cambridge University Press, 1998], 269 [interpolations in the French.—Tr.]). For Hölderlin, the human is human only if he unfolds a divine sphere that is also the sphere of spirit. But because spirit happens only by the "repetition" of effective life, it is not determined, no more than is God who is present in the finite sphere of a concrete life, as an already subsistent beyond, but rather as the "production" of the infinite from the finite.

12. Heidegger, *What Is Called Thinking?*, tr. J. G. Gray (New York: Harper Perennial, 1976), 15.

13. Heidegger states at Cerisy in 1955 that "there is no Heideggerian philosophy." There would thus not be, in the strict sense, "Heideggerians": no school or disciples, even less a "sect." *Not* to be the founder of any school or of any religion is what is proper to Socrates, who is perhaps the purest thinker of the West for this unique reason. Hegel, in his youthful writings from Berne, insisted on this point by opposing him to Christ: "Socrates, on the other hand, had all sorts of disciples—or rather, he had none at all. He was merely a teacher and master, just as every individual who distinguishes himself by means of exemplary integrity and superior reason is a teacher for all. . . . The number of his closer friends remains unspecified. The thirteenth, the fourteenth, etc., was as welcome as the preceding, provided only he was their equal in intellect and in heart. They were his friends, even his disciples—but in such a fashion that each remained what he was, without Socrates dwelling in each as the root from which they as branches obtained their vital fluids. . . . So although there were Socratics, there was never a Socratic guild such as the Masons, recognizable by their hammer and trowel; each of his pupils was a master in his own right, with many founding their own schools. A number of them became great generals, statesmen, and heroes of all sorts—but not heroes of one and the same stamp,

nor heroes in martyrdom and suffering; rather, each prospered in his own province of action and life. . . . . Socrates began with each one's handicraft and led him from hand to spirit"; G. W. F. Hegel, *Three Essays, 1793–1795: The Tübingen Essay, Berne Fragments, the Life of Jesus*, ed. and tr. P. Fuss and J. Dobbins (South Bend: Notre Dame University Press, 1984), 62–63.

14. Boss, *Einführung in die psychosomatische Medizin*, 79.

15. The phenomenological concept of motivations opposed to the scientific concept of causality is already invoked by Husserl in the first *Logical Investigation* (sections 2 and 3), as he recalls himself in *Ideas I* (section 47). In *Ideas II*, it serves to describe, in contrast to the natural attitude, the personalist attitude insofar as it is that of a "spiritual ego."

16. Heidegger, "On the Essence and Concept of *Physis*, in Aristotle's *Physics* B, 1 (1939)," in *Pathmarks*, 197.

17. Is not love the highest form of the relation to the other? This is the sense of Binswanger's objection that love cannot be understood on the basis of care. Heidegger vigorously claims the contrary in the *Seminars* (ZS, 227). In the "Letter on Humanism," he understands love as the taking in charge, the "adoption" (*Annahme*) of a thing or person, and as the power (in the original sense of *mögen*) of giving being (*das Wesen schenken*) and of letting something be unfolded ("*wesen*") in its provenance—that is, as *letting-be*. Love is thus nothing other than liberating care *par excellence*.

18. Such an alternative has meaning only if the other has the face of infinity and announces itself in a face-to-face without communion and without concern and in an irreducible dissymmetry. But is there an immediate experience of the infinite? And are not the finite and infinite always announced in a structural "coincidence"?

19. Medard Boss visited India several times and spoke very generally to Heidegger about "Indian thought." Heidegger seemed very interested in it, judging by what he wrote to Boss in November 1959: "The talk about India showed me at the same time that my attempts do not remain totally isolated." And a while later, in March 1960, he goes so far as to ask Boss to communicate to him, if he finds them, the Indian terms that designate the ontological difference, Being and being, non-occultation and forgetting (ZS, 254).

20. See "Gelassenheit," in Heidegger, *Discourse on Thinking*, tr. J. Anderson and E. H. Freund (New York: Harper and Row, 1966), 55–56. Of "in-dwelling," Heidegger says that it could be "the authentic essence of the spontaneity of thought." Is there not thought only where we persevere in the comportment of releasement (*Verhaltenheit der Gelassenhiet*) and where awaiting (*Erwartung*) is transformed into taking in guard and in giving care (*Warten*)?

21. Heidegger, "What Is Metaphysics?" (1929), in *Pathmarks*, 95.

22. Heidegger, *The Essence of Human Freedom: An Introduction to Philosophy*, tr. T. Sadler (London: Continuum, 2002), 93–95 [translation modified in accordance with Dastur's quotation in French].

8. Conscience: The Most Intimate Alterity (Ricoeur, Heidegger, Levinas)

1. Emmanuel Levinas, *Totality and Infinity: An Essay on Exteriority*, tr. A. Lingis (Pittsburgh: Duquesne University Press, 1969), 304.

2. LH, 271.

3. OA, 23.

4. Ibid., 318.

5. Ibid., 356.

6. Ibid.

7. Paul Ricoeur, "Existence and Hermeneutics," tr. K. McLaughlin, in *The Conflict of Interpretations*, ed. D. Ihde (Evanston: Northwestern University Press, 1974), 23–24.

8. Cf. Ernst Cassirer and Martin Heidegger, "Debate at Davos," in KM, 175: "For ontology is an index of finitude. God does not have it. And the human has *exhibitio* as the strongest proof of its finitude. For ontology requires only a finite creature."

9. "Davos Debate," in KM, 175.

10. OA, 352.

11. BT, 12.

12. KM, 129ff.

13. Ibid., 130.

14. Ibid., 156.

15. BT, 180.

16. Ibid.

17. OA, 337.

18. OA, 339.

19. KM, 156: "There is and must be something like Being only where finitude has come to exist." (Dergleichen wie Sein gibt es nur und muss nur geben, wo Endlichkeit existent geworden ist.)

20. BT, 39–40.

21. PCT, 317: "Wenn solche zugespitzten Formeln überhaupt etwas besagen, müsste die angemessene und das Dasein in seinem Sein bettreffende Aussage lauten: sum moribundus, un zwar nicht moribundus als Schwerkranker oder Verwundeter, sondern sofern ich bin, bin ich moribundus—das moribundus gibt dem sum allererst seinem Sinn."

22. Plato, *Phaedo* 81a, in *Five Dialogues*, tr. G. M. A. Grube (Indianapolis: Hackett, 2002), 119.

23. OA, 311–12n15 and 313n16.

24. BT, 78.

25. Ibid., 127.

26. See the interview with Paul Ricoeur in "A quoi pensent les philosophes?," in *Autrement* 102 (November 1988): 175.

27. See Jan Patočka, "Heidegger, penseur de l'humanité" (1974), *Epokhē* 2 (1991): 389.

28. Immanuel Kant, *Critique of Practical Reason*, section 7, tr. L. W. Beck (New York: Macmillan, 1956), 31.

29. OA, 22.

30. Ibid., 318.

31. Ibid., 342.

32. Ibid., 318.

33. Ibid., 342.

34. Ibid., 348.

35. Kant, *Critique of Practical Reason*, 93.

36. BT, 254.

37. Ibid.

38. "Davos Debate," in KM, 175.

39. BT, 251.

40. Ibid.

41. Maurice Merleau-Ponty, *The Prose of the World*, ed. C. Lefort, tr. J. O'Neill (Evanston: Northwestern University Press, 1973), 29–30.

42. OA, 351.

43. Hegel, "The Moral Vision of the World," in *Phenomenology of Spirit*, tr. A. V. Miller (Oxford: Oxford University Press, 1977), 365–73; see also Hegel, *Philosophy of Right*, section 135, tr. T. M. Knox (New York: Clarendon, 1952), 89–90.

44. LH, 239.

45. OA, 356.

46. See Chapter 7, on *Time and the Other*.

47. OA, 354–55.

48. Levinas, *Totality and Infinity*, 34.

49. Levinas, *Otherwise Than Being: or, Beyond Essence*, tr. A. Lingis (Dordrecht and Boston, Mass.: Kluwer, 1978), 141.

50. OA, 355.

9. Temporality and Existence (Merleau-Ponty between Husserl and Heidegger)

1. PhP, 497–98.

2. Ibid., 500.

3. Ibid., 477.

4. Ibid., 423.

5. Ibid., 476. The exergue reads, "Le temps est le sens de la vie (sens: comme on dit le sens d'un cours d'eau, le sens d'une phrase, le sens d'une étoffe, le sens de l'odorat)—Claudel, *Art Poétique*"; "Der Sinn des Daseins ist die Zeitlichkeit," Martin Heidegger, *Sein und Zeit*, 331; see also PhP, 487–88.

6. PhP, 502; my emphasis.

7. Ibid., 474: "The primary truth is indeed 'I think,' but only provided that we understand thereby as 'I am with myself, I am mine [*je suis à moi*]' while being in the world."

8. Ibid., 503.

9. The understanding requires by definition the relation to time in order to furnish knowledge, since the intermediary representations or schemas allowing the application of the categories to phenomena are defined by Kant as a priori determinations of time; see in this regard Martin Heidegger, *Phenomenological Interpretation of the Critique of Pure Reason*, tr. P. Emad and K. Maly (Bloomington: Indiana University Press, 1997), 221ff. Merleau-Ponty himself makes an allusion (PhP, 498) to the Kantian schematism "this art hidden in the depths of the human soul" by identifying it with Husserlian operant intentionality that is anterior to the merely objectivating intentionality of acts.

10. PhP, 477.

11. John Sallis, "Time, Subjectivity, and the Phenomenology of Perception," in *Modern Schoolman* 48 (November 1970).

12. PhP, 486. Merleau-Ponty remarks that this expression "is evidently not a solution, but an index to designate a problem," thus taking up Heidegger's remark concerning intentionality in his short preface to the *Lectures on Internal Time-Consciousness*, which he edited in 1928. See also PhP, 496: "A passive synthesis is a contradiction in terms if the synthesis is a process of composition, and if the passivity consists in being the recipient of multiplicity instead of its composer. What we meant by passive synthesis was that we make our way into multiplicity, but that we do not synthesize it. Now temporalization satisfies by its very nature these two conditions: it is indeed clear that I am not the creator of time any more than I make my heart beat. . . . Nevertheless this ceaseless welling up of time is not a simple fact to which I am passively subjected, for I can find a remedy against it in itself. . . . It tears me away from what I was going to be, but at the same time gives me the means to take hold of myself at a distance and to realize myself as ego."

13. See Heraclitus, Fragment 91. We would also have to cite Fragment 49a: "We step and do not step into the same rivers, we are and we are not," which expresses the "dialectic" of change and permanence, of discontinuity and continuity inherent in the experience of temporality.

14. PhP, 478.

15. Ibid., 477.

16. Ibid., 479–80.

17. Ibid., 481.

18. BT, section 65: 302.

19. PhP, 482.

20. Sallis, "Time, Subjectivity, and the Phenomenology of Perception," 350.

21. Gérard Granel, *Le sens du temps et de la perception chez Husserl* (Paris: Gallimard, 1968), 45. Here he speaks of "a temporality that *remains in* consciousness (*im-manet*) and consciousness that *remains in* temporality (*im-manet*)" in the nonreal and nonpsychological sense because this temporality instead expresses the result of short-circuiting objectivity.

22. VI, 94.

23. PhP, 482–83.

24. As Sallis shows well in "Time, Subjectivity, and the Phenomenology of Perception."

25. PhP, 486; see also Edmund Husserl, *Lectures on Internal Time Consciousness*, section 39, 84–88.

26. Jacques Derrida uses this term in *Speech and Phenomena*, tr. D. Allison (Evanston: Northwestern University Press, 1973), 35.

27. ITC, 88.

28. PhP, 495.

29. ITC, 85. "Longitudinal" intentionality is that intentionality that Husserl also calls "operant" in order to distinguish it from "mundane" intentionality, and that is constitutive of the subject itself. [Brough prefers to translate it as "horizontal" intentionality—Tr.]

30. See Heidegger, "On the Essence of Ground," in *Pathmarks*, ed. W. McNeill (Cambridge: Cambridge University Press, 1998), 108–9.

31. See Rudolph Boehm, "L'ambiguité des concepts husserliens de transcendance et d'immanence," *Revue Philosophique* 4 (1954).

32. Heidegger, *The Basic Problems of Phenomenology*, tr. A. Hofstadter (Bloomington: Indiana University Press, 1988), 63ff.

33. See BT, 33.

34. ITC, 4–5.

35. Ideas I, section 81, 216.

36. CM, 38.

37. See Françoise Dastur, "Monde, chair, vision," in *Chair et langage: Essais sur Merleau-Ponty* (La Versanne: Encre Marin, 2000), 69.

38. PhP, 492.

39. Derrida, *Voice and Phenomenon*, tr. L. Lawlor (Evanston: Northwestern University Press, 2010), 40.

40. Henri Bergson, "Life and Consciousness," in *Mind-Energy*, tr. H. W. Carr (New York: H. Holt, 1920), 7–8: "consciousness means, before everything else, memory. . . . A consciousness unable to conserve its past, forgetting itself unceasingly, would be a consciousness perishing and having to be reborn at each moment: and what is this but unconsciousness? When Leibniz said of matter that it is 'a momentary mind,' did he not declare it, whether he would or no, insensible? All consciousness, then, is memory,—conservation and accumulation of the past in the present."

41. PhP, 493. Merleau-Ponty borrows this grapheme from Henry Corbin, the first French translator of the first part of *Being and Time*, in order to underline the "effective gesture" of transcendence that Heideggerian *Existenz* implies.

42. VI, 250.

43. PhP, 493.

44. BT, 40.

45. Ibid., 12.

46. PhP, 483. [When Merleau-Ponty writes "en personne" in this context, he is translating Husserl's adverb *leibhaftig*; the English translator renders this as "unalloyed," which altogether misses the semantic texture of *Leib*, life, to which this belongs.]

47. Ibid., 487. [Note: the German word in question is *Übergangssynthesis*.]

48. Ibid., 491.

49. Ibid., 488.

50. Ibid., 489; see also ITC, 79.

51. VI, 104.

52. PhP, 491.

53. Ibid., 498 [translation modified—Tr.].

54. See BT, section 65.

55. "Seminar at Zähringen," in Heidegger, *Four Seminars*, tr. A. Mitchell and F. Raffoul (Bloomington: Indiana University Press, 2003), 80.

10. Phenomenology of the Event: Expectation and Surprise (Husserl and Heidegger)

1. See in this regard the remarkable article by Claude Romano, "Le possible et l'évènement," *Philosophie* 40 (December 1993) and 41 (March 1994), from which I draw much inspiration here.

2. PCT, 72.

3. Johann Wolfgang von Goethe, *The Theory of Colors*, ed. R. Matthaei and H. Aach (New York: Van Nostrand, 1971), 76: "Seek nothing beyond the phenomena; they are already the theory."

4. BT, 31.

5. IP, 68.

6. VI, 118.

7. Ibid., 232.

8. Immanuel Kant, *Critique of Pure Reason*, B 181, tr. N. K. Smith (New York: St. Martin's, 1929), 183.

9. Martin Heidegger, *Four Seminars*, tr. A. Mitchell and F. Raffoul (Bloomington: Indiana University Press, 2003), 80.

10. VI, 237; see also 225–27 and 281.

11. Recall that "accident" comes from the Latin *accido* (*ad-cado*), which means literally "fall on."

12. TO, 32. Diachronie is here determined as the "phenomenon of noncoincidence."

13. Crisis, section 9b: 31–32.

14. CM, 48.

15. See Heraclitus, fragment 18: "He who does not expect the unexpected will not discover it; for it is difficult to discover and unapproachable."

16. See the theme in Merleau-Ponty of "perceptual faith" in, e.g., VI, 3ff.

17. See Wolfgang Blankenburg, *La perte de l'evidence naturelle: Une contribution a la psychopathologie des schizophrenies pauci-symptomatiques* (Paris: PUF, 1991).

18. See Romano, "Le possible et l'évènement," *Philosophie* 41 (March 1994): 85.

19. VI, 221.

20. Henri Maldiney, *Penser l'homme et la folie* (Grenoble: J. Millon, 1994), 114.

21. ID, 30.

22. Ibid., 36–37.

23. See François Fédier, *Regarder voir* (Paris: Les Belles Lettres Archimbaud, 1995), 117: "If we look carefully, *Ereignis* names not the event but that which makes there be an event: the seeming that at first takes place (the seeming such and such a way, which it certainly comes from [*évient*], but firstly) so that an event may appear" (two pages earlier he makes reference to a text by Péguy, where we find the "astonishing hapax of the verb *évenir*").

11. Phenomenology and History (Dilthey, Husserl, Heidegger)

1. See Karl Marx, *The German Ideology*, as well as "The Holy Family," wherein we find the following passage: "History does nothing, it has no 'colossal riches,' it 'fights no battles'! Rather, it is man, real and living man who does all this, who possesses and fights: it is certainly not the case that 'history' is a separate person that uses men as a means to work and accomplish its own ends; on the contrary, history is nothing but the activity of man following his ends"; Marx, "The Holy Family," in *The Writings of the Young Marx*, tr. L. D. Easton and K. H. Guddat (Indianapolis: Hackett, 1997), 385.

2. See Alexandre Kojève, *Introduction to the Reading of Hegel*, tr. R. Queneau (Ithaca: Cornell University Press, 1980).

3. See Leonhard von Renthe-Fink, *Geschichtlichkeit: Zur terminologishche und begrifflicher Ursprung bei Hegel, Haym, Dilthey, und Yorck* (Göttingen: Vandenhoeck and Ruprecht, 1964).

4. Yorck von Wartenburg, *Bewusstseinstellung und Geschichte* (Tübingen: Niemeyer, 1956), 45.

5. See letter 127 from Yorck to Dilthey, in Wilhelm Dilthey and (Graf) Paul Yorck von Wartenburg, *Briefwechsel zwischen W. Dilthey und dem Grafen Paul Yorck von Wartenburg 1877–1897* (Halle: Niemeyer, 1923), 203: "Sein ist ein Derivat des Lebens, eine partikulare Lebens manifestation" (Being is a derivative of life, a particular manifestation of life). Martin Heidegger cites passages from the same letter in section 77 of *Being and Time* (tr. J. Stambaugh [Albany: SUNY Press, 1996]), in a section entirely dedicated to Dilthey and Yorck.

6. See Dilthey, *Gesammelte Schriften* (Stuttgart: Teubner, 1972), VII: 256: "Leben ist seinem Stoff nach eins mit der Geschichte" (Life is in its substance one with History).

7. See Gadamer, TM, 201, and Jean Hyppolite, "Vie et conscience de la vie dans la philosophie hégélienne d'Iéna," *Revue de Métaphysique et de Morale* (1938).

8. This is what Heidegger explains in his course from Summer Semester 1930–31 dedicated to Hegel; see Heidegger, *Hegel's Phenomenology of Spirit*, tr. P. Emad and K. Maly (Bloomington: Indiana University Press, 1988), 143 (GA 32:207): "Leben—das meint das sich aus sich erzeugende und in seiner Bewegung sich in sich erhaltende Sein" (Life means the *being* which produces *itself from out of itself*, and maintains itself in its movement).

9. See Gadamer, TM, 207.

10. Speaking of Husserlian teleology, Fink writes in "Welt und Geschichte" (World and History), a text originally published in 1959, that "this schema of the philosophy of history is not new. It is a 'phenomenology of the spirit' by the analytic means of an exegesis of intentional consciousness"; ND, 171.

11. [Appendix XXVI does not appear in the English translation of the *Crisis*—Tr.]

12. See in this regard Ante Pazanin, *Wissenschaft und Geschichte in der Phänomenologie E. Husserls* (The Hague: Nijhoff, 1972), 163ff.

13. This is, for example, Walter Biemel's case when, in "Les phases décisives dans le developpement de la philosophie de Husserl" (in *Husserl: Cahiers de Royaumont*, ed. W. Biemel [Paris: Minuit, 1959]), 58), he states that "Husserl's attempts to grasp history thematically can be considered failures."

14. See CM, sections 37 and 38: 75–80.

15. In the letter to Misch of 16 November 1930, Husserl gives a retrospective interpretation of his philosophical development, which, beginning with logical and ontological problems, culminates in the foundation of the theory of transcendental subjectivity and intersubjectivity. He writes, "For with the 'phenomenological reduction,' I had the conviction of having attained a finally concrete and actual subjectivity in the fullness of its being and its life, and of finding in it a universally (and not merely theoretically) effective life: absolute subjectivity in its historicity—subjectivity, science, world, culture, ethico-religious aspiration, etc.—all of it—in a new noema and a new meaning. The book that I've been preparing for ten years, which is only now truly in gestation, will bring, I hope, the most complete clarity as an entirely systematic edifice." This letter is cited by Alwin Diemer in his *Husserl* (Meisenheim am Glam: Anton Hain, 1956), 393–94.

16. See once again Fink, "Welt und Geschichte," in ND, 170: "the absolute subject, as long as it has not become certain of itself, takes itself as 'finite,' takes itself for a limited creature among other natural creatures. But when it becomes aware of its creative effectuation in the reduction, it tosses off this finitude like worn-out clothing."

17. EJ, section 64: 261: "The timelessness of objectivities of the understanding, their being 'everywhere and nowhere,' proves therefore to be a privileged form of temporality."

18. See the manuscripts cited by René Toulemont, in *L'essence de la société selon Husserl* (Paris: PUF, 1962), 270; see in particular Manuscript A V 22 (date not specified).

19. Ibid., Manuscript K III 6, dating from the end of August 1936.

20. See on this point Antonio Aguirre, *Genetische Phänomenologie und Reduktion* (The Hague: Nijhoff, 1970), 164.

21. Dilthey, *Gesammelte Schriften*, III: 241; VIII: 80.

22. This is the argument of Ernst Tugendhat, in *Der Wahrheitsbegriff bei Husserl und Heidegger* (Berlin: de Gruyter, 1967), 254.

23. BT, 353: "Authentic being-towards-death, that is, the finitude of temporality, is the concealed ground of the historicity of Da-sein."

24. See Husserl's notes on Heidegger's *Being and Time* and *Kant and the Problem of Metaphysics* in Edmund Husserl, *Psychological and Transcendental Phenomenology and the Confrontation with Heidegger (1927–1931)*, tr. T. Sheehan and R. Palmer (Dordrecht: Nijhoff, 1997), 263ff.

25. See Husserl, "The Origin of Geometry," in Crisis, esp. 370–72.

26. See Jacques Derrida, *Introduction to Husserl's "Origin of Geometry,"* tr. J. P. Leavy (Lincoln: University of Nebraska Press, 1974), 63–65.

27. See the "Vienna Conference," in Crisis, 279: "Scientific culture under the guidance of ideas of infinity means, then, a revolutionization of the whole culture, a revolutionization of the whole manner in which mankind creates culture. It also means a revolutionization of its historicity, which is now the history of the cutting-off of finite mankind's development as it becomes mankind with infinite tasks."

28. BT, 127: "The expression 'thrownness' is meant to suggest the facticity of its being delivered over" (Der Ausdruck Gerworfenheit soll die Faktizität der Überantwortung andeuten).

29. This expression is James Joyce's, cited by Derrida in his *Introduction to Husserl's "Origin of Geometry,"* 103.

30. BT, 351. [Stambaugh says "hand down" for "transmit" and "the retrieval" for "repetition," based on a very literal rendering of the German *Wiederholung*.]

31. Ibid., 349.

32. Ibid., 352.

33. Ibid.: "Repetition is explicit tradition" (Die Widerholung ist die ausdrückliche Überlieferung). [Note: Stambaugh says, "Retrieval is explicit handing down"—Tr.]

34. Ibid., 352–53: "Rather, repetition *responds* to the possibility of existence that has been there" (Die Widerholung *erwidert* vielmehr die Möglichkeit der dagewesenen Existenz).

35. Ibid., 358: "Authentic historicity includes history as the 'recurrence' of the possible" (Die eigentliche Geschichtlichkeit versteht die Geschichte als die "Widerkehr" des Möglichen).

36. Ibid., 242.

37. See Heidegger, "What Is Metaphysics?," in *Pathmarks*, ed. W. McNeill (Cambridge: Cambridge University Press, 1998), 95. It must be strongly emphasized that it is beginning with this text in 1929, and in reference to the Hegelian thesis of the idea of being and nothingness, that Heidegger comes to the fundamental idea of the finiteness of being itself and not only of Dasein.

38. BT, 196: "However, only as long as Da-sein is, as long as there is the ontic possibility of an understanding of being, 'is there' [*gibt es*] being" (Allerdings nur solange Dasein ist, das heisst die ontische Möglichkeit von Seinsverständnis, "gibt es" Sein).

39. LH, 249 and 271. As Heidegger pertinently underlines, a "turning" of thought can be made perceptible and comprehensible only if one tries first to express it in language.

40. Ibid., 273.

41. Ibid., 252. Compare with human being as the "placeholder" or "lieutenant" of nothing in "What Is Metaphysics?," in Heidegger, *Pathmarks*, 93.

42. ID, 36.

43. In Hegel, the epoch is a time of suspension (this is the sense of the Greek verb *epekein*) in which spirit is suspended as totality and takes on a particular face, that of the spirit of a people. Likewise for Heidegger there are epochs of being in which being is suspended or is forgotten, each time in a different manner.

44. Heidegger, "Nihilism as Determined by the History of Being," in *Nietzsche*, vol. 4, *Nihilism*, tr. D. F. Krell and F. A. Capuzzi (New York: Harper and Row, 1987), 238 [Dastur's interpolation in German.—Tr.].

45. Heidegger, "Recollection in Metaphysics," in *The End of Philosophy*, tr. J. Stambaugh (San Francisco: Harper and Row, 1973), 82.

46. Heidegger, "Nihilism as Determined by the History of Being," 242–43. [Dastur is glossing these essentially important paragraphs in this section of her essay. Note that "default," here and in what follows, translates "*demeurer-manquant*"—literally, to remain lacking.—Tr.].

47. Heidegger, "Nihilism as Determined by the History of Being," 244n.

48. Heidegger, *Die Geschichte des Seins* (38/40), GA 69: 93.

49. CTP, 207.

50. Heidegger, *Die Geschichte des Seins* (38/40), GA 69: 136.

51. EJ, section 64: 261.

52. BT, 208: "'There is' truth only insofar as and only so long as Dasein is."

53. Ibid., 208–9.

54. Ibid., 204–5.

55. Ibid., 211.

56. Ibid., 243.

12. History and Hermeneutics (Ricoeur and Gadamer)

1. David Carr, *Phenomenology and the Problem of History: A Study of Husserl's Transcendental Phenomenology* (Evanston: Northwestern University Press, 1974).

2. Carr, "Epistémologie et ontologie du récit," in *Paul Ricoeur: Les Métamorphoses de la raison herméneutique*, ed. J. Greisch and R. Kearney (Paris: Cerf, 1991), 205.

3. Thus Carr notes ("Epistémologie," 209) that, given that "for man, self-understanding is equal to self-constitution," "the notion of hermeneutics is transformed in the hands of Heidegger from an epistemological concept into an ontological concept," because "enrooted in human being, the interpretation of texts and other expressions in the human sciences is secondary and derived, a special application, so to speak, of human ontology."

4. TN III, 241.

5. TN I, 169.

6. Ibid., 186: "The poet works from a form of unification, while the historian works towards it. One produces, the other argues. And they argue because they know that they will be able to explain differently. They know this because, like the judge, they are in a situation of contestation and of trial, and because their plea is never finished."

7. Ibid., xi.

8. Carr, "Epistémologie," 206.

9. Ibid., 213.

10. TN III, 300f.

11. Ibid., 314f. Ricoeur evokes the discussion of historical continuity "interrupted at the moment that it shifted from epistemology to ontology."

12. TM, 251; cited by Ricoeur in TN III, 223.

13. TM, 250.

14. Ibid., 252–53.

15. Ibid., 253.

16. Wilhelm Dilthey, *Gesämmelte Schriften* (Stuttgart: Teubner, 1927), VII: 278; cited by Gadamer in TM, 196.

17. TM, 260.

18. Ibid., 341; my emphasis.

19. Idid., 321.

20. Ibid., 324: "I must allow tradition's claim to validity, not in the sense of simply acknowledging the past in its otherness, but in such a way that it has something to say to me."

21. Ibid.

22. TM, 263. This passage is also cited by Ricoeur in a note in TN III, 224.

23. TN III, 224; the passage refers to TM, 266.

24. TM, 266.

25. Ibid., 264.

26. Ibid.

27. Ibid., 267.

28. Ibid., 319.

29. Ibid.

30. Ibid.

31. Ibid., 321.
32. TN III, 217.
33. TM, 268–69.
34. TN III, 326n21.
35. TN III, 83.
36. MFL, 211. In support of this idea of an internal productivity of time, the model of which he finds in the Kantian theory of the transcendental imagination, Heidegger cites Heraclitus fragment 115, which defines the *psyche* as a *logos* growing from out of itself. [Sometimes this fragment is translated as "Soul has its own inner laws of growth"—Tr.]
37. From J. Droysen, *Historik*, section 8; cited by Gadamer in TM, 185.
38. TM, 185.
39. Ideas I, section 22: 88.
40. TN III, 217.
41. An expression that Heidegger takes up in SZ, 373. On this point, see the remarkable chapter that Gadamer devotes to Dilthey in TM, 192–213.
42. TN III, 219.
43. Michel Foucault, *Archaeology of Knowledge*, tr. A. M. Sheridan Smith (New York: Pantheon, 1972), 6; cited by Ricoeur in TN III, 217n29.
44. Foucault, *Archaeology*, 6; Ricoeur, TN III, 217n29.
45. TN III, 219
46. Ibid., 316; my emphasis.
47. Ibid., 219.
48. Ibid., 263.
49. Ibid., 223ff.
50. Ibid., 319–20.
51. Carr, "Epistémologie," 210.
52. Ibid., 211.

13. Phenomenology and the Question of Man (Patočka and Heidegger)

1. Jan Patočka, "Heidegger, penseur de l'humanité," text from 1976, translated from Czech into French by E. Abrams in *Epokhē* 2 (1991): 383–86, expressing the initial reaction of the Czech philosopher upon hearing the news of Heidegger's death. [This essay, like many works by Patočka, has currently not been translated into English; as such, I have had to rely on French and German translations of the original Czech for this chapter—Tr.]
2. Ibid., 384.
3. Ibid.
4. Ibid.," 386.
5. These seminars took place several times between 1959 and 1969 and were probably known to Patočka, who speaks abundantly of Medard Boss and his major work, *Grundriss der Medizin: Ansätze zu einer phänomenologischen Physiologie, Psychologie, Pathologie, Therapie und zu einer daseinsgemässen Präventiv-Medizin in der modernen Industrie-Gesellschaft* (Bern: Hans Huber,

1971), in a 1976 text, "Cartesianism and Phenomenology" dedicated to Karel Kosik; see *Jan Patočka: Philosophy and Selected Writings,* ed. and tr. E. Kohák (Chicago: University of Chicago Press, 1989), 285–326.

6. ZS, 123 (Seminar of 25 November 1965).

7. Ibid., 223; interview on 27 September 1968 with Boss.

8. "Heidegger is not an academic thinker. He is a thinker of the crisis in which we live—thinker of the twilight of Europe, thinker of the gathering of the time of catastrophe." These are the first phrases of a short text called "Heidegger" that Patočka published in Polish in 1974, tr. E. Adams, *Epokhē* 2 (1991): 387–91.

9. ZS, 212; interview of 7 July 1966.

10. Subtitle of Heidegger's course from Summer Semester 1923 (GA 63) on *Ontology—The Hermeneutics of Facticity*, tr. J. van Buren (Bloomington: Indiana University Press, 1999).

11. ZS, 109; seminar of 8 July 1965.

12. Martin Heidegger, *The Essence of Human Freedom: An Introduction to Philosophy*, Tr. T. Sadler (London: Continuum, 2002), 94–95.

13. ZS, 120, seminar of 23 November 1965.

14. Patočka, "Le subjectivisme de la phénoménologie husserlienne et la possibilité d'une phénoménologie 'asubjective,'" (1970), in *Qu'est-ce que la phénoménologie* (Grenoble: Millon, 1988), 214 [originally written in German as "Der Subjektivismus der Husserlschen und die Forderung einer asubjektiven Phänomenologie" and reprinted in Jan Patočka, *Ausgewählte Schriften IV: Die Bewegung der menschlichen Existenz; Phänomenologische Schriften II*, ed. K. Nellen, J. Nemec, and I. Srubar (Frankfurt: Verlag Kett-Cotta, 1991), 286–309.—Tr.].

15. Patočka, "Qu'est-ce que la phénoménologie," in *Qu'est-ce que la phénoménologie* (Grenoble: Millon, 1988), 265. [This text, originally written in German in 1976, is not translated into English, and is difficult to find in German; we therefore retain Dastur's references to the more readily available French translation.]

16. Ibid., 302.

17. See Hans-Georg Gadamer, "The Phenomenological Movement," in *Philosophical Hermeneutics*, ed. and tr. D. E. Linge (Berkeley: University of California Press, 1976), 134.

18. It is to the memory of Fink, who died in June 1975, that Heidegger dedicates volume 29/30 of the *Gesamtausgabe*, which contains the text from the Winter Semester 1929–30 course on the *Fundamental Concepts of Metaphysics*, and in particular the concept of world. Fink had attended this course and had frequently expressed his wish to see it published. In order to give an idea of Fink's singular position "between" Husserl and Heidegger, see the *Conversations with Husserl and Fink* (The Hague: Nijhoff, 1976) by Dorion Cairns, who had gone to study with Husserl in 1932.

19. See Patočka, "Erinnerung an Husserl," in *Festschrift für J. Patočka: Die Welt des Menschen; Die Welt der Philosophie*, ed. W. Biemel (Hague: Nijhoff,

1972), x; and "Interview zum 60: Geburtstag des Philosophen: Mit Jan Patočka über Philosophie und Philosophen' "; originally published in Czech in *Filosopficky casopis*, Jg. 15 (1967): 589.

20. See Ludwig Landgrebe, "Erinnerungen an meinem Freunde Jan Patočka: Ein Philosoph von Weltbedeutung," *Perspectiven der Philosophie* 3 (1977): 298.

21. Patočka, "Qu'est-ce que la phénoménologie," 265.

22. Heidegger, "The End of Philosophy and the Task of Thinking," in *Time and Being*, tr. J. Stambaugh (New York: Harper and Row, 1972), 61.

23. Patočka, *Heretical Essays in the Philosophy of History*, tr. J. Dodd and E. Kohák (Lasalle: Open Court, 1996), 28–29. [Hereafter, this work is designated as HE.]

24. Patočka, "Qu'est-ce que la phénoménologie," 279.

25. Patočka, "Cartesianism and Phenomenology," 320–21.

26. BT, 31.

27. Patočka, "Le subjectivisme," 243.

28. Ibid., 233.

29. Ibid., 46.

30. Ibid., 248.

31. Patočka, "Qu'est-ce que la phénoménologie," 283.

32. HE, 46.

33. BT, 40.

34. Ibid., 39.

35. HE, 47.

36. Patočka, "Qu'est-ce que la phénoménologie," 283.

37. LH, 271.

38. BT, 172.

39. Immanuel Kant, *Critique of Judgment*, section 82, tr. W. Pluhar (Indianapolis: Hackett, 1987), 312ff.

40. BT, 127.

41. Patočka, "Qu'est-ce que la phénoménologie," 284.

42. Patočka, "Heidegger," *Epokhē* 2 (1991):389–90.

43. Patočka, "Qu'est-ce que la phénoménologie," 285.

44. HE, 49.

45. Patočka, "Le subjectivisme," 247.

46. HE, 49.

47. Patočka, "Qu'est-ce que la phénoménologie," 287.

48. Ibid., 294.

49. BT, 129–30: "In attunement lies existentially a disclosive submission to world out of which things that matter to us can be encountered."

50. Patočka, "Qu'est-ce que la phénoménologie," 296.

51. HE, 51.

52. Patočka, "Le subjectivisme," 247.

53. HE, 51.

54. Patočka, "Heidegger," 388.

55. Patočka, *Le monde naturel et le mouvement de l'existence humaine*, ed. and tr. E. Abrams (Dordrecht: Kluwer, 1998), 99.

14. The Phenomenology of Finitude (Heidegger and Patočka)

1. This discovery followed the rhythm of publication of French translations of Patočka through the admirable work of Erika Abrams, the principal translator into French.

2. Patočka, *La crise du sens*, vol. 2, *Comte, Masaryk et l'action*, French translation of diverse writings by E. Abrams (Brussels: Ousia, 1986), 12. [Like most of Patočka's writings, the essays contained in this volume are largely unavailable in English—Tr.]

3. Ibid., 2: 20.

4. Ibid., 2: 18.

5. Ibid., 2: 31: "Thus: existentialism no, existence yes. Machovec's misunderstanding is to want to translate into the sphere of thought the *act* of Masaryk as an example of an existence that acts."

6. Ibid., 2: 29.

7. Ibid., 2: 22: "To say that Masaryk founded a state as a thinker is to say that the concern was not for the realization or guarantee of various interests, but rather, for a decision within which there is a chance for the human to gain access in some way to the authentic possibility of a responsible and conscientious life."

8. Ibid., 2: 44.

9. Ibid., 2: 26.

10. Ibid., 2: 12.

11. BT, 114–15. In this paragraph dedicated to coexistence with others, Heidegger opposes inauthentic concern, which consists in being substituted for the other and of taking the other into one's care, to authentic concern, which consists instead in helping the other assume responsibility for his own existence.

12. Patočka, *La crise du sens*, 2: 14.

13. Ibid., 2: 27.

14. Ibid., 2: 17.

15. Ibid.

16. BT, 211: "The contention that there are 'eternal truths,' as well as the confusion of the phenomenally based ideality of Dasein with an idealized absolute subject, belong to the remnants of Christian theology with the philosophical problematic that have not yet been radically eliminated." Here the Christianism in the form that Patočka will no doubt call "mythological" appears as this "Platonism for the people," of which Nietzsche spoke.

17. Patočka, *La crise du sens*, 2: 69.

18. Ibid., 2: 72: "Resoluteness is not the affair of the situation in general, but of such and such a situation."

19. In an article entitled, "Beiträge zu einer Phänomenologie des historischen Materialismus," published in 1928 in the first edition of *Philosophische Hefte*, entirely dedicated to an exegesis of *Being and Time*, Herbert Marcuse did not hesitate to elaborate a rapprochement between Heidegger and Marx.

20. The difference in the particle—*ent-* instead of *er-*—marks the passage from the state of openness (*Erschlossenheit*) to the "effective" taking in charge in resoluteness (*Entschlossenheit*) and access to "authenticity" (*Eigenlichkeit*)—that is, to the being-able-to-be most proper to Dasein that is understood from its birth and its death as finite existence.

21. BT, 275–76.

22. Ibid., 40. "The being with which this being is concerned in its being is always my own. Thus, Dasein is never to be understood ontologically as a case and instance of a genus of beings as objectively present."

23. Ibid., 311: "In resoluteness, the present is not only brought back from the dispersion in what is taken care of nearest at hand, but is held in the future and having-been. We call the *present* that is held in authentic temporality, and is thus *authentic*, the *Moment* [or instant]. This term must be understood in the active sense as an ecstasy. It means the resolute raptness of Dasein, which is yet *held* in resoluteness, in what is encountered as possibilities and circumstances to be taken care of in the situation. The phenomenon of the Moment can *in principle not* be clarified in terms of the *now*."

24. Patočka, *La crise du sens*, 2: 69.

25. Ibid., 2: 17.

26. Ibid., 2: 27: "The first pages of World Revolution are totally classic, it is only here that we see what in Masaryk the expression *sub specie aeterni* means, that it is not about a Platonism but rather about the irrevocability of what man does and what falls on him from above because he has called for it himself by claiming the possibility that he glimpses."

27. This short text by Patočka was published in French translation by E. Abrams in *Epokhē* 2 (1991): 383–86.

28. See Michel Haar, ed., *Martin Heidegger* (Paris: L'Herne, 1983), 94.

29. LH, 246–47.

30. Heidegger, *Logik, Die Frage nach der Wahrheit* (Frankfurt: Klostermann, 1976) (GA 21: 135); translation by T. Sheehan as *Logic—The Question of Truth* (Bloomington: Indiana University Press, 2010).

31. Martin Heidegger, "On the Essence of Truth," in *Pathmarks*, ed. W. McNeill (Cambridge: Cambridge University Press, 1998), 138.

32. BT, 20.

33. Recall that Dilthey was the only one to truly understand the meaning of the second volume when it appeared.

34. BT, 22.

35. Patočka, "Heidegger," tr. E. Adams, *Epokhē* 2 (1991): 387–91.

36. Ibid., 387.

37. See Ideas I, section 49: 139.

38. Patočka, "Heidegger," 388.

39. Ibid., 389.

40. Patočka, *Liberté et sacrifice: Ecrits politiques*, French tr. E. Abrams (Grenoble: Millon, 1990), 264. [This book comprises a series of articles on politics and political theory; the articles were published individually in a variety of journals and books, then collected together and translated by Erika Abrams in this French edition.—Tr.]

41. See Crisis, section 2, the title of which is "The 'Crisis' of Science as Loss of Its Meaning for Life [*Lebensbedeutsamkeit*]."

42. Patočka, *Liberté et sacrifice*, 269.

43. Heidegger, "The Question Concerning Technology," in *The Question Concerning Technology and Other Essays*, tr. W. Lovitt (New York: Harper and Row, 1977), 33.

44. Patočka, *Liberté et sacrifice*, 274.

45. Ibid., 271.

46. Ibid., 272.

47. Ibid., 274–75.

48. Ibid., 271. We also find the same idea in the tenth letter of Friedrich Schelling's "Letters on Dogmatism and Criticism," in *The Unconditional in Human Knowledge: Four Early Essays 1794–96*, ed. and tr. F. Marti (Lewisburg, Pa.: Bucknell University Press, 1980), and in Friedrich Hölderlin, "The Ground of Empedocles," in *The Death of Empedocles*, ed. and tr. D. F. Krell (Albany: SUNY Press, 2009).

49. Patočka, *Liberté et sacrifice*, 274.

50. Heidegger claimed as early as 1929 in "What Is Metaphysics?" that "being itself is essentially finite and manifests itself only in the transcendence of Dasein" (*Pathmarks*, 95). To renounce the infinity of being is therefore at the same time to reveal its undetachable co-belonging with the human. But if being needs the human and uses him, according to the formulae found in the later Heidegger, could we not then see Christianity (as Patočka underlines) as the religion constructed around the ideas of radical sacrifice and of the finitude of the divine, since its God must become human and undergo the ordeal of death? The young Heidegger saw the authentic experience of finite temporality in such "demythologized" Christianity (as Patočka calls it in *Liberté et sacrifice*, 272), which no longer rests on the myth of sacrifice understood as a human action that would obligate an infinite power with respect to humans—that is, in "phenomenological" Christianity, whose matrix it could be shown is already found in Hölderlin, where it is also restored to its existential truth and stripped of its theological vestments.

51. Heidegger, "The Question Concerning Technology," 28: "To save [*retten*] is: to fetch something home into essence, in order to bring the essence for the first time into its genuine appearing."

15. Worldliness and Mortality (Fink and Heidegger)

1. Martin Heidegger, *The Fundamental Concepts of Metaphysics: World, Finitude, Solitude*, tr. W. McNeill and N. Walker (Bloomington: Indiana University Press, 1995).

2. WE, 213–14.

3. Ibid., 19: "We name the distinction between world and intraworldly beings the cosmological difference."

4. See Eugen Fink, *Metaphysik und Tod* (Stuttgart: Kohlhammer, 1969).

5. GMD, 445: "The human as human is characterized and distinguished by the fact that he is the only being in the universe who is open to death and exists in work, play, love, and struggle for domination. Neither God nor the animal take part in these."

6. WE, 450.

7. MT, 208.

8. MT, 191.

9. SW, 231.

10. Ibid., 232.

11. Fink, "Vergegenwärtigung und Bild," in *Studien zur Phänomenologie* (The Hague: Nijhoff, 1954), 18.

12. SW, 234.

13. Fink, "Welt und Geschichte," in *Nähe und Distanz: Studien zur Phänomenologie* (Freiburg: Karl Alber, 1976), 176.

14. SW, 235.

15. Ibid., 235.

16. See Heidegger, "Postscript to 'What Is Metaphysics?,'" in *Pathmarks*, ed. W. McNeill (Cambridge: Cambridge University Press, 1998), 233: "As that which is altogether other than all beings, being is that which is not. But this nothing essentially prevails over Being" (Dies schlechthin Andere zu allem Seienden ist das Nicht-Seiende. Aber dieses Nichts west als das Sein).

17. AN, 30–31.

18. MFL, 210: "The World is the nothing that temporalizes itself primordially, that which simply arises in and with temporalization. We therefore call it the *nihil originarium*" (Die Welt ist das Nichts, das sich ursprünglich zeitigt, das in und mit der Zeitigung Entspringende schlechthin—wir nennen sie daher das *nihil originarium*).

19. ND, 176.

20. See Heidegger, "What Is Metaphysics?," 96.

21. Heidegger, *Parmenides*, tr. R. Rojcewicz (Bloomington: Indiana University Press, 1992).

22. See Heidegger, "The End of Philosophy and the Task of Thinking," in *On Time and Being*, tr. J. Stambaugh (New York: Harper and Row, 1972), 68. Here, Heidegger, taking up Fink's terms, defines *lēthē* "not as simple addition, not as shadow to light, but as the heart of *alētheia*."

23. Heidegger, "Time and Being," in ibid., 41.

24. See WE, 206: "the world must be thought and conceived as what accords" (Die Welt muss als das Gewähren gedacht und begriffen werden), and 207: "the world is what 'gives' everything, which means we can say that it is 'what there is' " (Welt ist dass, was alles "gibt," was alles schenkt, von dem wir dann sagen: "es gibt es.")

25. It should be stressed that the expression *Zeitraum*, which appears in 1962 in *On Time and Being,* already constitutes the object of a chapter of the work of the "turn," the *Contributions to Philosophy*, appropriately entitled "Der Zeit-Raum als der Ab-grund" (Space-time as Abyss).

26. ND, 176.

27. Ibid.

28. See WE, 153 and 171, where Fink declares, while speaking of "On the Essence of Ground": "For the problem of the world, this small work by Heidegger means the filling-in of a subjectivist conception of the world." But we must also immediately underline that he specifies that he is not thereby addressing a critique to Heidegger, because Heidegger's concern is only to bring a possibility to its end—that is, the one represented by the Kantian concept of the world.

29. MT, 191.

30. Heidegger, *What Is Called Thinking?*, tr. J. G. Gray (New York: Harper Perennial, 1968), 10.

31. MT, 192.

32. On this point, see Françoise Dastur, "La destruction heideggerienne de la logique," in *Études de philosophie ancienne et moderne*, ed. F. Dastur and C. Levy (Paris: L'Harmattan, 1999), 335–56.

33. It is with the citation from Heraclitus, fragment 50, which speaks of a *logos* "that does not belong to man" that Fink ends WE, 210.

34. MT, 193.

35. See chapter 25 of GMD, 420ff, entitled "Structure of Existential Anthropology."

36. Ibid., 442.

37. WE, 183.

38. Ibid., 189.

39. Ibid., 196.

40. Ibid., 195.

41. MT, 208.

42. WE, 195.

43. Ibid., 195.

44. Fragment 30. See the interpretation proposed by Fink in the seminar that he gave jointly with Heidegger during the winter 1966–67; Heidegger and Fink, *The Heraclitus Seminar* (Evanston: Northwestern University Press, 1993), 49ff.

45. WE, 196.

46. Ibid., 207.

47. SW, 241.

48. WE, 208.

49. GMD, 180–81. [Note that Dastur uses the term *esseulement*, which is the standard rendering of Heidegger's German term *Vereinzelung*, given in English as "individuation" (whereas the German emphasizes singularity as much as individuation, and the French evokes solitude). Elsewhere (including in the sentence following this one) Dastur uses the French word *individuation*.—Tr.]

50. Ibid., 185.

51. Ibid., 186 and 188.

52. Ibid., 193.

53. Ibid., 450.

54. Unlike German, which has but one word, *Endlichkeit*, for this purpose, the French language can distinguish finiteness [*finité*] from an assumed finitude.

55. WE, 209–10.

56. GMD, 333.

57. Nietzsche is invoked by Fink whenever he emphasizes what separates his anthropology from the formal and still idealist anthropology of the tradition; see GMD, 321, 334, 350, 350; and WE, 207, 208.

58. GMD, 194; here it is a question concerning the love of "knowing the infinity of human life through generation and birth."

59. We will have to take a look at this "glimpse" thrown on eternity with respect to what happens in the philosophy that, although not an "orphic possibility" (GMD, 202), can nevertheless be considered as both a "return" and a "repetition" of the mysteries; see on this subject Patočka's commentary on Fink's interpretation of Plato's allegory of the cave, in *Metaphysik der Erziehung im Weltverständnis von Plato und Aristoteles* (Frankfurt: Klostermann, 1970), and in his *Heretical Essays in the Philosophy of History*, tr. J. Dodd and E. Kohák (LaSalle: Open Court, 1996), 104ff. This is why one is allowed, even in Plato, to "cast a look to the outside, towards immortality and heroes," as Hölderlin says in his poem "Greece." This discourse on the true being of things, and what makes philosophy possible for him only on the basis of a situation of captivity in appearance, as Fink underlines in another short commentary on the allegory of the cave in *Nachdenkliches zur ontologishen Frühgeschichte von Raum-Zeit-Bewegung* (The Hague: Nijhoff, 1957), 78.

60. GMD, 347.

61. Ibid., 347–48.

62. Ibid., 349 and 351.

63. MT, 202.

64. Heidegger, "What Is Metaphysics?," 93.

65. See KM, 161.

66. MT, 203.

67. ND, 186.

68. MT, 192; see also ND, 276.

69. See the long and magnificent commentary that he gives of it in Fink, *Nachdenkliches zur ontologishen Frühgeschichte von Raum-Zeit-Bewegung*, 53–103.

70. SZ, 93.

71. Fink, *Nachdenkliches zur ontologishen Frühgeschichte von Raum-Zeit-Bewegung*, 50.

72. GMD, 137.

73. MT, 201.

74. GMD, 98; the title of chapter 8 is "*Jemeinigkeit* as Problem: The Finitude of the Self."

75. Ibid., 99 and 103.

76. Ibid., 154–55.

77. Ibid., 156.

78. MT, 208.

79. AN, 249.

80. Man is for Fink the *Todgeweihter*; see, for example, MT, 208, and *Heraclitus Seminar*, 98.

81. WE, 202.

82. MT, 208.

83. Fink's *Welt und Endlichkeit* ends with a commentary on the same late poem by Rilke, one of the *Duino Elegies*, which Heidegger had evoked at length in his text "Why Poets?" (1946), in *Off the Beaten Track*, tr. Julian Young and Kenneth Haynes (Cambridge: Cambridge University Press, 2002), 222ff.

16. The "Last God" of Phenomenology (Husserl and Heidegger)

1. See Johann Heinrich Lambert, "Phenomenology as Doctrine of Appearance," which is the title of the first article of the fourth part of his *Nouvel Organon* (1764). The *Nouvel Organon* is not translated into English, but a French translation of this article appears in *Alter* 5 (1997): 223–39.

2. See the French translation of this letter dated 2 September 1770, with a commentary, in Gérard Granel, *L'équivoque ontologique de la pensée kantienne* (Paris: Gallimard, 1970), 33–35.

3. See also Granel's translation of this letter, in ibid., 36–39.

4. Immanuel Kant, *Grounding for the Metaphysics of Morals*, tr. J. Ellington (Indianapolis: Hackett, 1981), 60–62.

5. KM, 22.

6. See Edmund Husserl's judgment on the First *Critique* in Ideas I, section 62: 166; see also Martin Heidegger's course on the *Phenomenological Interpretation of the Critique of Pure Reason*, tr. P. Emad and K. Maly (Bloomington: Indiana University Press. 1997).

7. Ideas I, section 43: 123.

8. Ibid., section 44: 125.

9. Ibid., section 150: 386.

10. Ibid., section 79: 210.

11. Ibid., section 79: 210n.

12. FTL, section 99: 251.

13. Ideas I, section 56: 155.

14. Ibid., section 58: 158.

15. Ibid., section 51: 142.

16. Ibid., section 58: 157–58.

17. See the manuscripts evoked by Emmanuel Housset in his chapter on the "religious soil," in *Personne et sujet selon Husserl* (Paris: PUF, 1997), 267–90.

18. Crisis, 288.

19. Ibid.

20. Ibid.

21. Manuscript from January 1930, cited by N. Depraz, in "L'incarnation phénoménologique, un problème non-théologique?," *Tijdschrift voor Filosofie* 3 (1993): 497.

22. See Edith Stein, *Par une moniale francaise* (Paris: Seuil, 1954), 113; cited by René Toulemont, *L'essence de la société chez Husserl* (Paris: PUF, 1962), 303.

23. Also cited by Toulemont, *L'essence*, 278.

24. Crisis, 66.

25. Husserl, *Aufsätze und Vorträge.* 1922–1937, ed. T. Nenon and H. R. Sepp (The Hague: Kluwer, 1988), 59.

26. See Crisis, 62.

27. This is the expression used by Housset, *Personne et sujet selon Husserl*, 266.

28. BT, 31.

29. Heidegger, *The Phenomenology of Religious Life*, tr. M. Fritsch and J. Gosetti-Ferencei (Bloomington: Indiana University Press, 2004); see in particular the Winter Semester 1920–21 course, 3–111. Concerning the relations between Heideggerian thought and theology, see Françoise Dastur, "Heidegger et la théologie," *Revue Philosophique de Louvain*, 92, nos. 2–3 (1994): 226–45.

30. Heidegger, *Phenomenological Interpretations of Aristotle: Initiation into Phenomenological Research*, tr. R. Rojcewicz (Bloomington: Indiana University Press, 2001), 28.

31. See Heidegger, "Phenomenology and Theology," in *Pathmarks*, 53.

32. Heidegger, *Schelling's Treatise on Human Freedom*, tr. J. Stambaugh (Athens: University of Ohio Press, 1985), 50–51.

33. LH, 267.

34. ID, 72.

35. CTP, 290–91.

36. Ibid., 18.

37. Ibid., 283.

38. Ibid., 285–86.

39. Ibid., 289.

40. Ibid., 288.

41. Heidegger, "What Is Metaphysics?," in *Pathmarks*, 95.

42. CTP, 288.

43. Heidegger, *Four Seminars*, tr. A. Mitchell and F. Raffoul (Bloomington: Indiana University Press, 2003), 80.

Bibliography

Aguirre, Antonio. *Genetische Phänomenologie und Reduktion*. The Hague: Nijhoff, 1970.

Aristotle. "Metaphysics" and "On the Soul." In *The Basic Works of Aristotle*, edited and translated by R. McKeon. New York: Random House, 1941.

Bachelard, Suzanne. *A Study of Husserl's Formal and Transcendental Logic*. Translated by L. Embree. Evanston: Northwestern University Press, 1990.

Bergson, Henri. "Life and Consciousness." In *Mind-Energy*, translated by H. W. Carr. New York: H. Holt, 1920.

———. *Oeuvres*. Paris: PUF, 1963.

Biemel, Walter. "Les phases décisives dans le developpement de la philosophie de Husserl." In *Husserl: Cahiers de Royaumont*, edited by W. Biemel. Paris: Minuit, 1959.

Blankenburg, Wolfgang. *La perte de l'évidence naturelle: Une contribution à la psychopathologie des schizophrenies pauci-symptomatiques*. Paris: PUF, 1991.

Boehm, Rudolph. "L'ambiguité des concepts husserliens de transcendence et d'immanence." *Revue Philosophique* 4 (1954).

———. "Deux points de vue: Husserl et Nietzsche." *Archivio di Filosophia* 3 (1962): 167–81.

Boss, Medard. *Einführung in die psychosomatische Medizin*. Bern: Hans Huber, 1954. Translated into French as *Introduction à la médicine psychosomatique*. Paris: PUF, 1959.

———. *Existential Foundations of Medicine and Psychology*. Translated by Stephen Conway and Anne Cleaves. Introduction by Paul J. Stern. New York: Jason Aronson, 1979.

———. *Grundriss der Medizin: Ansätze zu einer phänomenologischen Physiologie, Psychologie, Pathologie, Therapie und zu einer daseinsgemässen Präventiv-Medizin in der modernen Industrie-Gesellschaft*. Bern: Hans Huber, 1971.

———. "Zollikoner Seminare." In *Erinnerung an Martin Heidegger*. Pfullingen: Neske, 1977.

Cairns, Dorion. *Conversations with Husserl and Fink*. The Hague: Nijhoff, 1976.

Carr, David. "Epistémologie et ontologie du récit." In *Paul Ricoeur: Les métamorphoses de la raison herméneutique*, edited by J. Greisch and R. Kearney. Paris: Cerf, 1991.

———. *Phenomenology and the Problem of History: A Study of Husserl's Transcendental Phenomenology*. Evanston: Northwestern University Press, 1974.

Cassirer, Ernst, and Martin Heidegger. "Davos Debate." In Heidegger, *Kant and the Problem of Metaphysics*, Translated by R. Taft. Bloomington: Indiana University Press, 1990.

Char, René. *Oeuvres Complètes*. Paris: Gallimard, 1983.

Chomsky, Noam. *Cartesian Linguistics: A Chapter in the History of Rational Thought*. New York: University Press of America, 1966.

Dastur, Françoise. *Death: An Essay on Finitude*. Translated by J. Llewelyn. London: Athlone Press, 1996.

———. "La destruction heideggerienne de la logique." In *Études de philosophie ancienne et moderne*, edited by F. Dastur and C. Levy. Paris: L'Harmattan, 1999.

———. "Heidegger et la théologie." *Revue philosophique de Louvain* 92, nos. 2–3 (May–August 1994): 226–45.

———. "Heidegger et le ton de retenue de la pensée." *Epokhē* 2 (1991): 309–24.

———. "World, Flesh, Vision." In *Chiasms: Merleau-Ponty's Notion of the Flesh*, edited by L. Lawler and F. Evans, 23–50. Albany: SUNY Press, 1994. Also published in "Monde, chair, vision." In *Chair et langage: Essais sur Merleau-Ponty*, 69–107. La Versanne: Encre Marine, 2001.

Depraz, N. "L'incarnation phénoménologique, un problème non-théologique?" *Tijdschrift voor Filosofie* 3 (1993): 497.

Derrida, Jacques. "Geschlecht I: Sexual Difference, Ontological Difference." In *Psyche: Invention of the Other*, edited and translated by P. Kamuf and E. Rottenberg, 2:19–23. Stanford: Stanford University Press, 2008.

———. *Introduction to Husserl's "Origin of Geometry."* Translated by J. P. Leavy. Lincoln: University of Nebraska Press, 1974.

———. *Margins: of Philosophy*. Translated by A. Bass. Chicago: University of Chicago Press, 1982.

———. *Of Spirit: Heidegger and the Question*. Translated by G. Bennington and R. Bowlby. Chicago: University of Chicago Press, 1991.

———. *Speech and Phenomena, and Other Essays on Husserl's Theory of Signs*. Translated by D. Allison. Evanston: Northwestern University Press, 1973.

———. *Voice and Phenomenon*. Translated by L. Lawlor. Evanston: Northwestern University Press, 2010.

———. *La voix et le phenomena*. Paris: PUF, 1967.

de Waehlens, Alphonse. *Phénoménologie et vérité: Essai sur l'evolution de l'idée de vérité chez Husserl et Heidegger*. Paris: PUF, 1957.

Diemer, Alwin. *Husserl*. Meisenheim am Glam: Anton Hain, 1956.

Dilthey, Wilhelm. *Gesammelte Schriften*. Bd. 7. Stuttgart: Teubner, 1927.

Dilthey, Wilhelm, and (Graf) Paul Yorck von Wartenburg. *Briefwechsel zwischen Wilhelm Dilthey und dem Grafen Paul Yorck v. Wartenburg, 1877–1897*. Halle: Niemeyer, 1923.

Edie, James M. "Husserl's Conception of 'The Grammatical' and Contemporary Linguistics." In Mohanty, *Readings on Edmund Husserl's "Logical Investigations,"* edited by J. N. Mohanty. The Hague: Nijhoff, 1977.

Fédier, François. *Regarder voir*. Paris: Les Belles Lettres Archimbaud, 1995.

Fink, Eugen. *Alles und Nichts*. The Hague: Nijhoff, 1959.

———. "Les concepts opératoires dans la phénoménologie de Husserl." In *Husserl, Cahiers de Royaumont*. Paris: Minuit, 1959. See also in Fink, *Nähe und Distanz: Studien zur Phänomenologie*. Freiburg: Alber Karl, 2008.

———. *Grundphänomene des menschlichen Daseins*. Freiburg: Karl Alber, 1979.

———. *Metaphysik und Tod*. Stuttgart: Kohlhammer, 1969.

———. *Nachdenkliches zur ontologischen Frühgeschichte von Raum-Zeit-Bewegung*. The Hague: Nijhoff, 1957.

———. "Phenomenological Philosophy of Edmund Husserl and Contemporary Criticism." In *Husserl: Critical Assessments of Leading Philosophers*, edited by R. Bernet, D. Wellton, and G. Zavota. New York: Routledge, 2005.

———. "Vergegenwärtigung und Bild." In *Studien zur Phänomenologie*. The Hague: Nijhoff, 1954.

———. *Welt und Endlichkeit*. Würzburg: Koenigshausen and Neumann, 1990.

———. "Welt und Geschichte." In *Nähe und Distanz: Studien zur Phänomenologie*. Freiburg: Karl Alber, 2008.

Foucault, Michel. *Archaeology of Knowledge*. Translated by A. Sheridan. New York: Pantheon, 1972.

Gadamer, Hans-Georg. "The Phenomenological Movement (1963)." In *Philosophical Hermeneutics*, edited and translated by D. E. Linge. Berkeley: University of California Press, 1976.

———. *Truth and Method*. New York: Crossroads, 1988.

Goethe, Johann Wolfgang von. *The Theory of Colors*. Edited by R Matthaei and H. Aach. New York: Van Nostrand, 1971.

Granel, Gérard. *L'équivoque ontologique de la pensée kantienne*. Paris: Gallimard, 1970.

———. *Le sens du temps et de la perception chez E. Husserl*. Paris: Gallimard, 1968.

Haar, Michel, ed. *Martin Heidegger*. Paris: L'Herne, 1983.

Hegel, G. W. F. "The Moral Vision of the World." In *Phenomenology of Spirit*, translated by A. V. Miller. Oxford: Oxford University Press, 1977.

———. *Philosophy of Right*. Translated by T. M. Knox. New York: Clarendon, 1952.

———. *Three Essays, 1793–1795: The Tübingen Essay, Berne Fragments, the Life of Jesus*. Edited and translated by P. Fuss and J. Dobbins. South Bend: Notre Dame University Press, 1984.

Heidegger, Martin. *Gesamtausgabe*. Frankfurt: Klostermann, 1916–.

———. *The Basic Problems of Phenomenology*. Translated by A. Hofstadter. Bloomington: Indiana University Press, 1988.

———. *Basic Questions of Philosophy: Selected "Problems" of "Logic."* Translated by R. Rojcewicz and A. Schuwer. Bloomington: Indiana University Press, 1994.

———. "Building, Dwelling, Thinking." In *Basic Writings of Heidegger*, edited by D. F. Krell. New York: Harper, 1977.

———. *The Concept of Time*. Translated by W. McNeill. London: Blackwell, 1992.

———. *Contributions to Philosophy: From Enowning*. Translated by P. Emad and K. Maly. Bloomington: Indiana University Press, 2000.

———. "A Dialogue on Language." In *On the Way to Language*. Translated by P. D. Hertz. New York: Harper and Row, 1971.

———. "The End of Philosophy and the Task of Thinking." In *On Time and Being*, translated by J. Stambaugh. New York: Harper and Row, 1972.

———. *The Essence of Human Freedom: An Introduction to Philosophy*. Translated by T. Sadler. London: Continuum, 2002.

———. *Frühe Schriften*. Edited by F. von Herrmann. Frankfurt: Klosterman, 1972.

———. *The Fundamental Concepts of Metaphysics: World, Finitude, Solitude*. Translated by W. McNeill and N. Walker. Bloomington: Indiana University Press, 1995.

———. "Gelassenheit." In *Discourse on Thinking*, translated by J. Anderson and E. H. Freund. New York: Harper and Row, 1966.

———. *Die Geschichte des Seins* (1938/40). Frankfurt: Klostermann, 1998.

———. *Hegel's Phenomenology of Spirit*. Translated by P. Emad and K. Maly. Bloomington: Indiana University Press, 1988.

———. *History of the Concept of Time: Prolegomena*. Translated by T. Kisiel. Bloomington: Indiana University Press, 1992.

———. *Identity and Difference*. Translated by J. Stambaugh. Chicago: University of Chicago Press, 2002.

———. *Kant and the Problem of Metaphysics*. Translated by R. Taft. Bloomington: Indiana University Press, 1990.

———. "Letter on 'Humanism'" (1946). Translated by F. Capuzzi. In *Pathmarks*, edited by W. McNeill. Cambridge: Cambridge University Press, 1998.

———. "Letter to Richardson." In *Heidegger: Through Phenomenology to Thought*, by William Richardson. 4th ed. New York: Fordham University Press, 2003.

———. *Logic: The Question of Truth.* Translated by T. Sheehan. Bloomington: Indiana University Press, 2010. Originally published as *Logik, die Frage nach der Wahrheit.* Frankfurt: Klostermann, 1976 (GA 21).

———. "Mein Weg in die Phänomenologie." In *Zur Sache des Denkens*, edited by F. W. von Herrmann. Frankfurt: Klostermann, 2007.

———. *The Metaphysical Foundations of Logic.* Translated by M. Heim. Bloomington: Indiana University Press, 1984.

———. "My Way into Phenomenology." In *Being and Time*, translated by J. Stambaugh. Albany: SUNY Press, 1996.

———. *Nietzsche.* Vols. 1 and 2. Translated by D. Krell. San Francisco: Harper Collins, 1991.

———. *Nietzsche.* Vols. 3 and 4. Translated by D. F. Krell and F. A. Capuzzi. New York: Harper and Rowe, 1987.

———. "Nihilism as Determined by the History of Being," in *Nietzsche*, vol. 4, *Nihilism*, tr. D. F. Krell and F. A. Capuzzi (New York: Harper and Row, 1987), 238 [Dastur's interpolation in German.—Tr.].

———. *Off the Beaten Track.* Translated by Julian Young and Kenneth Haynes. Cambridge: Cambridge University Press, 2002.

———. "On the Essence of Ground." Translated by J. Sallis. In *Pathmarks*, edited by W. McNeill. Cambridge: Cambridge University Press, 1998.

———. "On the Essence of Truth," in *Pathmarks*, edited by W. McNeill. Cambridge: Cambridge University Press, 1998.

———. *On Time and Being.* Translated by J. Stambaugh. New York: Harper and Row, 1972.

———. *Ontology: The Hermeneutics of Facticity.* Translated by J. van Buren. Bloomington: Indiana University Press, 1999.

———. *Parmenides.* Translated by R. Rojcewicz. Bloomington: Indiana University Press, 1992.

———. *Pathmarks.* Edited by W. McNeill. Cambridge: Cambridge University Press, 1998.

———. *The Principle of Reason.* Translated by R. Lilly. Bloomington: Indiana University Press, 1991.

———. *Phenomenological Interpretation of the Critique of Pure Reason.* Translated by P. Emad and K. Maly. Bloomington: Indiana University Press. 1997.

———. *Phenomenological Interpretations of Aristotle: Initiation into Phenomenological Research.* Translated by R. Rojcewicz. Bloomington: Indiana University Press, 2001.

———. "Phenomenology and Theology." In *Pathmarks*, translated by W. McNeill. Cambridge: Cambridge University Press, 1998.

———. *The Phenomenology of Religious Life.* Translated by M. Fritsch and J. Gosetti-Ferencei. Bloomington: Indiana University Press, 2004.
———. *The Question of Being.* Translated by J. Wilde and W. Kluback. New York: Rowman and Littlefield, 1958.
———. "Recollection in Metaphysics." In *The End of Philosophy,* translated by J. Stambaugh. San Francisco: Harper and Row, 1973.
———. *The Question Concerning Technology and Other Essays.* Translated by W. Lovitt. New York: Harper and Row, 1977.
———. *Schelling's Treatise on Human Freedom.* Translated by J. Stambaugh. Athens: University of Ohio Press, 1985.
———. "The Self-Assertion of the German University." Translated by W. S. Lewis. In *The Heidegger Controversy: A Critical Reader,* edited by R. Wolin, 33–34. Cambridge, Mass.: MIT Press, 1993.
———. "Seminar at Zähringen." In *Four Seminars,* translated by A. Mitchell and F. Raffoul. Bloomington: Indiana University Press, 2003.
———. *Towards the Definition of Philosophy.* Translated by T. Sadler. London: Continuum, 2003.
———. "The Turning." In *The Question Concerning Technology and Other Essays,* translated by W. Lovitt. New York: Harper and Row, 1977.
———. *What Is Called Thinking?* Translated by J. G. Gray. New York: Harper Perennial, 1968.
———. "What Is Metaphysics? (1929)." In *Pathmarks,* edited by W. McNeill. Cambridge: Cambridge University Press, 1998.
———. *What Is Philosophy?* Translated by J. Wilde and W. Kluback. Albany: NCUP, 1956.
———. *The Zollikon Seminars: Protocols, Conversations, Letters.* Edited by M. Boss. Translated by F. Mayr and R. Askay. Evanston: Northwestern University Press, 2001.
———. *Zollikoner Seminare.* Edited by Medard Boss. Frankfurt: Klostermann, 1987.
Heidegger, Martin, and Eugen Fink. *The Heraclitus Seminar.* Evanston: Northwestern University Press, 1993.
Held, Klaus. *Die Lebendige Gegenwart.* Cologne: Springer, 1963.
Hölderlin, Friedrich. "The Ground of Empedocles." In *The Death of Empedocles,* edited and translated by D. F. Krell. Albany: SUNY Press, 2009.
Housset, Emmanuel. *Personne et sujet selon Husserl.* Paris: PUF, 1997.
Husserl, Edmund. *Analyses Concerning Passive and Active Synthesis: Lectures on Transcendental Logic.* Translated by A. Steinbock. Dordrecht: Kluwer, 2001.
———. *Aufsätze und Vorträge, 1922–1937.* Edited by T. Nenon and H. R. Sepp. The Hague: Kluwer, 1988.
———. *The Basic Problems of Phenomenology: From the Lectures, Winter Semester, 1910–1911.* Translated by I. Farin and J. G. Hart. Dordrecht: Nijhoff, 2006.
———. *Briefwechsel 9.* Dordrecht: Kluwer, 1994.

———. *Cartesian Meditations: An Introduction to Phenomenology.* Translated by D. Cairns. Dordrecht: Nijhoff, 1988.

———. *The Crisis of European Sciences and Transcendental Phenomenology.* Translated by D. Carr. Evanston: Northwestern University Press, 1970.

———. "A Draft of a Preface to *Logical Investigations.*" In *Introduction to the Logical Investigations*, edited by E. Fink, translated by P. J. Bossert and C. H. Peters. The Hague: Nijhoff, 1975.

———. *Erste Philosophie (1923/24).* Zweiter Teil, *Theorie der phänomenologischen Reduktion.* Translated by R. Boehm. The Hague: Nijhoff, 1959.

———. *Experience and Judgment.* Translated by J. Churchill, J. Spencer, and K. Ameriks. Evanston: Northwestern University Press, 1973.

———. *Formal and Transcendental Logic.* Edited and translated by D. Cairns. Dordrecht: Nijhoff, 1969.

———. *The Idea of Phenomenology.* Translated by L. Hardy. Dordrecht: Nijhoff, 1999.

———. *Ideas: General Introduction to Pure Phenomenology.* Translated by W. R. Gibson. New York: Collier, 1962.

———. *Ideas Pertaining to a Pure Phenomenology and to a Phenomenological Philosophy.* Second Book, *Studies in the Phenomenology of Constitution.* Translated by R. Rojcewicz and A. Schuwer. Dordrecht: Kluwer, 1989.

———. *Logical Investigations.* Vol. 1. Translated by J. N. Findlay. London: Routledge, 1970.

———. *Logical Investigations.* Vol. 2. Translated by J. N. Findlay. London: Routledge, 1970.

———. *On the Phenomenology of the Consciousness of Internal Time (1893–1917).* Translated by J. Brough. The Hague: Nijhoff, 1991.

———. *Phenomenological and Transcendental Psychology and the Confrontation with Heidegger.* Translated and edited by T. Sheehan and R. Palmer. Dordrecht: Kluwer, 1997.

———. *Phenomenological Psychology: Lectures, Summer Semester, 1925.* The Hague: Nijhoff, 1977.

———. "Présentation des Recherches logiques (1901)." In *Articles sur la logique*, translated by Jacques English, section 2. Paris: PUF, 1975.

———. *Psychological and Transcendental Phenomenology and the Confrontation with Heidegger (1927–1931).* Translated by T. Sheehan and R. Palmer. Dordrecht: Nijhoff, 1997.

———. "Review of Melchior Palagyi's *Der Streit der Psychologisten und Formalisten in der Modernen Logik.*" Translated by D. Willard. In *Early Writings in the Philosophy of Logic and Mathematics.* Dordrecht: Kluwer, 1994.

———. *Zur Phänomenologie der Intersubjektivität: Texte Aus Dem Nachlass.* Dritter Teil, *1929–1935.* Edited by I. Kern. The Hague: Nijhoff, 1973.

Hyppolite, Jean. "Vie et conscience de la vie dans la philosophie hegélienne d'Iéna." *Revue de Métaphysique et de Morale* (1938).

Kant, Immanuel. *Critique of Judgment.* Translated by W. Pluhar. Indianapolis: Hackett, 1987.

———. *Critique of Practical Reason.* Section 7. Translated by L. W. Beck. New York: Macmillan, 1956.

———. *Critique of Pure Reason.* Translated by N. K. Smith. New York: St. Martin's, 1929.

———. *Grounding for the Metaphysics of Morals.* Translated by J. Ellington. Indianapolis: Hackett, 1981.

Kern, Iso. "Die drei Wege zur transzendental-phänomenologischen Reduktion in der Philosophie Edmund Husserls." *Tijdschrift vor Filosofie* 4, no. 2 (1962): 303–49.

Kockelmans, Joseph J. *On Heidegger and Language.* Evanston: Northwestern University Press, 1980.

Kojève, Alexandre. *Introduction to the Reading of Hegel.* Translated by R. Queneau. Ithaca: Cornell University Press, 1980.

Lambert, Johann Heinrich. *Neues Organo.* Liepzig: Johann Mendler, 1764.

Landgrebe, Ludwig. "Erinnerungen an meinem Freund Jan Patočka: Ein Philosoph von Weltbedeutung." *Perspectiven der Philosophie* 3 (1977).

Landgrebe, Ludwig, and Edmund Husserl. *Der Weg der Phänomenologie: Das Problem einer ursprünglichen Erfahrung.* Gütersloh: Mohn, 1963.

Leibniz, Gottfried Wilhelm. *Principles of Nature and Grace.* In "*Philosophical Papers and Letters*," edited by Leroy E. Loemker, 636–42. Dordrecht: Kluwer, 1989.

Levinas, Emmanuel. *On Escape.* Translated by B. G. Bergo. Stanford: Stanford University Press, 2003.

———. *Otherwise Than Being: or, Beyond Essence.* Translated by A. Lingis. Dordrecht and Boston, Mass.: Kluwer, 1978.

———. *Time and the Other.* Translated by R. Cohen. Pittsburgh: Duquesne University Press, 1987.

———. *Totality and Infinity: An Essay on Exteriority.* Translated by A. Lingis. Pittsburgh: Duquesne University Press, 1969.

Lohmann, Johannes. "M. Heidegger's 'Ontological Difference' and Speech." In *On Heidegger and Language,* edited and translated by J. Kockelmans, 303–63. Evanston: Northwestern University Press, 1972. Originally published as "M. Heideggers 'ontologische Differenz' und die Sprache." *Lexis* 1 (1948): 49–106.

Lotze, R. Hermann. *Logic: In Three Books.* Translated by B. Bosanquet. 2 vols. Oxford: Clarendon, 1888.

Lowit, Alexandre. "*L'epokhē* de Husserl et le doute de Descartes." *Revue de metaphysique et morale* (1957).

Macann, Christopher E. *Martin Heidegger: Critical Assessments.* Vol. 3. London: Routledge, 1992.

Maldiney, Henri. *Penser l'homme et la folie.* Grenoble: J. Millon, 1991.

Marx, Karl. "The Holy Family." In *The Writings of the Young Marx*, translated by L. D. Easton and K. H. Guddat. Indianapolis: Hackett, 1997.

Marx, Werner. "Les mortels." In *Le Cahier du College International de Philosophie* 8 (1989).

Merleau-Ponty, Maurice. *Notes de cours 1959–1961*. Paris: Gallimard, 1996.

———. "On the Phenomenology of Language," In *Signs*. Evanston: Northwestern University Press, 1972.

———. *Phenomenology of Perception*. Translated by C. Smith. London: Routledge, 2002.

———. *The Prose of the World*. Edited by C. Lefort. Translated by J. O'Neill. Evanston: Northwestern University Press, 1973.

———. *The Visible and the Invisible*. Edited by C. Lefort. Translated by A. Lingis. Evanston: Northwestern University Press, 1968.

Mohanty, Jitendra Nath. *Edmund Husserl's "Theory of Meaning."* The Hague: Nijhoff, 1976.

———. *Readings on Edmund Husserl's "Logical Investigations."* The Hague: Nijhoff, 1977.

Patočka, Jan. "Cartesianism and Phenomenology." In *Jan Patočka: Philosophy and Selected Writings*, edited and translated by E. Kohák. Chicago: University of Chicago Press, 1989.

———. *La crise du sens*. Vol. 2, *Comte, Masaryk et l'action*. Brussels: Ousia, 1986.

———. "Erinnerungen an Husserl." In *Festschrift für Patočka: Die Welt des Menschen; Die Welt der Philosophie*, edited by W. Biemel, x–. *Phaenomenologica* 72. The Hague: Nijhoff, 1972.

———. "Heidegger, penseur de l'humanité" (1974). *Epokhē* 2 (1991): 383–86.

———. *Heretical Essays in the Philosophy of History*. Translated by J. Dodd and E. Kohák. LaSalle: Open Court, 1996.

———. *Liberté et sacrifice: Écrits politiques*. Translated by E. Abrams. Grenoble: Millon, 1990.

———. *Le monde naturel et le movement de l'existence humaine*. Edited and translated by E. Abrams. Dordrecht: Kuwer, 1998.

———. *Metaphysik der Erziehung im Weltverständnis von Plato und Aristoteles*. Frankfurt: Klostermann, 1970.

———. " 'The Movement of Human Existence': A Selection from *Body, Community, Language, World* (1968–1969)." In *Jan Patočka: Philosophy and Selected Writings*, by Erazim V.Kohák. Chicago: University of Chicago Press, 1989.

———. "Qu'est-ce que la phenomenology." In *Qu'est-ce que la phénoménologie?* Grenoble: Millon, 1988.

———. "Le subjectivisme de la phénoménologie husserlienne et la possibilité d'une phénoménologie 'asubjective.' " In *Qu'est-ce que la phénoménologie?* Grenoble: Millon, 1988.

———. "Der Subjektivismus der Husserlschen und die Forderung einer asubjektiven Phänomenologie." In *Ausgewählte Schriften IV: Die Bewegung der Menschlichen Existenz; Phänomenologische Schriften II*, edited by K. Nellen, J. Nemec, and I. Srubar. Frankfurt: Verlag Kett-Cotta, 1991.

Pazanin, Ante. *Wissenschaft und Geschichte in der Phänomenologie E. Husserls.* The Hague: Nijhoff, 1972.

Picht, Georg. "Die Macht des Denkens." In *Erinnerung an Martin Heidegger.* Pfullingen: Neske, 1977.

Plato. "Phaedo." In *Five Dialogues*, translated by G. M. A. Grube. Indianapolis: Hackett, 2002.

———. *Plato: Collected Dialogues.* Edited by E. Hamilton and H. Cairns. Princeton: Princeton University Press, 1961.

———. *Symposium.* Translated by S. Benardete. Chicago: University of Chicago, 1993.

Renthe-Fink, Leonhard von. *Geschichtlichkeit: Zur terminologischer und begrifflicher Ursprung bei Hegel, Haym, Dilthey und Yorck.* Göttingen: Vandenhoeck and Ruprecht, 1964.

Ricoeur, Paul. "À quoi pensent les philosophes?" *Autrement* 102 (November 1988).

———. *The Conflict of Interpretations.* Translated by D. Ihde. Evanston: Northwestern University Press, 1974.

———. *Oneself as Another.* Translated by K. Blamey. Chicago: University of Chicago Press, 1995.

———. *Time and Narrative.* Vol. 1. Translated by K. Blamey and D. Pellauer. Chicago: University of Chicago Press, 1990.

———. *Time and Narrative.* Vol. 3. Translated by K. Blamey and D. Pellauer. Chicago: University of Chicago Press, 1990.

Romano, Claude. "Le possible et l'événement." *Philosophie* 40 (December 1993) and 41 (March 1994).

Sallis, John. "Time, Subjectivity, and the *Phenomenology of Perception.*" *Modern Schoolman* 48 (November 1970).

Schelling, Friedrich Wilhelm Josef. "Letters on Dogmatism and Criticism." In *The Unconditional in Human Knowledge: Four Early Essays 1794–96*, edited and translated by F. Marti. Lewisburg, Pa.: Bucknell University Press, 1980.

———. "Of the I." In *The Unconditional in Human Knowledge: Four Early Essays 1794–96*, edited and translated by F. Marti. Lewisburg, Pa.: Bucknell University Press, 1980.

Schérer, René. *La phénoménologie des "Recherches Logiques" de Husserl.* Paris: PUF, 1967.

Serrus, Charles. *Le parallélisme logico-grammatical.* Paris: Alcan, 1938.

Sokolowski, Robert. "The Logic of Parts and Wholes in Husserl's *Investigations.*" In *Readings on Edmund Husserl's Logical Investigations*, edited by J. N. Mohanty, 94–111. The Hague: Nijhoff, 1977.

Stein, Edith. *Par une moniale française.* Paris: Seuil, 1954.

Taminiaux, Jacques. *Dialectic and Difference.* Edited and translated by J. Decker and R. Crease. Atlantic Highlands, N.J.: Humanities Press International, 1985.

Toulemont, René. *L'essence de la société selon Husserl.* Paris: PUF, 1962.

Tugendhat, Ernst. *Der Wahrheitsbegriff bei Husserl und Heidegger.* Berlin: Walter de Gruyter, 1967.

Villela-Petit, Maria. "Recéptivité antéprédicative et familiarité typique." *Archives de Philosophie* 58 (1995): 603–15.

Wartenburg, Paul Yorck von. *Bewusstseinstellung und Geschichte.* Tübingen: Niemeyer, 1956.

Index of Names

Perspectives in Continental Philosophy
John D. Caputo, series editor

Recent titles:

Emmanuel Alloa, *Resistance of the Sensible World: An Introduction to Merleau-Ponty.* Translated by Jane Marie Todd. Foreword by Renaud Barbaras.

Françoise Dastur, *Questions of Phenomenology: Language, Alterity, Temporality, Finitude.* Translated by Robert Vallier.

Jean-Luc Marion, *Believing in Order to See: On the Rationality of Revelation and the Irrationality of Some Believers.* Translated by Christina M. Gschwandtner.

Adam Y. Wells, ed., *Phenomenologies of Scripture.*

An Yountae, *The Decolonial Abyss: Mysticism and Cosmopolitics from the Ruins.*

Jean Wahl, *Transcendence and the Concrete: Selected Writings.* Edited and with an Introduction by Alan D. Schrift and Ian Alexander Moore.

Colby Dickinson, *Words Fail: Theology, Poetry, and the Challenge of Representation.*

Emmanuel Falque, *The Wedding Feast of the Lamb: Eros, the Body, and the Eucharist.* Translated by George Hughes.

Emmanuel Falque, *Crossing the Rubicon: The Borderlands of Philosophy and Theology.* Translated by Reuben Shank. Introduction by Matthew Farley.

Colby Dickinson and Stéphane Symons (eds.), *Walter Benjamin and Theology.*

Don Ihde, *Husserl's Missing Technologies.*

William S. Allen, *Aesthetics of Negativity: Blanchot, Adorno, and Autonomy.*

Jeremy Biles and Kent L. Brintnall, eds., *Georges Bataille and the Study of Religion.*

Tarek R. Dika and W. Chris Hackett, *Quiet Powers of the Possible: Interviews in Contemporary French Phenomenology*. Foreword by Richard Kearney.

Richard Kearney and Brian Treanor, eds., *Carnal Hermeneutics*.

Aaron T. Looney, *Vladimir Jankélévitch: The Time of Forgiveness*.

Vanessa Lemm, ed., *Nietzsche and the Becoming of Life*.

Edward Baring and Peter E. Gordon, eds., *The Trace of God: Derrida and Religion*.

Jean-Louis Chrétien, *Under the Gaze of the Bible*. Translated by John Marson Dunaway.

Michael Naas, *The End of the World and Other Teachable Moments: Jacques Derrida's Final Seminar*.

Noëlle Vahanian, *The Rebellious No: Variations on a Secular Theology of Language*.

A complete list of titles is available at http://fordhampress.com.